MARIANNE THORNTON
A Domestic Biography

BOOKS BY E. M. FORSTER

Novels

WHERE ANGELS FEAR TO TREAD
THE LONGEST JOURNEY
A ROOM WITH A VIEW
HOWARDS END
A PASSAGE TO INDIA

Short Stories

THE COLLECTED SHORT STORIES

Biography

GOLDSWORTHY LOWES DICKINSON
THE HILL OF DEVI

Essays and Criticism

ASPECTS OF THE NOVEL
ABINGER HARVEST
TWO CHEERS FOR DEMOCRACY
PHAROS AND PHARILLON

Marianne Thornton, July 1873
by George Richmond

Marianne Thornton

A DOMESTIC BIOGRAPHY

1797-1887

by E. M. FORSTER

HARCOURT, BRACE AND COMPANY · NEW YORK

TO MY MOTHER

Preface

THIS BIOGRAPHY is based almost entirely upon family papers. It is only concerned with them in their domestic aspect, but scholars (both English and American) who have looked at them report that they are also interesting in other ways. I have therefore arranged that they shall be accessible after my death. They are so miscellaneous that classification has been difficult. Here is an attempt:

I. *First Vellum Book*. About 650 pages. The opening 434 pages are in Marianne Thornton's handwriting. She transcribes the short autobiography of her father, Henry Thornton, also family letters down to the death of her parents in 1815. From page 435 the "Family Chronicle" is continued by my aunt, Miss Laura Forster: she transcribes Marianne Thornton's "Recollections" and further letters.

II. *Second Vellum Book*. About 360 pages. Continuation by Laura Forster, bringing letters copied down to 1852. A few Forster letters, copied in by myself, at the end.

III. *Ten Small Volumes*. Begun for me by Marianne Thornton in her old age, and continued by my mother. Largely a replica of the early part of the First Vellum Book with some additional matter.

IV. *The "Wigan" Book*. A large bound volume in the Public Library at Wigan. Copied in by some unknown scribe for Lucy Thornton, Marianne's sister. Contains all the matter in the early part of the First Vellum Book, together with many other letters of the period. Catalogue description: Edward Hall M.S. Coll. Wigan Public Library. M.786.

V. *Small Green Book.* 110 pages. Copies in an early hand of some additional early letters.

VI. *Henry Thornton's Diary.* 180 pages. Entries in his handwriting from 1795 to 1814.

VII. *Recollections of Miss Laura Forster.* About 280 pages of typescript. Bound vellum volume. References to events from about 1830 to 1880.

VIII. Various letters, MS. brochures, diaries, notes, etc., dating from about 1750 to 1900. Originally they filled ten tin boxes, which have been reduced in the course of the years to the Sibylline number of three. None of the earlier stuff has been destroyed and there will be no further destruction.

I have many acknowledgements to make. My thanks are due in the first place to my cousin Sir Hugh Thornton and to Lady Thornton for their constant help and encouragement; also to my cousins and connections Mr. John Acland-Troyte, Mrs. Demarest, the Earl of Leven and Melville, Mr. Ronald Southey, Mrs. Ernest Sykes and Mr. John Thornton (the present head of the Thornton family); also to Mr. E. K. Bennett, Dr. G. S. R. Kitson Clark, Mr. B. W. Fagan, Mr. D. M. Joslin, Lady Keynes, Professor G. R. Owst, Miss Eirene Skilbeck, Dr. G. M. Trevelyan, and the Directors of Messrs. Williams Deacon's Bank.

Owing to its domestic character, the Biography falls naturally into the four sections of Daughter, Sister, Aunt, and Great Aunt.

E. M. F.

Cambridge, 1956

Contents

Illustrations

ILLUSTRATIONS

DAUGHTER

1797-1815

A detailed "Pedigree of Thornton of Birkin" was compiled in 1874. The subjoined diagram merely indicates a few of the characters mentioned in this biography. The names of the more important are in *italics*.

Henry Thornton m. *Marianne Sykes*

Marianne	*Henry*	Lucy	Watson	Isabella	Sophia	Henrietta	*Laura*	Charles
	m. (i) Harriet Dealtry. Two *ds.*: *Harti* m. Ruthven Pym; *Emmy* m. Cam Sykes (ii) *Emily Dealtry*		His *d.* Marion m. Reginald Southey	m. Archdeacon Harrison	m. John Melville, afterwards Earl of Leven and Melville	m. Richard Synnot. Two *c.*: son *Inglis* m. *Mary Preston* (*Maimie*); daughter *Henrietta* never married	m. *Rev. Charles Forster.* Ten children including *Laura,* and *Edward* who m. my mother *Alice Clara Whichelo*	

It will be noticed that there are going to be two Henry Thorntons, two Henrietta Synnots and two Laura Forsters. Confusion shall be avoided as far as possible.

ONE

Battersea Rise

Battersea Rise,
Friday morning,
June 20th, 1806.

Pray can you tell me daughter dear
What day's the longest in the year?
Doubtless you'll answer very soon
And say the 21st of June.
But I can prove on grounds the strongest
The twentieth day is now the longest
For since I now am living here
Robbed of my five poor children dear,
Robbed of my valued wife beside
At once my pleasure and my pride,
The twentieth day seems long indeed.
But if you will but make good speed
And come this evening as thou oughtest
Thou'lt make the longest day the shortest.

THESE PRETTY little verses were addressed by Henry Thornton M.P., to his daughter Marianne, then nine years old. They are not characteristic of him. When she was only four he had addressed her and her baby brother in a sterner strain and had warned them in a prose exhortation against the dangers of this life. When she was six he had analysed her faults, and counselled her how to correct them. His exhortations were sincere, like everything else he wrote or did, and the anxieties expressed were genuine. But the words he used—like many of the words then used—will not travel. Whereas the pretty little verses, though they have no literary merit and are a hundred and fifty years old, can still be heard by those who sit quiet. Their affectionate gaiety provides a good approach to one who was herself affectionate and gay, and who loved her father and mother, her brothers and sisters, her nephews and nieces, and, finally, at the end of her long life, her great-nephew, namely myself.

Battersea Rise, the home to which she returned that summer evening, was originally a compact brick house of the age of Queen Anne: three stories high with a front door in the middle, which opened on to a passage running through the house to the garden door at the back. It stood at the west side of Clapham Common, then a wild and marshy tract. Henry Thornton bought it in 1792; he was a prosperous banker who was already hoping for marriage and a family. He started enlarging it and soon trebled its size. To the right and the left of the Queen Anne block he threw out additions—only two stories high, but the rooms were so lofty that the roof-line nearly attained the height of the central block. The front, which was reached by a small "sweep," faced north and remained forbidding. The back became charming. There was a prospect over a great grassed garden, planted with trees, and beyond the garden were fields, cows, horses, and all the amenities of semicountrified life. The Clapham area had become civilised, there was no longer danger from highwaymen, the merchants and politicians who were beginning to settle there could leave their families in safety when they drove the four or five miles up to Westminster, or to the City.

[4]

This was not the end of his building. Close by he built two houses of similar style and rented them to his friends. He shared his own house for four years with William Wilberforce, the abolitionist—of whom there will be much to say. Then he married and filled it with children; Marianne Thornton, the subject of this memoir, was born there in 1797, Henry Sykes Thornton was born there in 1800, Lucy in 1801, Watson in 1802, Isabella (1803), Sophia (1805), Henrietta (1807), Laura (1809), Charles (1810). To them it was a perfect playground and in after years a sacred shrine. It satisfied in them that longing for a particular place, a home, which is common amongst our upper and middle classes, and some of them transmitted that longing to their descendants, who have lived on into an age where it cannot be gratified. There will never be another Battersea Rise, and the modest imitations of it which lasted into the present century and became more and more difficult to staff have also disappeared.

The heart of the house was a fine oval library. This was the most important feature of the Henry Thornton additions, and had been designed for him by his political chief, William Pitt. Several water-colour drawings of the library exist, made by the children when they had grown up; they drew well, Henrietta especially. It had an "Adams" mantelpiece, over which hung the excellent Hoppner portrait of Henry; it had an "Adams" ceiling, busts of Pitt and of Fox, curved bookcases at one end, and at the other end large glass doors, giving on to the garden. To the left of the fireplace was a dignified settee, upholstered in green with red pipings. It had a high back and arms, and against each arm was pressed a sausage-shaped cushion tightly stuffed. When they were children it appears in their macabre caricatures: teeth would be extracted, fits fallen into, ghosts seen in the settee, and later on Marianne was depicted there as a middle-aged lady at her sewing or knitting.

Upstairs there were thirty-four bedrooms. Also the nursery—facing north. I possess the nursery table. It is the one relic of the establishment that has come my way—an oval of dark walnut, six feet by four, resting on a central column, which rests on four strong spreading legs. The oval swivels on a hinge, which can be released by a catch, and each leg is fitted with an easily running caster. Consequently, though the table looks impressive and is indeed my valued dining table, it slides about easily and can even be coaxed along a landing and up a flight of stairs. Underneath the oval, close to the hinge, a small brass plate has been inserted by one of my aunts. "Bought about 1798 for the nursery, Battersea Rise, by Henry Thornton M.P." the inscription runs, and if this is correct the table arrived when Marianne was one year old. It was bought under Nurse Hunter's guidance, for she would have "no table with nasty corners for her children to knock their heads against." She must have sat at it, nursery maids sewn at it, children, not very naughty ones, must have played, eaten, and banged. It passed to Laura Thornton, my grandmother, at her marriage: more playing, eating, banging, by not very naughty children, but not so many nursery maids. Now I sit at it.

The children retained happy memories of the nursery and their loved Nurse Hunter. But it was the prospect from the library into the garden that really captured their imagination. To stand in the noble bow window with the great room behind them, to look out through the high glass door, upon the magnificent tulip tree, became a ritual, and almost a pretaste of heaven. Marianne was to write: "To the day of my death I shall think nothing so lovely as the trees and the lawn at Battersea Rise." Laura, recalling the sad days when their father was dead and their mother dying, was to write: "She used to sit before the library windows and one day she called me and asked if it was I who had been picking branches from the willow tree. I said I had and she said 'Don't ever pick one again. I love that tree because it grows over the urn so beautifully.' And she made me come and stand before her and see how lovely it looked. And I then saw she chose that place to watch the urn." And later on in the century the daughter of that Laura, Laura Forster, stood in the same place as her mother, and she was to write:

I doubt if I was three years old, for we walked about the house at a very early age, and what I remember is being carried into the library at Battersea Rise one cold morning, and being put down by the glass door to watch the men rolling great balls of snow on the lawn and leaving green paths behind them as they went. It was a most fascinating sight and I stood entranced, balancing myself with outspread hands on the glass, and I remember a feeling of acute disappointment, and of being baulked, when someone came behind me and gently took my hands from the window, saying I should get them too cold if I kept them there. I obeyed but felt the men and the great snow-balls were no longer so close to me as before. I have no doubt that my parents were in the group of people breakfasting at the round table in the Library, and I remember the pleasant smell of coffee and toast when I was carried to the window, but I do not know in whose arms I was borne, nor which aunt made me take my hands off the window panes but I feel sure it was not my mother. I believe that I should have said 'Need I?' to her, and that her sympathy would have set me free to stand as I liked. The wide lawn and snow-covered trees glittering in the sun with the men plodding steadily on, rolling the great snow-ball before them, is the very first of many beautiful landscapes that hang like pictures in my memory.

The above is to my mind the great moment in the library-garden ritual, the passage which concentrates the diffused emotions of a hundred years. But there are other references. Marianne herself, in a letter to my mother, has evoked a moment when William Wilberforce was ravished:

He used to go into ecstacies especially about flowers. When staying with us at the time of wicked Queen Caroline's trial [*i.e.*, in 1820] he was one of a deputation of three from the House of Commons to persuade her to give up being crowned, for a large annual allowance. She was half drunk I believe when they got there and she all but kicked them downstairs. Mr Wilberforce came back very low and dispirited, thinking indeed that she would upset the monarchy; when stepping out of the library window before dinner he caught sight of a gorgeous moss-rose that grew up the wall, and seeing how it transfixed him I gathered it. Oh the beauty of it, Oh the goodness of God in giving us such alleviations in this hard world. The bell rang for dinner, there was a large assemblage of notables to meet him, but there was no getting him to go in while he stood worshipping his flower and when he had lavished all other endearments and admiration he ended with 'And Oh how unlike the Queen's countenance'.

And my cousin Dorothy Pym, in her *Battersea Rise*,* has charmingly expressed the enthusiasm of a younger generation. I myself was once taken to the house as a very small boy, and I can just remember a pair of globes. I cannot remember either the library or the garden. The ritual has ended.

Such, so far as I can construct it, was the outward scene, for over a hundred years. Henry Thornton's Battersea Rise did not vary. The grounds behind it were so extensive, the front opposite to Clapham Common so tight and strong that

* Published by Jonathan Cape, 1934.

The Library, Battersea Rise, looking toward the garden

it kept out London until it fell and it fell suddenly. The estate was broken up in 1907. I have identified the area with difficulty. It is completely covered with very small two-storied houses. A couple of roads run through it, north to south, intersected by crossroads. The site was cleared at a time when development was unusually ruthless. Not one tree survives. Clapham Common survives, but so messed about, so full of roads and railings and notices and huts and facilities and infelicities, that Marianne and her mama would not recognise it for the countrified tract through which they drove down on that faraway evening. The pretty little poem, received up in London that morning, would be in the carriage with them, the coachman would wear a flaxen wig and the horses orange and purple election ribbons. Mr. Harrison, the butler (sometimes called "Cuckoo") would open the heavy front door, and Papa himself would be within to greet his "daughter dear."

TWO

The Parents

HER PAPA was of Yorkshire stock. Ancestors had been rectors of Birkin, near York, in the seventeenth century and there is a memorial to them in its church. In 1709 John her great-great-grandfather bought a fine house in Hull, now known as Wilberforce House. Then came the migration to Clapham. Robert, her great-grandfather, moved there in 1735. He was a Director of the Bank of England and a merchant in the Russian trade and it was probably he who bought land extensively at the south side of the Common. This, not Battersea Rise, is the family nucleus. The estate lay close to the present tube-station. Several family houses were built on it. The most important of them survived till 1945, but at present no Thornton memorial can be found in the area except a dilapidated "orangery," to which I will return.

Marianne's grandfather, John (1720-1790) spent most of his life in the house above mentioned. By then the estate had been added to and it was beautifully laid out: the circuit of the grounds measured over two miles. John was, like Robert, a Director of the Bank of England and in the Russian trade. Prosperous and pious, he devoted his great wealth to the promotion of Evangelicalism: he purchased advowsons and installed suitable incumbents; he was the friend of the

Rev. John Newton—I have many of his letters to Newton, and they are beautifully written though not readable otherwise; he was the friend and protector of William Cowper:

> Thee, therefore, of commercial fame but more
> Famed for thy probity from shore to shore—
> Thee Thornton! worthy in some page to shine,
> As honest and more eloquent than mine
> I mourn,

sang the poet at John's death. He promoted the spiritual welfare of seamen, and his portrait was painted for the Royal Marine Society by Gainsborough—by a Gainsborough who was thoroughly bored. Slumped and potbellied, John sits. In another version of the picture he is attended by a soldier and a sailor, to each of whom he hands a copy of the Scriptures.

Henry Thornton was critical of both his parents, and his references to his father are notably unfilial and cool. He censures old John for being "rough, vehement and eager," for his indifference to education, for his incorrectness of speech, for allotting too little time to secret prayer, and for being a Jack-of-all-trades. He admits that he improved, that he gave up hunting, was not self-indulgent, walked out of the room when an improper toast was sung, and spent between £2,000 and £3,000 on the extension of Gospel knowledge. But a dissatisfied tone persists. Of his mother (nee Lucy Watson) he says less. I would like to know more. She too was both wealthy and religious. I possess a poignant fragment of her diary, in which she sees, with terrible clarity, that the time must come when it will not be known that Lucy Thornton ever lived. She stands on the brink of an oblivion which frightened her: it doesn't frighten us now—we are used to it. In fantastic contrast to her diary is her MS.

cookery book. It is a vellum-bound volume, dated 1756, and full of rich recipes in her handwriting and in the handwritings of friends and of housekeepers. The Thorntons deplored luxury but insisted on having enough to eat. Prayers before plenty. But plenty!

Marianne never knew these worthy grandparents—they died too soon. But she became well acquainted with the next generation: with her uncles Samuel and Robert, with her Aunt Jane, and above all with her own papa.

Henry (1760-1815) was the youngest son. He had been born over in the family house. He had left a journal and some reminiscences behind him, so his early career can be followed. He was critical of his home and of his Wandsworth school, but enjoyed a visit to Paris; there he saw Queen Marie Antoinette "in all her beauty" and stood close to her—a strange thrill for so sedate a boy. On his return his parents insisted on his attending the English court also, for they believed in British liberties, and sent him and his brother unsuitably dressed: the poor children wore their school suits—blue clothes with blue buttons—and felt miserable. Then he attended another school, which was better, though some of the West Indian scholars were "very vicious," and he returned to his parents' house at nineteen; imperfectly educated.

Thereafter he began to get upsides with life. He took himself in hand. The family aptitude for money-making developed in him, and after apprenticeship in the counting-houses of a cousin and of his father he joined, at twenty-four, the banking house of Down, Thornton & Free. He also found himself religions. To the ill-regulated piety of his parents there succeeded a piety that satisfied him, and found vent in constructive charity. In 1790 he gave away over £2,000; in

Henry Thornton, M.P.
by John Hoppner (about 1814)

1793 over £6,000. Parliament attracted him, because that way he might do good. He worked with his second cousin and close friend, William Wilberforce, to abolish the slave trade. He became Chairman of the Sierra Leone Company, first President of the Sunday School Society, etc., but he was never (as is sometimes stated) Governor of the Bank of England. After an attempt to stand for Hull, he was elected member for Southwark in 1782, to be re-elected seven or eight times. He was a close friend of Hannah More and supported her educational schemes. He published *An Enquiry into the Nature and Effects of the Paper Credit of Great Britain*— a work which after a period of oblivion has now a high reputation among economists. (His *Family Prayers* were published posthumously.) He comes out as a typical Thornton, pious, benevolent, industrious, serious, wealthy, shrewd. What distinguishes him from the rest of them was his outstanding intellect. This appears not only in his important public career but in his private letters. He never pens a sentence that is clumsy or feeble, and he knows exactly what he wants to say. What a contrast is the portrait of him, by Hoppner, to his father's portrait! Cold, intellectual, public-spirited, fastidious, and full of integrity, Henry stands, and his hand rests upon a parliamentary bill.*

Such was Papa. What of Mama?

The portrait of Miss Mary Ann (or Marianne) Sykes of West Ella near Hull looks down on me as I write. It is by Sir George Chalmers, a Scottish baronet who was then living in Hull; it is signed by him and is dated 1777. The charming girl is in fancy dress—for what else could that

---

* The original is a fine piece of work, of which no idea can be gained from the engraving in the House of Commons. A crimson background and a dark blue coat emphasise the pallor and the severity of the face most impressively.

high frothy white turban denote, what else that low-cut blue
bodice with short sleeves? Her brown hair is cut straight
across her forehead like a boy's, ringlets behind mingling
with the tassels that depend from the turban. Her expression
is discreet and happy. She fondles a spaniel on a plinth,
strokes its head, holds its paw, and its free paw scratches at
her bodice. That's my great-grandmother, that's Marianne's
beloved Mama. She looks seventeen, but if the date is correct she can only be twelve. That very year she wrote to her
father from Lichfield:

Yes Papa, I am very happy at Litchfield. I read practice get
by heart talk laugh play at cards and eat oysters. . . . I am
going with Miss Seward to a party of commerce of grown ladies. I have finished Cornaro and the Turk and have began
Milton's morning hymn. My love and duty where it is due and
where I hope I shall always pay it. Your dutiful daughter
Marianne Sykes.

Her parents, the Joseph Sykeses, were of precisely the
same social class as the Thorntons, equally pious, similarly
rich, and more thoroughly Yorkshire. Her father was a merchant in the Russian trade. He had given her a sound education, and the Miss Seward mentioned above—the famous
Swan of Lichfield—had been her governess and had indeed
tried to be her sister-in-law. It is difficult to estimate her
character for the reason that it soon resembled her husband's. She became moon to his sun. He first met her during
his unsuccessful election campaign at Hull. From his autobiography:

I called on many of the principal gentlemen of Hull and was
well received. It is worthy of being recorded that I for the first
time visited that house at West Ella where the future partner

of my life was then residing. I well remember to have enquired before I went to the door, after the usual manner of a canvasser whether Mr Sykes had any family. I also recollect that I was told (I forget by whom) that beside his sons he had one daughter and that she was reckoned a very sensible young woman. I saw her sitting in the large bow room, she being then probably about 14 years old. How wonderful are the ways of Providence! The person whom I then accosted in those terms of general civility which I was then lavishing upon a multitude of others has at the time at which I now write been 7 years my wife.

In 1790, Miss Sykes went to Buxton with her brother Dan, who had been unwell, and she wrote to her mother about her future husband as follows:

Daniel's attack has been a slight one and he is now I think better than when we left West Ella. I have hired a pony to attend him in his rides when I can, and we discuss and talk nonsense as much as ever. Sometimes Mr H. Thornton brings a book and reads to us and last night he set me to read to them—when I tell you the book you will not think it too rigid: it was the Loves of the Plants. . . . Surely nothing short of witchcraft could inform you I was unwell—the truth is this horrid water has disagreed with me. Mr H. T. gives me lectures on the duty of preserving my health. . . . Time does not hang very heavy on my hands for when Daniel does not want me I ramble over these bleak moors in quest of misery, poverty I always meet with but generally so much content as makes me blush—their simplicity pleases me and a few shillings gratifies them, and I leave them I hope not unimproved by the acquaintance. I have never admitted Mr H. T. to be of my party but once, and then I could not well decline it for he had dined with us on the Sunday, and as we were the only Spa people at church in the afternoon and as he earnestly requested it I thought he might as well come with me as walk home with him to the Crescent in full view of everybody. He has just called.

Six years later he makes his proposal of marriage. It is a touching letter, with its mixture of the tender and the formal, and it can be best understood by readers who tolerate an outmoded approach to love. Writing from Battersea Rise, he reminds her of her encouraging behaviour to him some time back, and explains that he received it with the greater reserve because "it was so clear a point in my mind that I ought not then to change my situation in life" or "allow myself to entertain any immediate thoughts of a more intimate connection with you." The reference is to his father's last illness, which had greatly occupied him. A reference then follows to another suitor, whose attentions he had thought it not right to disturb. He can speak freely now, and he does so with delicacy and with strength.

To talk much of my attachment in this letter is perhaps more than I ought to presume to do—but I must add that before my inclinations were allowed to guide me, my judgement led me to prefer you to any woman I had ever seen, and now that I feel at liberty to exercise my inclinations, I find that if you do not forbid them, together with everything else that I am able to give you, you will certainly have my heart.

I will tell you fairly, and thus early that my own views of this life and the happiness of it, even in the best situations, are very moderate, and it is in the pleasing certainty of your being one that will help my everlasting interests, and one whom I may hope to meet in a better world that I look on you with the most complacency.

He wrote this letter on a Saturday. Miss Sykes, who was then in London, replied to it on the Sunday. She expressed her regret at being obliged to write a letter on such a day and she declined his proposal. On Tuesday she accepted it. In the following month they were married. So sudden an end to so leisurely an acquaintance may be explained by the ill health of her mother: they desired the happy event to take place in her lifetime. Neither bride nor bridegroom was now young, and each entered matrimony with a good understanding of the other's character. There were no surprises. And there was no penury. The bride was amply dowered and her husband had amassed a substantial fortune. Writing to her father shortly before the wedding she says:

Mr T. tells me that in my Settlement he has merely consulted established custom because it is right in these sort of matters to go with the world, but in case of my surviving him all his worldly possessions devolve to me—one grand motive of his attachment being that striking similarity in many of our sentiments which will necessarily incline me to dispose of my income just as he does at present. His present *domestic* expenses are about £3000 per ann. and he thinks the additional establishment of carriages and horses proper for my accommodation will not amount to quite £1000 more. I will send Mary [her Yorkshire servant] down when opportunity offers, for as Mr T. has already a house-keeper and 4 other female servants in each of his houses, it would be absurd to introduce any more, especially as he wishes the present two mistresses of his establishments to wait on my person. Battersea Rise I have not yet seen, but the house in town where I dined the other day is so large that it banished all apprehensions of closeness.*

To her mother:

Mr T. tells me we must do good both to the bodies and souls of men and to gain an influence over the minds of our equals is

* The town house at that date was in King's Yard, Coleman Street, near Birchin Lane and the Bank. Later on it was at Palace Yard, Westminster, close to the Houses of Parliament.

perhaps most necessary, which cannot be done if we are not equally free from austerity and ostentation. Laying this down as a general rule, I am going this morning about my clothes. Moderation and modesty is to be the order of the day, but yet my dress is to be elegant and fashionable.

Marriage promised harmony and fulfilled its promise despite the French Revolution and Napoleonic wars. Fate held no major surprises for the prosperous couple: an occasional stillborn child, a disputed election, an absconding servant, Henry's irritability and poor health—that is all that they seem to have had to face. I say "seem to have had" because their letters and the Thornton papers generally have been tidied up by pious editresses. The copies on which I have often to rely may conceal omissions. That the marriage was happy cannot however be doubted. In all the letters that pass between Henry Thornton and his wife there is gratitude and quiet confidence. Sixteen years after marriage he can write to her: "And now before I close my Sunday's scrawl let me tell you, my dear M, how much I think of you and associate you in all my cares temporal and spiritual, May God bless you for all your kindness to me and above all for giving me your helping hand on the way to Heaven." And in his private journal: "Her conversation is on subjects of Importance. I think I have known no woman whose topics are better chosen and more suitably treated."

An expected event approached. At the end of 1796 Henry writes to his father-in-law:

There is one piece of information which I have been slow in giving you because I feared it might increase your anxiety. Marianne is then likely to become a mother within no very long period if it pleases God to continue her present health. . . . I cannot too strongly express the confidence I feel that she will

Marianne Sykes (Mrs. Henry Thornton)
by Sir George Chalmers (1777)

fulfil every new relative duty in life in a Christian manner tho' in this as in other matters she retains her usual diffidence.

In February 1797 Mrs. Thornton writes to Hannah More, the friend and counsellor of her husband, with whom she herself had become friends after some diffidence—and perhaps after some jealousy. She "cannot forbear to seize one of the last gleams of health that may be left to me to express to you once more my thanks for the warm and lively interest you have taken in my happiness. It seems to me as if there were but a faint probability that we shall meet again in this world." She finds "the very prospect of suffering and danger" a blessing since it may rouse her mind from earthly to eternal matters, she has listened to the "soothing and persuasive sermons" of the rector of Clapham, John Venn, and "whenever I have been assailed by gloomy fears Mr H. T. has been at hand to dispel them by sound arguments and to pray with me and for me." The event followed, and on March 10, 1797, Marianne Thornton was born.

Henry Thornton to his father-in-law:

My dear Sir—It is with the utmost satisfaction that I write to tell you that my dear M. at 4. o'clock this morning gave me a fine little girl and both she and the child are doing extremely well. I have just been talking to her for half an hour and her mind is calm and happy, so much so that she is at present only afraid of giving vent to the joyful and grateful feelings which are ready to agitate her. I will not add more than my assurance (which I trust is superfluous) that I shall take great care of her and not suffer too much company to come near her, till her strength is a little restored. She hopes to nurse her little girl herself and the prospect gives her great pleasure.—

Yrs ever very aff. H. T.

[*19*]

To Hannah More:

I am just returned from the House like a labourer after his week's work, and am receiving my pay in the smiles of my wife and little girl, both of whom are doing well. I have been truly fagged this week or two and they tell me I rather grow thin upon it, but thank God I feel tolerably. . . . I am not without a little ray of hope of peace [with France] but it is a very little one. I have been going thro' long examinations of the Bank affairs and I am now going to return to the labours of my own committee where I know not when I shall have done sitting.

Such was the atmosphere, such the household, into which Marianne Thornton was born: affections, comfort, piety, integrity, intelligence, public activity, private benevolence: and transcending them all an unshaken belief in a future life where the members of the household would meet again and would recognise each other and be happy eternally. It is this belief that makes the "Clapham Sect" seem remote today, even to Christians. Personal immortality today may not be denied by orthodoxy, but it is played down, it is felt to be self-centred and antisocial, it is seldom conceived as a changeless background for family life as it was at Battersea Rise. Our hopes of continuance, when we entertain them, are arguably more spiritual. Then, they were a solid possession, to be maintained by prayers, self-questionings, and good deeds, and to be confirmed finally through the mercy of God.

THREE

On Clapham Common

WHEN MARIANNE was sixty years old and had left Battersea
Rise under painful circumstances, she wrote down some recollections of her childhood. They begin as follows:

I think that I must naturally have been very timid, for I can
remember suffering intensely from all sorts of terrors. There
were parts of the Battersea Rise garden I dared not visit alone.
I could not endure being left in the dark, and being bathed in
the sea almost killed me with fright, and I believe there was
hardly any quality my father valued so much as courage, and
he possessed it himself in an eminent degree. But I was never
laughed at and never scolded for my fancies, but soothed, and
indulged, as some people would have thought, in consequence.
I was never put to bed in the dark, but my mother often used
to place a new toy, or some fruit or sugar plums in an adjoining dark room first shewing me there was nothing there that
could hurt me, and then told me if I liked to fetch it I might
have it. One corner of the dark walk where I had once been
frightened by a dog was made into a little garden for me, and
after playing there all day with my nurse I forgot the horror
I had of passing it. Then at the sea my own dear nurse undressed and went into the water with me, letting me at first only
play with it. I had the greatest fear of horses but very gradually I was induced to mount a donkey, then to sit before my
father while he cantered his horse about the field, and by the

time I was six years old I had a pony of my own and enjoyed beyond measure riding nearly into London every day with my father and escorted by an old coachman who brought me back.

The "Recollections" continue with a portrait of Nurse Hunter:

We were much less indebted to our governesses for our education than to dear old nurse Hunter. Not that she was old then. I can recollect her the most lively, active, healthy personification of a nurse, never weary, never irritable, never overdone by the sick babies by night, or the well ones by day. There never was such a temper with such warm glowing affections. We all felt indescribable confidence in her sense of right and wrong, and in her sympathy with us all combined with the strongest feeling of justice. Our delight in her society increased with our age. She was a woman of great talent and sagacity, though she had scarcely any learning as she used to say, for she had gone to service at 11, and a capital servant I have no doubt she then made. She never opened any book except her Bible on Sundays, and her letters, tho' very clever, were scarcely legible from the bad spelling and writing. Every visitor who came much to the house treated her quite as a friend, but she never forgot her place, and was very indignant at what she thought the disrespectful manners of modern times. But she always talked about 'our money' and 'our children' just as if they were joint property. There was a sort of feudal feeling about her which made her quite incapable of separating her interests from ours during the 52 years she lived in our house, and all that time she never asked for a holiday. 'I hate the nurses' she said 'who can bear to leave their precious children.'

She was excessively untidy which she maintained was needful if you wished children to be happy, and her untidiness did not prevent her from being extremely clean. We might bring flowers stones and playthings into the nursery till the floor was strewn with them without a remonstrance from her, but ceaseless were the scrubbings and sweepings and shakings that the floor and carpet underwent every day in consequence. She had a great dislike to needlework and was fond of a story of Mr Venn's nurse, who, when knitting stockings when walking out with her children, let little Maria Venn fall into the water. She thought 'the girls' as she called all nursery maids, the proper people to sit sewing, but the care of the children, body and mind, she would share with no one. No hands except her own put each child in succession into its tub of water every morning, and soaped and rubbed and dried them, turning each out for a walk when the weather was tolerable. To no one but 'Nursey' could we say our prayers comfortably, nor could any one else tuck us up to our satisfaction. Indeed she continued to undress me until within ten years of her death, when she became too infirm to sit up late, but until I was forty no one else had ever put me to bed. I always enjoyed having her for the sake of conversation with her. She was the safest possible confidante on all topics and for this reason was wonderfully entrusted with all our secrets. Her sayings, expressed in strange quaint words, had great weight with us, and remain as proverbs amongst us, to this day.

Some of Nurse Hunter's sayings have been preserved. They now seem insufficiently quaint. "What's the use of a Judge and wig when you *know* a man has done a thing? You should just take and hang him" is a slogan which has become all too familiar to the twentieth century. Nor is one impressed by her advice about choosing a housemaid: "Well there's but one choice: the pretty ones the men are after and the ugly ones are after the men." Wiser was her "Try and let it pass my dear" when a quarrel was beating up in the nursery.

From the nursery we pass to the schoolroom, and to Henry Thornton's ideas on education:

[*23*]

My father had a strong idea that half the naughtiness of little children arose from want of employment, and that they have a very early perception of the difference between amusing themselves and doing something that saved trouble to others. As soon as I could speak so as to be understood I used to be their waiter at breakfast and was sent to the butler to ask for whatever was wanted instead of ringing the bell. I had to put the chairs and books in their places, and to put by my own playthings whenever I was tired of playing with them, and when I could work at all I had to sew strings on my bonnet and pinafores, and do many odd jobs that are usually left to a nursery maid.

When I could write legibly I was made a sort of secretary to my father whose friends must have been astonished at receiving notes of invitation written in a child's round text hand. I copied his MS. instead of writing copies and in the same manner when I could do sums my earliest lessons in arithmetic consisted in adding up the house accounts for my mother, and when a little older I was employed in various calculations relating to the household expenses, such as how much bread, meat, &c., were consumed weekly by each person, what was the cost of the board of a servant, &c. My father never made the least mystery with me about his expenditure, every year he calculated to what sum each head in his account book should amount, and if one became larger than he expected he reduced another in proportion. All this amused and interested me extremely and gave me a pleasant idea of the meaning of the word economy, which he often explained did not mean saving but a right distribution of property. Amongst other amusements I was allowed to churn some butter for the library breakfast every morning by shaking cream in a wide mouthed bottle, in the garden in summer, in the dining room in winter; it was good exercise before breakfast and I liked it but I believe my governesses were not a little surprised by what they considered the menial occupations that were given me. But being three years older than Henry I was in some measure like an only child, and was therefore employed in many ways not customary in a nursery full of children.

As soon as I could do so intelligently I had to read the *Morning Chronicle* every morning whilst my father and mother breakfasted. Those were days of great interest, when we were all in hourly fear of invasion, owing to Bonaparte's successes, and as children we were all taught to care much about public events. My father wrote a paper on the duty of interesting young pepole in such matters, in the *Christian Observer*. He even tried to make me understand a little about paper-credit and the bullion question, as I had many papers on these subjects to copy for him. When we lived in Palace Yard I heard so much about the debates in the House of Commons, that he sometimes came to my bedside when he returned and told me what had been the Division. He was not afraid of my becoming hot on such subjects, I suppose his own opinions were so calm and dispassionate. The contested elections in the Borough of Southwark, of which he had to undergo I think eight, were always made an occasion for giving us useful lessons.

Here is the attitude towards "the Staff":

Nothing could exceed the kindness of my father and mother to all their servants and their families. They objected strongly to the usual restriction of 'no followers allowed' and used to say that a servant who would consent to cut all connection with her friends and relations could not be worth having. They were told when and how they could see their friends, and were encouraged to tell all their family circumstances. Many a country girl was allowed to invite her old father and mother to stay for a few days, and a present made towards their journey. Many a younger sister has come to our house to find a place and remained till she could hear of a promising one. Married man servants were preferred to single. My father used to give them higher wages because he thought they were steadier and less likely to leave their situation and he thought it a duty to give the good wages for sobriety and steadiness that are usually only given for superior dexterity and knowledge of their work. Both he and my mother paid peculiar attention to the lower servants, such as the underhousemaid and the kitchen maid, the helper in the stables and washer woman in the laundry, fancying these were often overworked and tyranically treated by the upper servants. There were not so many conveyances to London as there are now. If they missed Harriet Butler's coach in the morning there was no chance of getting there that day, and if it was a case of illness, or a maid had been promised a holiday, or any reason of that sort it seemed a natural arrangement that the carriage should take her. If the roads were heavy it was thought cruel to drive even to town with only a pair. The four were driven by our old coachman who lived for forty years in the house, and wore a flaxen wig and cocked hat, the horses with cockades of blue and orange, my father's election colours, yet the whole excited no more attention than a one-horse fly would now.

The above reminiscences show that Battersea Rise was anything but a "Victorian" establishment and that charges of narrowness and stuffiness must be brought against it with caution. It appears, rather, as a blend of feudal loyalty and eighteenth-century enlightenment, as a home where the nursery could visit the schoolroom, the schoolroom the library, and all of them the pantry without self-consciousness. For an intelligent, good-tempered child life there must have been very pleasant, and in after days, with the nineteenth century cramping her, she looked back on it as golden.

Let us now advance on to Clapham Common and see what is happening there. What was later called the "Clapham Sect" had come into being. Wherever she walked the child found herself surrounded by assorted saints. It was not a

closed sainthood, there were no entry tests, no esoteric hush-
hush, but the members of it shared so many interests that
they hung together, and lived as near to each other as they
could.

Nearest in kinship were the two uncles who lived in grandeur on the great family estate at the south side of the Common—Uncle Sam and Uncle Robert. As regards each of
these there was, however, a reservation.

In the case of Uncle Sam the reservation is difficult to de-
fine, for he was a pious Evangelical, he was a banker and
an M.P., he was head of the family and entitled to respect
on that count, he was benevolent, and he had children of the
same age as the little Henry Thorntons. And there was ade-
quate intercourse between the two families, particularly
while the Samuels stayed at Clapham. But an undertone of
disapproval, such as we have already noticed in Henry's references to his father, comes into Marianne's "Recollections."

My uncle Mr Samuel Thornton was anxious to connect himself with fashionable people. He quitted his house on Clapham
Common and bought Albury Park, became M.P. for Surrey
and certainly looked down on my father whose society consisted of people who were his associates in his works of benevolence and charity, and who were his companions in political affairs. He often smiled at his brother's ideas of the importance
of the Thornton family. 'We are all City people and connected
with merchants, and nothing but merchants on every side,' he
used to say and if we reminded him of the Levens, he did not
scruple to tell us that the only thing that his father had ever
done that he much lamented was allowing his daughter to marry
Lord Leven.

Samuel's diary has been preserved and been privately
printed. It covers the years 1774-1838. Its tone is sober and
charitable.

In the case of Uncle Robert, Marianne's "Recollections" are more explicit, and more sympathetic.

We were very fond of our Uncle Robert. He was a most agreeable, lively and pleasant man, but my father was always very anxious about him, and he at length got into difficulties which obliged him to leave the country, and he died many years afterwards under a feigned name in New York. He had embellished the grounds of his villa on Clapham Common, built an exquisite greenhouse, and had the most expensive gardens in this vicinity. He also spent large sums on Books and prints and became intimate with some of the Royal Dukes, the sons of George the 3rd., particularly the Duke of Cumberland, a very bad man who afterwards became King of Hanover. My uncle gave a breakfast at his house on Clapham Common to Queen Charlotte and her daughters, and I with some difficulty persuaded my father to let my sister Lucy and myself go to it, though he and my mother would not be present themselves, and he stipulated there should be no expensive dresses for the occasion. I remember we did wear only our Sunday white frocks and blue sashes, no bonnets, our hair was always cut short as little boys are now. He took us up to the Queen who very goodnaturedly observed that she supposed we were always delighted to walk in our Uncle's beautiful garden on which I was so rude as to reply that ours was more beautiful still, which sounded like boasting on my part. But it was the plain truth for then and now and to the day of my death I shall always think nothing so lovely as the trees and the lawn at Battersea Rise. I fancy that my father and mother would not go to this fête because they disapproved of the expense, and my aunt, Mrs Robert Thornton, who disliked the whole thing, took to her bed on the occasion.

The grand breakfast referred to took place in 1808: there is a gratified notice about it in the Parish Register. But in 1810 Uncle Robert had to sell his property, in 1814 he vanished, leaving a disconsolate wife, no children and many debts.

A detailed account of this disaster is given in a letter from Mrs. Thornton to a Miss Patty Smith; Miss Smith, a member of another pious banking family, became in later years a friend and correspondent of Marianne's.

The story is indeed a bad one as must ever be the case in gambling transactions, but probably it is far less atrocious than malice will represent it. His account to Mr H. T. (the only human being whom he would see since the affair became public) is nearly as follows. That he has been long sick of the world, that he had a half formed intention of quitting the India House and also Parl^t and his Place, but this would not be done without an independence, that he had gained his share of omnium * £10,000, and with that gain *only* he would speculate in the Stocks. At first he was very successful & gained 30 or 40,000. This very success proved fatal, for enamoured of his own sagacity he went on venturing more and more, till the depression in the Stocks annihilated all his gains & in the true spirit of a gambler he attempted to retrieve this loss by desperate efforts & at last foiled and disappointed in every effort he became a defaulter to the amount of 45,000. Many of his private debts he half and some entirely liquidated by giving his prints or plates or minerals, to others he gave nothing, in this distribution he attended more to feeling than to justice, and those Creditors who get nothing are justly angry. By this time he has left the Kingdom.

His story is very affecting & very instructive. With 40 or 50,000£ from his father, a kind & generous heart & a very fine temper what a wreck has he made of Life! Now a fugitive,

---

* At that period, when the Government issued a loan, the subscribers received mixed amounts of various types of stock. These were known as an "Omnium." When the loan was fully paid up, the Omnium was converted into its component stocks. I am indebted to Mr. David Joslin for this information and for other facts about Robert Thornton's public career.

without character, without money & friendless as the most forlorn of human Beings! He happily has no arrears due as Marshal. I wish you would ask your father what he thinks of his resigning or retaining the Place & wht is likely to be said about it in Parl^t. I know it is the wish of Mr H. T. that he should not keep it, *confidentially* he offered to allow him some hundreds p^r an if he would not take it, but one great fault in R. T. has been obstinate adherence to his own plans. Poor Mrs R. T. is much to be pitied, but that she has called for. May God in his great mercy pardon the faults of both, & reconcile them to each other before that final separation which must embitter the heart of the survivor with recollections that sorrow cannot efface nor future good resolutions do away. I have never seen Mr. H. T. so deeply affected by an event as this.

The virtuous Henry behaved well over the scandal: not one touch of smugness, only affection, concern for his brother's health, and desire to help him. Robert lived till March 1826 and according to their brother Samuel "through Divine grace terminated a life of variable anxiety in peace and in comfort." I should like to think so, and I have sometimes wondered whether he may not have founded a Thornton family in the United States. He sounds capable of it, and his wife had failed to accompany him into exile. There are two memorials of Robert on this side: firstly the exquisite greenhouse or "orangery" where he entertained Queen Charlotte, an elegant classical building with seven columns and a pediment—that is to say, it was elegant until recently: it looks death and desolation now in the midst of an L.C.C. housing estate, and ironic is the quotation from the Georgics on it, promising summer in winter and eternal spring.

Hic ver assiduum atque alienis mensibus aestas.

The other relic is his "town house," 6 Grafton Street, W.1—a sombre solid building which he occupied from 1792 to

1814; it is the only house that survives from that generation of Thorntons.

Marianne's aunt Jane—who had married the Earl of Leven and Melville—seldom occurs in her annals. The Levens spent most of their time up in Scotland. There was a close banking connection between the two families, and further marriages were to connect them in the future.

Next to be mentioned by Marianne in the "Recollections" are the Venns, the beloved family at the Rectory.

My great friends from my infancy were the Venns, and they have remained so till this day. Every feeling of love and reverence that ought to be felt towards a clergyman was his. As a little child I can recollect how his entrance into the room seemed to brighten everybody and everything in it, how my father and mother enjoyed his conversation and looked up to him for advice and welcomed his pastoral ministration. His children were chiefly educated by himself, and I was continually sent to the Rectory for the day when my mother was going out, and shared in his instructions and in his hospitalities, for it was the most hospitable house on the Common. His daughters were very remarkable as children; in Emilia there was a degree of originality and shrewdness, a power of seizing on the truth of any subject, and I must add a power of putting everything in the most amusing light that I have never seen equalled. (For many years her unrivalled powers have been devoted to doing good in her brother's parish.)

The first time I realized the fact that this is a world of sorrow was when Mr Venn died. I was a great deal there, and their sorrow was beyond all control. They were to leave their home at Clapham and be under the care of an aunt whom they did not then much like, and they had lost their most loved father. It seemed to me then a degree of misery no one could survive, and I remember my father saying to me 'This is your first experience that death has entered into the world, may you learn from it how unsafe it is to rest in it for all our happiness,' and the thought rushed me could it be possible that I too should ever be called to suffer such agony.

John Venn had been born in Clapham and had been given the living by the trustees of old John Thornton. He was a founder of the Church Missionary Society. Doctrinally as well as personally he was all that Battersea Rise could desire. The church where he ministered for twenty years is the one on Clapham Common, Holy Trinity. Too ponderous to be quaint, it is now a depressing object. Bombs in a World War have not romanticised it, and rarely does the visitor try to people its heavy interior with the heavy families who once worshipped there. The power of the Church over the Thorntons was moral rather than mystic. They were indifferent to ceremony, their references to Holy Communion are temperate, and though they desired sound doctrine they were not upset by deviations from it. What did excite them was Mr. Venn's sermons. They listened to sermons with avidity, copied them out and posted them to each other. They also preached and had prayers in their own home: Henry Thornton's *Family Prayers* are composed for that very purpose. Battersea Rise library with the united family kneeling seemed more sacred to them than any consecrated edifice. The Venns too were a family and had family prayers at the Rectory. The enduring link was here.

The Grants lived close to us, and in nearly every confinement Mrs Grant came to nurse my mother, and she generally brought over some of her daughters. The youngest was then some years older than I was, but my earliest recollections of them all was their continually stealing me away from our garden and playing with me. They lived where the Horners do now, and our houses and grounds were almost common property.

The girls used to teach me poetry, and tell me fairy tales and amuse themselves and me by taking me long walks and pretending we were heroes or heroines in such tales as Tom Thumb, or sometimes the Pilgrim's Progress. My father and mother delighted in the Grants more than in any other family with whom they were acquainted as their letters abundantly shew. There was a refinement about them almost amounting to fastidiousness which was not so common amongst the higher ranks as it is now, and which peculiarly suited my father and mother. The second daughter Charamile was their great favourite, but no words of mine can describe her. When she died I remember Sir Thos. Acland saying 'she had all Robert's wit and all Charles's eloquence' alluding to her two brothers; and Mme de Stael said of her that she came nearer to her idea of her own Corinne than any one she had ever met. Though ten years older than I was from my very infancy she exercised a sort of witchery over me. The Lay of the Last Minstrel I first heard when it came out by her repeating it to me after I was in bed. Fairy tales, old ballads, romances of ancient times were familiar words to her, and as I grew older the masters of mighty song were all made known to me by her. Perhaps she made me rather too impatient of dullness, and led me to be too much disgusted by vulgarity and to fancy too much that all the world was wrong and we were right, still there were few people so gifted. I thought so then and I am sure of it now. She captivated every one that she wished to please, but perhaps that was not saying much, for the Grants were not generally popular and really did not wish to be so. They were devotedly attached to each other and to a small circle of friends who they thought appreciated them. There I am now sure they were wrong, and many of them now survive to think so too. It is true that it is bad to have crowds of acquaintances and no friends, but it is wrong also to shut oneself up in a home circle where all we say or do is sure to be admired.

But with all their faults there was an indescribable charm about the Grants. The majestic old head of the family 'the

Director' as his children called him kept us all rather in awe, but he was too much occupied in governing the India House, and in House of Commons business to be much with his family. Mrs Grant was the loveliest sweetest type of an Indian mother, I mean of a woman who had married in India and had a large family around her, every one of whom leant upon her for comfort and advice and sympathy in a way I hardly ever saw in any other household. She adopted all of us from love to my mother as if we had been her own. Their house was always open to us, and every event of joy or sorrow that occurred in ours brought her to us, and when the last and saddest days of sickness and separation drew nearer Mrs Grant was at her post 'surely sent into this world to soothe the sick and the dying, so soft so gentle, so unwearied'.

Also next door for a time lived the friend of friends, William Wilberforce. He and Hannah More were the two whom she took over from her parents when they died, and Wilberforce had the advantage of belonging to Clapham; he had even lived at Battersea Rise once. It is with the saintly, gay, and innocent side of his character that her "Recollections" deal; they ignore the cleverness and astuteness which are evident in his public life and sometimes remind us of Gandhi:

Mr Wilberforce seemed so entirely one of our family that I cannot describe my *first* impression of him any more than of my own father, indeed I can remember having a game of play with him earlier than with any one. He was as restless and as volatile as a child himself, and during the long and grave discussions that went on between him and my father and others, he was most thankful to refresh himself by throwing a ball or a bunch of flowers at me, or opening the glass door and going off with me for a race on the lawn 'to warm his feet'. I know one of my first lessons was I must never disturb Papa when he was talking or reading, but no such prohibition existed with Mr Wilberforce. His love for, and enjoyment in, all children was remarkable, and he had a strong reason for his affection for all of us. My grandfather Mr Joseph Sykes of West Ella had been his guardian, and as a boy he spent his holidays at his house, and of course became as intimate as a brother with my mother and her brothers. His delight at her marriage afterwards with 'the dearest friend he had in the world' he expressed most warmly, and up to the day of her death his affection for her never varied.

I once heard him say that the union between her and my father gave him such a delightful idea of domestic life that it made him determined to marry also, but he was not equally fortunate in his choice. He fell in love very suddenly with a Miss Barbara Spooner, the only religious member of a worldly family, and she confided to Mr Wilberforce all her persecutions and difficulties. She was extremely handsome and in some ways very clever, but very deficient in common sense, a woman with narrow views and selfish aims, that is if selfishness can be so called when it took the shape of idolatry of her husband, and thinking everything in the world ought to give way to what she thought expedient for him. Instead of helping him forward in the great works which it appeared Providence had given him to do, she always considered she was hardly used when he left her side, and instead of making his home attractive to the crowds of superior people that he invited, her love of economy made her anything but a hospitable hostess. Yet the oddity and queerness of the scenes that went on there often made up, especially to young people, for all other deficiencies.

The passage continues with reminiscences which relate to a later period—and continues to be sub-acid on the topic of Mrs. Wilberforce.

One of Mr Wilberforce's constant inmates was Dr Milner the Dean of Carlisle, the most enormous man it was ever my fate to see in a drawing-room. He was a rough loud and rather coarse man, but he used to say all he thought and ask for all

he wanted, in a way no one else ever ventured to do, in the
many Wilberforce homes he visited. The real bond of union
between him and Mr Wilberforce was that he was a deeply religious man, and how clever he was the records of Cambridge
honours shew. 'Now Wilberforce listen, for no power will make
me repeat what I am going to say' used to be his rough exclamation when Mr W. was flitting after a child, a cat, a flower
or a new book, when they had met to discuss some important
point. At the Wilberforce breakfasts, when he chiefly received
company, there was the most extraordinary mixture of guests,
and an equally strange want of the common usages of life. To
use a Yorkshire expression of his—everyone was expected to
fend for themselves. He was so short-sighted he could see nothing beyond his own plate, which Mrs W. took care to supply
with all he wanted till the Dean's stentorian voice was heard
roaring 'there was nothing on earth to eat', and desiring the
servants to bring some bread and butter, he would add 'and
bring plenty without limit', while Mr W. would join in with
'thank you, thank you kindly Milner, for seeing to these things,
Mrs Wilberforce is not strong eno' to meddle much in domestic
matters'. I remember my mother saying to some one who wished
he had married a different woman 'that no one would have
known how much of the angel there was in him if they had not
seen his behaviour to one whose different tastes must have tried
his patience so much'. But never for a moment did it fail, he
was always throwing his shield over her, bringing forward her
best points and trying to persuade other people that if they
knew her well they would value her more. It was one of the
bright parts of my mother's character that she was always so
kind to Mrs Wilberforce. In a fearful infectious fever my
mother nursed her like a sister, and always shewed her affection
for her old friend by doing all she could for his wife, and taking the whole party into our house whenever they could come,
which was often.

At the other end of the Common, near the present public house of the Plough, lived a family who were to become as famous as the Wilberforces: the Macaulays. Zachary Macaulay—friend and ally of Henry Thornton in the anti-slavery campaign and founder of the Sierra Leone colony and editor of the *Christian Observer*—was a familiar figure. His wife had been a protégée of Hannah More, and one of their daughters—Marianne's lifelong friend—bore Hannah's name. The son—the world-famous Tom—was born in 1800, and there is extant a letter in which Mrs. Thornton commiserates Mrs. Macaulay on the child not being a girl. Tom visited Battersea Rise as a baby and almost died there, for little Marianne gave him an appalling cold: Mrs. Thornton abounds in pious consolations and sound remedies. He recovered and young Henry Sykes Thornton, then also a baby, became his great friend. The Macaulays figure constantly in correspondence, but there is no reference to them in the "Recollections" beyond the following:

Another frequenter of our house was Mr Babington brother-in-law to Mr Zachary Macaulay. How clearly do I see now his rather wooden face, his country gentleman figure, his odd husky utterance, weighing so fairly and clearly every side of every question, and putting down Mr Wilberforce's airy flights by his facts and dates and figures; a sort of moral and mental arithmetician to be referred to at any moment. No man ever gave one a stronger belief that he was acting from conscientious motives on every occasion, small or great, or a more firm conviction of his truth. Some years later when I went with my eldest brother to stay at his house, Rothley Temple in Leicestershire, Henry told him that he feared, as his house was very full, our coming might be inconvenient. 'I do not deny', said Mr Babington 'that your coming has put us to considerable inconvenience, but the pleasure of your society quite outweighs it', and so satisfied were we with his sincerity that we stayed.

Near the Macaulays lived Lord Teignmouth and his family. Teignmouth (as Sir John Shore) had been Governor General of India. On his return to England he became the first president of the British and Foreign Bible Society. With him and with the alarming and able Stephen family the Clapham Circle is complete. Two things are notable about it. The first is its homogeneity. With the exception of the Macaulays, all its members were wealthy, and all of them without exception were devoted to good works, and were intellectual rather than artistic. Their earnestness and their pious phraseology make them fair game for the satirists, but neither Thackeray in *The Newcomes* nor Disraeli in an unfinished novel gets down to their depths. The second point about them is that though they came to be called the Clapham Sect, few of them remained long at Clapham. The Thorntons themselves continued at Battersea Rise, but most of the neighbours whom Marianne lists had moved to London or elsewhere by the time of her parents' death. In the golden period nearly all the people she loved were around her.

Not all. There was Hannah More down in Somerset.

Since Dr. M. G. Jones's excellent book on Hannah More, it has been possible to get a clearer view of that "bishop in petticoats" and to realise her warmth and charm. Marianne adored her. There is an extensive passage in the "Recollections."

But I have yet said nothing of the friend par excellence of my mother, the woman who held that rare place of having been my father's nearest associate and most confidential counsellor before his marriage, and then become the nearest and dearest tie she had out of her own family, to my mother. I mean Mrs Hannah More. I should add Hannah More and her sisters for my parents loved them all, and though Hannah More was the

most celebrated, they always thought Patty her equal in talent
and goodness. 'May is coming and then Hannah will be with
us,' was one of the earliest hopes of my childhood, and when
she did arrive I always felt I had a fresh companion just my
own age, and ready to sympathize with all my pleasures and
troubles. Her health was always very bad and often prevented
her going out for weeks together, and when this was the case
and I was too young to go to Church, I was delighted at being
left under her care on a Sunday. How well I remember sitting
on her bed whilst she discoursed to me about Joseph and his
brethren, and all the wonderful adventures of the children of
Israel with such eloquence and force that I fancied she must
have lived amongst them herself. She was in many ways a
charming companion for children, but she had very little power
of resisting either persuasion or fun, and I early found I had
much more influence over her than I had over my mother. As I
grew older I learnt not to take advantage of this. I have this
year [1857] revisited that Paradise of my childhood, Barley
Wood, and fancied I could once more see the venerable forms,
and hear the kind greetings of the 5 hospitable sisters.

Surely there never was such a house, so full of intellect and
piety and active benevolence. They lived in such uninterrupted
harmony with each other, were so full of their separate pur-
suits, enjoyed with such interest and vivacity all the pleasures
of their beautiful home, or wholly laid aside all the forms of
society that were irksome, that young or old one felt oneself in
a brighter and happier world, alloyed indeed by the most fearful attacks of illness occasionally, but even when these occurred
the patience and cheerfulness of both patient and nurses never
failed. I can now imagine our arrival at the door covered with
roses, and 'the ladies' as they were always called, rushing out
to cover us with kisses, and then take us into the kitchen to
exhibit us to Mary and Charles, the housemaid and coachman,
then running themselves to fetch the tea things, Mrs Patty allowing no one but herself to fry the eggs for 'the darling', the

brown loaf brought out, the colour of a mahogany table, baked only once a week, of enormous size but excellent taste. Then the 2 cats called 'Non-resistance' and 'Passive obedience' who were fed by us all day long, and then the next day crowns of flowers were made for ourselves, garlands for the sheep; the peas we were set to pick, and then shell, perched upon the kitchen dresser, while Sally made the room resound with some of her merry stories of the cottagers round, and then we were sent off by ourselves or with some village child to buy chickens at the next farm, and when we returned dragging along our purchases, how we were fed with strawberries and cream, and told to lie down in the hay whilst Charles the coachman, gardener bailiff and carpenter, made us a syllabub under the cow. Then came Sunday—when they were younger 'the ladies' rode behind Charles on horseback to the school they meant to visit, but in my time they always went in some odd conveyance on wheels. In those small parishes the service was seldom performed twice in the day and after going with the children to church we dined at some farmer's who was proud to take us in, and then proceeded to the school.

How Bell and Lancaster [educationists] were unknown then, and to read their Bible was the highest summit of knowledge to which they aspired. I chiefly recollect Mrs Hannah's or Mrs Patty's eloquent exhortations made to the whole school in the most familiar homely language, full of anecdotes of the people round them, as well as of the good people who lived in old times, and full of practical piety brought down to such minute details one never hears now. I particularly remember how she explained the fifth commandment, enjoined us to 'do errands for mother not saucily or lazily or stupidly' amongst many other small duties that she enumerated. Hannah More was always ready to talk about the literary set with whom she passed her youth. Many an evening has she amused me by describing Johnson and Burke, Horace Walpole, Mrs Montagu and the many personages I had read of in Boswell, and for this reason I suppose no period in history interests me so much. At our last two visits to Barley Wood she was alone living of all the band of sisters. She was too ill even to leave her bedroom, but her flow of spirits never failed, her sufferings of body seemed conquered by her cheerfulness, and her love of all she had ever known, her interest in their welfare, her enjoyment of their society was as great as ever. One night her maid came to send me out of her room, saying her mistress would be tired, and must be put to bed, she being then confined to it the greater part of the day. While Mary went down for something, Mrs H. More said 'We have not had half our talk out, and it does not tire me a bit, hide behind the window curtain and come out when Mary fancies she has shut me up.' No girl of 16 could have enjoyed the trick more. But she too is now lying in Wrington Churchyard by her sisters and Barley Wood has passed into other hands, but God has indeed given them a better name than sons and daughters.

The "Recollections" have extended beyond childhood, for Hannah More lived until 1833. Marianne made a symbol of her. Unlike Wilberforce, she never married and so she never altered. She represented continuity. It is significant that the final sentence about the Mores ("God has indeed given them a better name than sons and daughters") should be a quotation from Henry Thornton's journal. Childless herself, she became the family life that does not die with death. Her cult (to use an overemphatic word) went on till my own time. A garden I once owned had a grass slope in it which had been made to imitate a slope at Barley Wood.

After this glance at the Clapham Circle through Marianne's eyes, we must return to her babyhood, and must accompany her at the age of five months on a holiday to Lancing. Mrs. Thornton wrote long accounts of it and of similar outings to her sister-in-law, the pious Aunt Robert, and they are well worth quoting; they show how people of sense and substance organised a summer holiday during the French wars, and they are comparable with the jauntings of Jane Austen.

On this occasion (August 1797) mother, baby, and Nurse Hunter set out in an open carriage and drove along the south coast in search of a suitable house. A carriage-full of servants followed. A servant was sent forward to prospect at Worthing, failed there, but reported favourably on a house at Lancing.

So on the Saturday morning we and our servants of the second division from B. Rise arrived here and in a few hours we were all as comfortably settled as we could wish.—Worthing seems to be very much as you described it and both for our sakes and for our servants' morality I am glad that we are not there.—Lancing is a pretty rural village at the foot of the great Hill, and from thence to Worthing it is flat and can possess no charms for a Painter's Eye, but here I feel quite at home for it resembles many of the little villages at the foot of the Yorkshire wolds. The harvest adds much to the pleasantness of the scene and I have never seen any peasants' dress so picturesque as these; it consists generally of a brown or light blue linen frock (for the men) with a straw hat bound with black ribbon.

The exterior however is all that is worthy of praise for those of the Inhabitants of Lancing with whom I have got acquainted are very ignorant and very discontented with their lot—very few of the women can read and hardly any of the children. The *Clerk's* daughter I have hired to attend in the house: she is eighteen and does not know her letters, she is ignorant of the existence of a God and of all the common precepts of right and wrong, and what is more lamentable she has six brothers and sisters equally ignorant with herself. There is fine scope if one

stays a summer amongst these people but I am not very sanguine as to any effects that can be produced by us during our
stay.

We have the great comfort of bathing here instead of going
to *exhibit* at Worthing, and I have great hopes that it will
be of service to Mr H. T. I bathe in the sea but it is merely for
the pleasure of it, for I am extremely strong and well. Little
Marianne takes *due pains with her complexion* and braves the
sea breezes which have been rather strong since we came for
about five or six hours every day. . . . I find our open carriages very pleasant and useful here. We are about a quarter
of a mile from the sea and after an early dinner Mr T. and I
take a book with us to the sands where we stroll about until
we are tired of walking. In a morning after breakfast we are
chiefly *at work* till dinner: in the afternoon we read Shakespeare
or some such author and in an evening History: this is what
Mr T. calls a fine idle life and I term it quite a holiday because
I see so much of him, but we both agree that it must only be
considered as a sort of preparative for harder duty when we
return to the field of action.

The letter then reports that Battersea Rise has been lent
to some people with awful nerves so that the Grant children
from next door have been forbidden to come and skip on the
lawn; "how thankful ought we to be who are free from such
heavy trials." When they return there themselves, there is
trouble: their next child dies at birth, and as to "my dear
little Marianne: I rather grieve to see how nervous she is;
in part I wish to attribute it to the intense heat of the
weather and in part to her ceasing to take hemlock. When
anything has frightened her during the day she starts up
often at night in her sleep saying out in a most piteous tone
Go away, Go away."

In 1799 there was another seaside holiday at Christchurch.
The political situation was acute "and it was not till near 9

o'clock that I knew Mr Pitt would allow us to set off the next morning." Hannah More joined them. There was extended bathing:

Marianne grows plump and round, and bathes twice a week with very respectable fortitude.—The nymph of the waves is however rather terrific and Nurse who is all good humour takes off her own shoes and stockings and walks into the sea with her charge who comes out so rosy and in such riotous spirits that you would not know her.

1800 brought them to Bognor Rocks where they bathed more than ever. There is an important addition to the party: the son and heir has been born and has been christened Henry Sykes Thornton:

I like Bognor much more than any sea-bathing place on this coast that I have yet seen. The bathing is quite delicious and the accommodation of every kind *good enough.* There being no place of general rendezvous for the Company makes it very quiet and free from form, so that we may sit down with our Book just where we please.

Our visits have been among the cottagers who as to temporal things are better provided than any poor I have yet known but as to spirituals it is a barren land indeed. Marianne has bathed a few times and behaves really very well about it. She allows herself one short cry and then it is all over. She is well and appears to me grown even since she came here. She complains of the difficulty of being good and says 'I try and I try Ma but I *can't* be good'.

Bognor was the last bathing holiday that Marianne had to endure. It ended disastrously, owing to the misfortunes and the tiresomenesses of the Wilberforces. They had taken a house too, in order to remain close to the Thorntons, and Mrs. Wilberforce fell dangerously ill. Mrs. Thornton had to send the baby back to Battersea Rise, and to settle Marianne elsewhere, and she remained organising the large-scale confusion.

Mrs W. is perfectly rational but deaf and indisposed to talk. She has had two good nights with opium and her appetite is very well, but we starve her for her strongest food is veal-tea, anything beyond that raises her pulse in a few minutes. . . . It has been a very awful and distressing scene, and while we only had the Apothecary I did not know whether the medecine she took might kill or might cure her, and when I had got my two poor babes out of the house and settled safely I found I had lost my only two attendants. . . . I shall come home like a soldier from a foreign expedition, somewhat battered and bruised. If however it has been the means of detaching me from the world I shall have cause to rejoice in it as long as I live. . . .

I continue bathing and feel much refreshed by it.—I have been very careful of myself and never sit up at nights, but it has been rather worrying, for our family in two houses has consisted of *32*—many of them extremely particular about their diet—and half the servants not mine—that to have the table right, the servants quiet and submissive—Mrs W's room always in perfect order and she never without two attendants has required some exertion.

In 1803—the year of the invasion threat—mother and daughter went to visit old Mr. Joseph Sykes in Yorkshire: not without adventure.

We had an uncommonly pleasant journey till we embarked on the Humber and then I more than half feared that Mrs Thornton Astall's old chaise and I should never be heard of more. Poor Marianne was much terrified but I could not prevail on her to leave me in the chaise which was the only place

[*45*]

of danger, and I hesitated in much doubt which to prefer, sitting in a carriage which was placed across a small boat to which it could not be fastened in a high wind and a rough sea, or standing almost ancle deep in wet straw with an east wind and a heavy rain. Somehow I picked up a little cold which the sharp northern air did not at once drive away.

Mr. Sykes had had a stroke, and looking round the old house where she had once been a child with other children, Mrs. Thornton reflects that a similar desolation might one day afflict even Battersea Rise. No such forebodings visit Marianne:

Marianne looks *charmingly* and is of course much admired for her merriment &ct. If she is thought to be grown fat when she returns home I shall bid adieu to all systems of diet and management for added to hot rolls muffins &ct. I have seen her eat a roasted pigeon and a gooseberry tart by way of desert. The air here is very keen and sharp and she runs about a great deal and so I suppose it does not harm her. I feel her being so well a great cause of thankfulness.

Meanwhile Henry Thornton was passing through grave public anxieties. The Peace of Amiens had not held, and the second Napoleonic war had begun. He had opposed our entry to it in Parliament, partly because he loved peace, partly because he expected disaster. From his journal:

I now write (31 July 1803) in the apprehension of an invasion. My wife is advised by some of our friends to leave London for the sake of avoiding the danger of being surrounded by French soldiery, and I am hearing day by day new accounts of slaughter and insurrection in Ireland. Perhaps however the war was not finally to be avoided. I myself suspect that it was not but I was anxious to take at least the best chance of avoiding it. May I and mine be preserved from the perils which surround us, and may we perform our part in sustaining the spirit of the country, and in deprecating that wrath of God which there is too much reason to fear may be denounced against us.

His health was already impaired by overwork. Later in the year he went to take the waters at Bath, accompanied by his growing family. Little Lucy, a newish arrival, took the lime-light. Escaping into the street, she announced to a strange lady: "Here me in my blue coat and my new buff shoes" and accepted an invitation to dine and sleep. Marianne, aged six, was more sedately employed: "She gets on fast with her writing and arithmetic and admires her master here as much as the one at Clapham," Mrs. Thornton reports.

In a letter of 1806 she gives a pleasant picture of the two little girls.

Marianne and Lucy are very well and the latter is much caressed by the village and will hardly know her place when she returns to the nursery. For their credit and mine I must tell you that we travelled from Saturday to Tuesday without Maid or Footman and that *we lost nothing:* they dressed each other at the Inns and Marianne packed and unpacked their things all the way on the road. As we did not go more than forty miles any one day there was abundance of time for all this, and had we taken a maid we must have hired another chaise.

They were bound for Buxton which had been recommended to Henry Thornton as a cure. On his arrival there he wrote Charles Grant a letter of unusual interest, for it reports one of his rare contacts with industrialism.

We bought a grey pony on which my little girl has cantered many a half stage by my side, & I have to thank the pony for having made me much better acquainted with my Daughter than I was before. We have also gone together to see a variety of Manufactures and have been learning to feel for those who

dig in Mines, who toil in Quarries, perspire in Salt works, wear
out their Eyes in looking at Furnaces, or pass their morning
noon and Even in the limited Employment of putting on the
head of a Pin, or drawing over and over the same pattern on a
piece of China. I fear that the less pleasant part of Education
has been neglected. I trust however that seeing the world in
this sense will prove very useful. It has also not a little entertained Mrs. T. & I trust that the View which we have taken of
our fellow creatures has inspired some thankfulness for the temporal as well as spiritual Advantages of our condition.

Were I writing not a domestic biography but a public
one I should have much to say about this letter. For it neatly
illustrates the weakness in the Thornton-Wilberforce outlook—the weakness that has been mercilessly exposed by the
Hammonds and other critics. Marianne's parents would
have behaved very differently if they had encountered a
slave gang. They would have tried both to free the gang
and to discover the causes of slavery, so that it might be
eliminated. By legislation in Parliament, by supervision of
cargoes, by agreements with other countries and with
African chiefs they would have persisted until abolition was
total. When the slavery was industrial they did nothing and
had no thought of doing anything; they regarded it as
something "natural," to encounter it was an educational experience, and an opportunity for smug thankfulness. Misery
might be alleviated at the soup-kitchen level, but to do more
might make the workers unruly and even un-Christian.
Hence Hannah More's tracts, recommending industry, fru-
gality, obedience, and harder and still harder work. Hence
Wilberforce's unsatisfactory record in Parliament when it
came to Home Affairs—his support of the Combination
Acts, his approval of the Peterloo massacre—and hence

Francis Place's description of him as "an ugly epitome of the devil."

I agree with the above line of criticism. But I do not share the moral indignation that sometime accompanies it. The really bad people, it seems to me, are those who do no good anywhere and help no one either at home or abroad. There are plenty of them about, and when they are clever as well as selfish they often manage to slip through their lives un-noticed, and so escape the censure of historians.

The year of the industrial encounter is the very year in which Henry Thornton wrote the pretty little verses with which this biography starts. His daughter dear was nine years old. She was already distinct to him as one whom he could educate to be his companion. She had intelligence, high spirits, high principles. She had also her faults, and he did not cease to remind her and himself of them, and to analyse her character, and to hope that she would grow up to be less diffident with strangers and less easily bored. He ana-lysed the other children too, but Marianne occupied most space. As soon as possible he interested her in his parlia-mentary career and in politics generally. Nothing, in his judgement, should remain unknown or half known, and the mysteries of the Constitution, like the economics of her home, were explained to her at an early age. His own elec-tions were the starting point; they excited her, as they would any loyal child. From her "Recollections":

He was generally the unpopular candidate with the mob, and was hissed and hooted sometimes not listened to by the popu-lace. I remember crying partly from fright and partly from vexation when he took me with him in his carriage on one of those occasions, and how, small as I was, he explained how these people disliked him because he would not vote as they wished, and that they were not to be blamed because they knew no better than to desire things which were not good for them; that we should not regret unpopularity when we were doing right nor 'hate and detest' as I proposed, all the people who were so unkind as to hiss and hoot my papa. Though to a certain extent a Reformer, and though a great enemy to corruption jobs and peculation he never was liked by the mob in Southwark, however he was re-elected in eight successive Parliaments, though not always at the head of the Poll. I remember however being delighted at a song which was sung at the door of our carriage of which I only recollect one verse.

> No place or pension ere got he
> For self or for connection
> We shall not tax the Treasury
> By Thornton's re-election.

He was most scrupulous about the money spent on these occasions, and at that time it was not common to care how or what amount was given if the election was secured. He stood very nearly alone in refusing to give the 'guinea a head' to each voter, which was then continually done and not considered to be breaking the bribery laws because every candidate gave it. Some of his supporters complained of his stiffness on these points and said it was astonishing he was ever elected at all with such scrupulous notions. When the battle was fought and won, he was chaired as it was called, and a very pretty sight it was. We always went to a window in the Town Hall to see him pass. He sat in his open Landau drawn by horses quite covered with orange and purple ribbons, the old coachman driving the 1st four. His friends and supporters carriages followed in procession with flags and music. The winning candidates were always well received and the shouts of 'Thornton for ever' delighted me, but he never failed to tell us afterwards how little such applause was worth. 'I would rather have a shake of the hand from good old John Newton' he said, 'than

[50]

the cheers of all that foolish mob who praise one they don't know why.'

She does not explain why, despite this Coriolanus attitude, he always got in. He seems to have achieved the best of both worlds here. No one liked him outside his personal friends. Outwardly he was cold, and his integrity sometimes passed into censoriousness. Ludicrously inappropriate is another election song:

> Here's a health to the man whom with rapture we sing,
> To the friend of our Church of our Country and King!
> Then cheerly my boys drain the bowls as they pass,
> And Thornton forever shall hang in the glass.

The boys would have received but a slight acknowledgement from the reserved dignified figure at the head of the table. He wanted to get away from their meaningless applause and perform his duties in Parliament—duties they were incapable of understanding.

Mrs. Thornton furnishes further details about the Southwark election that left such an impression on her daughter. Parliament had been dissolved suddenly, and a discredited and discreditable candidate had presented himself. To Hannah More:

> We fully expected that at the nomination the show of hands would have been completely in favour of Mr T. and we drove into the midst of the people before the hustings, took off our horses and sat in the coach. The first thing that caught my eye was the Calvert ribbon on more than half the mob. The next was Calvert himself, attended by music, marrow bones and cleavers, and every sort of noise that patriotism or licentiousness ever invented. Only a few respectable men attended Mr T.

She tried to rally "our gentlemen" in her husband's cause, but first they said there was no danger and then no hope and the purity of his record had caused so much irritation that they were reluctant to canvass. Tumult continued for five days. Thornton hung in the balance as well as the glass. He got in, thanks to a "white collar" vote: the clerks connected with the India Office, etc., were rallied to his support by the Grants. Through the favour of the High Sheriff she and the two children were admitted on to the hustings to hear the victorious candidate: "hissed and abused and threatened by the mob with all sorts of horrors, but he went on unmoved till he had distinctly made his charge heard, that Calvert had 'treated' and broke the law. This scene did worry my nerves a little, but it furnished me with a useful topic for Marianne and Henry." The scene was further enlivened by "Mendoza the Jew boxer" who kept shaking his fist at Mr. T. and crying "No popery! no popery," in a highly irrational way. The children became overexcited during the triumphal drive, and she could only trust they had received more good than harm from the experience.

Life at Battersea Rise was certainly never dull. Not only was there this recurrent political excitement, but streams of interesting visitors kept passing through the house. For instance, one summer a young Mohawk came to stop. He was gentle and good looking. Mrs. Thornton found him altogether delightful, and so did the children, for he was persuaded to sing and dance. The library can seldom have witnessed a stranger scene: "he began gracefully, by degrees his tones became louder and his actions more vehement, till at last he seemed transported with rage and fury and stabbed his foe with horrid shrieks and yells then in an instant resumed his calmness and said the English coat was very inconvenient for that kind of amusement." He was "more than half a Christian," and he was also half Scotch, for his mother had "followed our army to America and instead of returning as a widow had married one of our allies." He had come over to settle the boundaries between the Five Nations and Canada. Besides the Mohawk there were Africans from Sierra Leone, who came with or in consequence of Zachary Macaulay; little black boys would wander over Clapham Common and be beckoned into houses by the delighted inhabitants. The great world was expanding. It brought no mystery, no feeling for poetry. But it was an increasing field for curiosity and for missionary effort.

And there were the children's parties. "Our philosophic fête with the aid of a splendid plum cake went off very well," Mrs. Thornton thought. An electrical machine played a hundred tricks, and a mechanical machine demonstrated the properties of the lever. She was never interested in science and entertained herself by a more familiar sport: she examined the characters of the audience. Young William Wilberforce, the son of their beloved friend, "attended to nothing, dashed at all, was often right and then triumphed playing a thousand monkey tricks the whole time, spinning cup and ball, holding a flower by the stalk by curling down his under lip, &ct." Lord Teignmouth's boy "was generally right and blushed whether right or wrong." Another "knew little, thought he knew all and was very cheerful." Her own young Henry "was considerate, the subject being new to him, made two guesses and was each time right." Tom Macaulay on the other hand was "terrified at electricity, fell asleep over mechanics." And her nephew Sam Thornton (afterwards an admiral) "groans under all intellectual employment and amused himself with mischief." The party ended in a puppet show, script by Mrs. Hannah More, narrator Henry Thornton. And that same month (Jan. 1808) Lord Teignmouth gave a Twelfth Night party. The same company attended but the emphasis was literary. Young Wilberforce went as the Pope, Tom Macaulay as Bonaparte, Marianne as Mrs. Slipslop, "in an old satin gown with treble ruffles, an apron and a mob of the housekeeper's, "Lucy as a shepherdess "in a green jacket with a painted trimming of flowers, a garland of ivy and holly round her hair," and she carried a crook to which a bunch of real roses was tied. Henry was Don Quixote, Watson, Sancho Panza with a wallet full of apples. All had been provided with lines by Henry Thornton and said them very well, with the exception of the Wilberforce boy who lost his head. They were welcomed by two of Lord Teignmouth's children, who sat in a bower of plants, flowers, and lights at the farther end of the dining room. The King arose with admirable grace, "stepped from his throne, threw away his sceptre and repeated capitally some excellent lines expressive of his abhorrence of superiority. . . . Then supper and a magic lantern and at 9.0. we all came home."

There was nothing contrary to principle in these diversions. The Thorntons were not ascetic, and though all was subordinated to duty they held that "this is a world in which some amusement is necessary to enable us to perform our duties." So the children amused themselves with good conscience and their elders often forgot that enjoyment is only a means. When ill health came, the balance shifted: remorse and repentance weighed in, and when they kept journals and examined themselves in solitude, there was also a shift. On the whole the way of life they discovered worked, and they could pursue it to the glory of their God without self-torture or torturing others. Compare Marianne's easy if supervised childhood with the torments inflicted forty years later on Augustus Hare. Deep in the Thorntons' character, deeper even than they suspected, was the disinclination to inflict pain.

The children also had some private diversions, more difficult to classify. I am thinking of some curious water-colour drawings. There are about thirty of them, done on both sides of rough pieces of paper. They are not reasonable or instructive or edifying, and some of them go beyond the blugginess natural to the young into a very strange country. I will catalogue a few, adding the name of the artist, where known, in brackets.

Serpent round boy. He kneels, dressed in blue. Coil round his knee, face pressed against his. Another boy in red feebly untwists tail. Background of trees [Henrietta].

Apoplexy. Victim at one end of the family-settee, with attendants. At the other end a genteel lady holds a fan [Laura].

"The papa hanging his children." Fine figure of a man suspending pretty child in blue, boy in trousers, child in maroon from a single rod [Henrietta].

Child eaten by lion. It stretches out its hands to its mother who stretches out hers. In the background a second lion looks on: it has the face of a man.

Boy over precipice. Alpine scene. Handsome boy. Regretful relatives [Sophia].

Gig over precipice. Father pulls, mother screams in magenta, child struggles in green. All are lost [Henrietta].

"Bonassus." Bull with human face and protruding tongue pursues man over a precipice [Charles].

Ogre. Terrifying. Oversized face, venerable white beard, red lips, sharp teeth, green eyes, his head is humped on his shoulders, he hugs three shrieking children, he wears a bright yellow dressing-gown spotted with red. All this could be borne, but look at his tiny scaled feet and tremble [Henrietta].

"Laura feeding the hens with ham-sandwiches and potatoes." Inoffensive caricature of my grandmother and her
long neck employed as stated.

"Marianne asleep," or "Industry." Again the library
settee. A thickset wench with her feet up [Henrietta].

Marianne and her sage elder brothers took no part in this
orgy. Indeed I do not think she could draw, and Lucy, who
could, also held aloof. It was the work of their juniors. No
one thought the collection bizarre. It passed into the possession of Henrietta, the leading artist, then to her daughter,
then to an aunt of mine, and so reached Freud and me. None
of the children "went wrong." The collection is useless as
a horoscope. All it does is to suggest that there was at the
time an emotional stress, perhaps induced by the Napoleonic
menace; thanks to high principles the stress eased.

Napoleon certainly did hang over Battersea Rise. At any
moment he might arrive, perhaps had already arrived,
and he would cut down the tulip tree upon the lawn, Marianne said; that was why the French fleet was assembled at
Boulogne. Tom Macaulay, with his truer sense of history
corrected her: Napoleon when he arrived would merely stab
all the little children in their beds. Their fears bring them
close to us. It is the security of the Victorian era that we
find so remote. Napoleon, as it might be the Kaiser, never
landed, but some years later Napoleon, as it might be Hitler,
tried a second time. In the year of the Battle of Nations
little Laura had a terrible fright. She had gone out before
breakfast to visit a litter of puppies in the loft. There was
not much light, and before she could get to their corner she
saw, sticking out from under a truss of hay, a man's leg. She
rushed back to the trap door shrieking, scrambled down the

ladder and announced that "Bonaparty" had come and was hiding. A search party set out, and discovered the top boot of a groom. Behind the comfort and piety and philanthropy there was always this fear. It peeps out in their parents' letters, it lies behind the political repressions of Pitt, and behind the children's scrawls.

On a rational level, Napoleon was coldly judged. When Mrs. Thornton was displeased with some house decorators who had "made us look gay and pretty, but we fear they are dishonest," she reflects that "Bonaparte is a villain of a more magnificent size and surrounded with splendours but in the eye of the Almighty he is but a sinner of a still worse class," and she buys a good map on which to study his downfall. In 1814 this seemed to have occurred. Foreign potentates visited London for the rejoicings, and she took up Marianne and some of the others to see them. Her impressions were unfavourable. To Hannah More:

Tell Miss Patty I think she lost not much by refusing to come to town. The Emperor of Russia looks dull and at least not magnanimous, and the King of Prussia seemed at once unhappy and ignorant but perhaps his ignorance of English might give him that appearance. I saw him at the H. of Lords where to give those foreigners some idea of our constitution it was agreed that the Commons should appear at the bar and some bills be past by the Lords. The Emperor did not come and nothing could exceed the apparent inattention of the Prussians and Germans, tho' Lord Liverpool was explaining to them the whole time. We saw them on various occasions but I think the impression was always the same. They were not very refined or very intellectual nor very great in any way.

The following year brought the Hundred Days, Waterloo, St. Helena, and the end of terror for the tulip tree and for England.

During the whole of this exhausting period Henry Thornton continued to educate his eldest daughter. An entry in his journal states:

I discovered that to possess a strong interest in a subject and some previous acquaintance with it rendered a long continued attention easy and operates almost like inspiration. I make this observation for the benefit of my eldest daughter in particular. I perceive that she is easily discouraged and is too much disposed to desist from some attempt owing to the difficulties in the entrance. She is likewise eager as I was. Probably some of my other children may resemble her. I . . . advise them all to endeavour to divert their mental powers to various subjects while very young, to beware of that false shame which makes us ashamed of the discredit attending our first feeble efforts, and, looking to the approbation of God rather than to that of man, to lay out their talents, whatever these may be, for the public good, and to the glory of Him who gave them.

The results of so much advice might have been disastrous, for he had a strong personality, and he was so sure that he knew what was right that a female caricature of Papa might have resulted. Fortunately Marianne too had a strong nature, and her gaiety and warmth transformed his teachings into something individual. As time went on he was fertile in devices for improving her. He worried endlessly about her—about whom was he not now worried? High principles had been reinforced by low health. To his wife:

In this world of bustle it is soothing to reflect on that intimate and fast friend at home who is presiding over the domestic matters and the education of an interesting generation of children and it is melancholy to contemplate the case of those who are without this counterpoise to their public cares. Marianne should learn to bear dullness, for she must endure much of it hereafter if she will fulfil her duties, and yet her turn is naturally so active that in reflecting as I have done on this subject I have thought that I could endeavour to find her animating employment, and thus exercise her powers of giving animation to others, hoping that a tender conscience will, either sooner or later and more or less, supply a disposition constantly to turn her activity to a profitable and benevolent account.

The "animating employment" he devised was that of amanuensis to himself. He appointed her formally in 1812. The following letter to her is surprisingly adult in tone and indicates with precision what he expects her to know and to understand:

My dear M.—I must not fail to answer your letter since I am very ambitious to begin to make you act as a substitute for M. T. senior, and as this is the first act the young adventurer ought to be very particularly encouraged. My reply though is that I really am now thinking of my journey to you in good earnest. . . . 'Nil mihi rescribas attamen ipse veni'. Can you construe that Latin pentameter verse? Attamen is almost the same as sed. It is a line of Ovid written by some daughter like you to some such father as me from some such place as Bath and on some such occasion as that on which you have written. I am now scribbling in Birchin Lane [the Banking House]. . . . I am going to the India House while Henry and Watson get shod. Then I mean to call with them at Newgate on the poor clerk who robbed us. The impression of the sad consequences of sin which this interview will give them, by the blessing of God may do them good. I want to mix mercy with judgment. He sends word he shall be put in irons if we do not afford him a guinea to give the jailor, May God preserve us all from those dispositions of mind which ultimately lead to these scenes of misery.

[*59*]

Henry and Watson being at that date twelve and ten years of age. The transition from the atmosphere of Ovid to that of the Fairchild family is abrupt: nowhere else does Henry Thornton go so far in either direction. Marianne was all enthusiasm, and after learning some shorthand (Gurney's Method), she entered on her secretarial duties. The following letter is an early example of them; it involves her papa and herself in some funny tangles.

Battersea Rise, Sunday.

Dear Mamma: Although it is Sunday, Papa thinks he may dictate a letter to you since it is not a letter of business but upon subjects not ill suited to the day. Papa arrived here yesterday about 5 o'clock, having called at Mrs Bewicke. The good old lady said she had never been at Church since Papa went and had seen but few people. Papa says that in a visit of 5 minutes, during which however he was rather cold and hungry, he communicated to the old lady more happiness than had been derived in the preceding half hour from all the pork chops upon the table. She was delighted to hear that you were better but above all at the news that the only daughter of the late John Thornton [Lady Leven] was then in town.

The children were beaming with joy when Papa arrived. Charles looks fat and promising. Sophy is growing up to be a giant. Watson looks pale and shabby. He has been moralizing in his usual way and seems likely to be a universalist in knowledge. When Papa told him of the possibility of war with America and the cause of it, he said that we had always claimed a right to take all the ships at sea that we could meet, and when driven from that ground asked whether the Americans were not all infidels. Papa says that by keeping company that will instruct him, and by perseverance in enquiry, he trusts he will abound with important and useful knowledge.

Papa says the little children are rather troublesome, though for the most part not at all blameable on that account since it has pleased God to give them great activity which is evidently subservient to the purposes of promoting their health and the improvement of their minds. Charles [aged 2] has been travelling round the room in search of every kind of prey, and Marianne's work box would have had its inside completely shattered if Papa had not interposed. It was pleasant to see the progress that he made in learning to open the sliding top in the little box within, but Papa attempted in vain to perfect him in this lesson, in the art of shutting it.

We heard today an excellent sermon from Mr Venn, 'The Night Cometh', &ct. He pointed out the many duties as well as tempers to which we have to attend, and also urged the great general duty of taking care of our souls, and particularly not to let even the occupation of doing good so engross our minds as to afford us no opportunity of cultivating 'a devotional spirit'. Papa dines tomorrow with Mr Stephens and Mr Wilberforce,

Yours affectly HENRY THORNTON.

Another letter, also written in 1812, to her aunt Mrs. Dan Sykes, is more natural in its tone and more logical in its sequences, but no more assured in its style. It is a voluble, "festive" letter, like so many letters written by ladies to ladies throughout the century, and though it marks a stage in her literary development it is not worth quoting.

The sympathy between father and daughter increased rapidly. When ill and feverish he had a long rambling dream of which he wrote an account. He, and she after him, were to suffer but little from the onslaughts of the imagination, so the dream is worth preserving. It began in a mail coach "driving full 80 miles an hour," from which he dismounted to hang over the edge of a sublime precipice: thence was he transferred to a valley by a roadside where several young ladies sat, "the neatness of whose shoes I perfectly remember for I touched one of them," and where a number of scattered dolls lay about, also very nice images of carved wood, and "a lady whose foot trod on a beautiful bird which I seized informed me that they all belonged to a Mr Philips." Hence to the House of Commons—no, to the House of Lords —no, to the road between Parliament and his town house, where a great debate was proceeding in darkness etc., etc.

He had been taking laudanum and his dream recalls the contemporary and more agitating dreams of George Crabbe. But for him sleep opened no doors into evil or poetry. He proceeds to draw useful conclusions: "Happily for us when the wild faculty of the imagination is deceiving us in dreams the body does not follow that adventurous leader." Except for "a few unlucky perambulators" who jump out of window, all are safe. It is the waking imagination which must be mistrusted: it is a little too like the sleeping one "and hence more than half the kicks and cuffs and broken bones or rather the broken hearts and spirits which we must meet with in our terrestrial journey. We imagine things to be in part only as they are not. But this error in part makes a wonderful difference in the happiness of our poor minds and bodies, for they follow our waking imaginations exactly." He then takes the usual run through his children. Lucy is still far too imaginative, so is Watson; Marianne herself improves but gradually; only Henry "is escaping fast out of that foggy region," which makes many of us "err long and much from the truth."

For Marianne, as for her father, the terrestrial world became entirely tangible and behind it, equally reliable in another and a superior way, stood God. For her, as for him, imagination is dangerous because it makes us behave in an unreal way to people, which may hurt them. But she had a wider outlook than his, and more external warmth, she was fonder of fun and even loved nonsense, and she allowed considerable liberty to imagination's henchman, fancy.

FOUR

The Deathbeds

HENRY THORNTON'S HEALTH did not break up until the autumn of 1814, but he had never been robust. All his life he had overworked. He suffered from headaches, irritability, and sleeplessness, and took laudanum and opium constantly. Tuberculosis developed. He has "laboured under a cough for these ten days," he is tempted out by a bright October afternoon, the sun goes in, the feverishness returns, the doctor orders him to rub his neck with laudanum, he cannot eat but manages some sago and wine which warms him.

The full story of his death and of her mother's death is related by Marianne in a document which might be called a Pronouncement. It is twice as long as her "Recollections" —over sixty pages in her close, firm handwriting, stitched up into notebook form. I do not know at what date she wrote it. It came to me by the same route as the children's drawings. The opening sentence in it is "It was on Thursday 17th Oct. 1814 that we were all at Brighton except my father who had gone to Town on business when on returning from a walk to Preston with my mother we found a letter from him begging we would come to London the next day as he was not well." After which I will paraphrase. The Pronouncement is not merely wordy: it is far removed from us in spirit. He was ill. He died. His family and his friends were with him. Why cannot his daughter leave it there—keeping the rest in her heart?

She and her mother left Brighton the next day: Mrs. Thornton longed to leave immediately, but would not out of deference to her husband's wishes, and had scarcely slept. They travelled by coach and found reassuring letters from the invalid awaiting them at each stage, and at Sutton their own carriage met them. Marianne fell asleep in it to be woken by the church clock striking 8:00 on Clapham Common: strange not to be turning into Battersea Rise, but it was in his town house in Palace Yard that her father had collapsed. Mr. Harrison, the butler, and Sage, the housekeeper, were on the steps both saying "he is better, much better today," and they found him on a sofa, looking much as usual.

A fortnight later all the other children arrived from Brighton, he managed to get to his Bank at Birchin Lane, and he spent a long day there going into his private affairs: he realised that he was going to die. He also got down to Battersea Rise and "went immediately into the garden and I walked a little way with him on the lawn. How little did I think it was the last walk he would ever take in that Garden he was so fond of, when I had so often worked with him when I was a little child amongst the trees he had planted and the flowers he had admired so much." Parliament opened; he tried to attend, collapsed, and a graver phase began. "As I sat by his bedside he said to me 'Don't look grave about this, this life cannot be the smiling scene always that you have hitherto found it, but God will take care of us all.'" Two things worried him. One was the fate of his much-loved brother in America. When his pleasant meals were brought he would say "Oh if my poor brother Robert had any tender

nurses or any good food . . . but he is an outcaste and a
wanderer and may be dying all alone." He even managed to
write a long letter and Robert answered it, but not satisfactorily.

His other worry was financial; he had discovered some
alarming losses at the Bank during his recent researches:
but realising he could do nothing he dismissed them from
his mind, exerted his moral strength and read no more newspapers, or anything that was not of a religious character.
To Marianne he said, "I have something I want you to do
for me—to take my place at dinner, and also to give my
Chestnut Horse a little work. He has been a faithful servant
to me but his present idleness will hurt his conscience—so
do you take him . . . and keep him" he added as she was
leaving the room.

Their London return was not to Palace Yard but to Wilberforce's house at 4 Kensington Gore, where he finally died
"in a large gloomy green bedroom." On goes her sad narra-
tive, gently, relentlessly, as if the spirit of the age, which
adored deathbeds, was speaking through her lips. Nothing
is insincere, nothing strained or in bad taste, but on it goes,
on . . . "Nurse, nurse, give me air," and Nurse Hunter
answers, "Yes, sir, I will." Little Laura tries to warm his
hands and says, "Papa, I should like to be an Angel and go
with you." Little Charles is carried in by young Henry, but
his spirits were so high that he had to be taken away again.
"Papa opened his eyes at the sound of his merry voice and
said Poor little Charles and closed them again." Doctors,
consultations, relapses, prayers, sufferings. He still dictated
letters. To an acquaintance:

Dr Baillie still gives me assurances of safety but in a case
of such protracted weakness there cannot be much certainty in

their hopes. However through the great mercy of God I hope
I may be a little emerging from the depression in which I have
been during the last few weeks.—But Dr Baillie has just forbid
my speaking any more, and I can therefore only request you
my dear Sir to let me have an interest in your prayers.

He died on January 16, 1815, at the age of fifty. The final
scene shall be quoted in full. Slowness gathers up beauty.

Towards evening the breathing became slower and rather
more difficult. 'My Marianne' we now often heard and mama
gently answering 'I am here.' The room became almost dark
and the ticking of the watch—*his* watch—as it lay on the
Table was the only sound for some minutes when Sage who was
close to his head suddenly stood up made some sign to Nurse,
and then sate down again. I had not the least idea that the last
moments could be so quiet and unmarked by the least struggle,
and so had no idea all was over till Nurse stirred the fire to
give more light and still we heard not the slightest sound. His
countenance had the expression of 'ever deepening repose'
which comforted those who had so often seen him in pain. His
attitude was so composed and quiet that if I had seen him so a
week before, I should have rejoiced to see him in so sweet a
slumber. Suddenly mama burst into tears, saying 'He is sleeping in Jesus' and bending down she kissed him. 'One more before
it is all cold in death' she said and then Mrs Grant drew her
away. I staid a little longer still holding his hand, till Robert
Melville came to say she wanted me in the next room—where
she was sitting near Mrs Grant by the fire, several of the children on the bed crying most bitterly.

In half an hour Watson was sent in by Nurse to say we might
return, and Mrs Grant mama and I went in. But we only took
one glance—it was all so sadly altered. Before it looked like the
living image—now the low bed and the white cloths and all the
other arrangements looked like death indeed—and mama ex-

claimed 'I cannot bear this'. Mrs Grant took her away and she
never entered the room again nor did I.

The Pronouncement proceeds through the minutiae of
grief and burial and then describes—in equal detail—the
illness and death of her mother. I shall give no account of
that or of the many other deathbeds which will line this pro-
cessional way. They must be realised by all who would understand the full implications of family life, but Henry
Thornton's is a sufficient epitome of them. He was buried
in the family vault in the Old Church, and his wife soon
joined him there. His memorial urn in the Battersea Rise
garden became her memorial too, and remained until all was
destroyed.

Mrs. Thornton died of grief, that is to say grief weakened
her, and she developed her husband's disease: Marianne
rightly surmised that she had caught it from him. Her end
was less exemplary, for she worried about money. Sometimes
she thought there would be enough for the children. At other
times she panicked and persuaded a Sykes aunt to leave each
of them £1,000. At yet other times she declared that poverty
was a blessing in disguise: "My children *will* be blessed, and
wealth and patronage and the sunshine of their honoured
Father's Protection and his popularity would have ob-
structed their path to heaven." She is mortified that none
of them will have any further interest in the Banking House
(save an annuity for herself), and that her sons are not to
be partners: adding "I see so clearly the hand of God in
this that I could not wish it otherwise." She was also puzzled
by some of her husband's testamentary dispositions. She
herself was sole executrix and guardian of the nine children,
and in the event of her death her brother Dan and others
whom she trusted would become executors. But who would

then become guardian? A young couple of the name of Inglis had been appointed. None of the family knew these Inglises well. Were they suitable? Distracted with such problems, moving constantly between worldliness and piety, and resting in neither, the sick woman wore her life away. Only one thing remained for her in the flux: Marianne, "My eldest daughter is everything to me . . . with judgement beyond her years and warm affection in the bloom of youth, she devotes herself to the comfort and aid of her sorrowing mother." She died on October 15, 1815 at Brighton, whither she had been removed in the hope of alleviating her malady.

Then sorrow broke out again with accumulated force. To convey it is difficult—not through lack of material but through superabundance. The bereaved and their comforters all write enormous letters, symptoms are dwelt on, dying speeches and death moments repeated and extended, the Will of God is bowed to again and again, sorrow is so persistently exhibited as joy that both become meaningless. The twentieth-century observer has to remind himself that inside all this cocoonery of words there was love, there was pain. It was the technique of the age and of a section of the middle class; it lasted, as far as my own family were concerned, into the 1850's. After that the technique of mourning shortens; it is now very brief and some sensible people cut out mourning altogether. With it they cut down pain, which has practical advantages, and with pain they cut down love. People today love each other from moment to moment as much as ever their ancestors did, but loyalty of soul, such as the elder Thorntons possessed, is on the decrease.

A typical ejaculation, from Hannah More:

"Blessing and honour and glory and power be unto Him that sitteth upon the throne and unto the Lamb for ever and ever!"

[69]

My dearest Marianne

What an honour, what a privelege to have had two such parents! What a joy unspeakable in the midst of heart-rending sorrow to see them bear their dying testimony to the faithfulness and truth of God, and enabled to give such incontestable proofs of the reality of the Christian religion! She is now united to him whom she so tenderly loved on earth. She now makes one of the glorious society in Heaven of the spirits of the just made perfect. Though our souls are sorrowful yet let them be thankful also. Though your father and your mother have forsaken you, the Lord will take you up.

God bless and console you all

H. M.

The children had good friends and relatives in Clapham and Yorkshire, they had health and position and brains, they were not penniless, and they deserve no special sympathy. But the double bereavement was staggering. They had been completely dependent on their parents and in less than a year both were gone. It seemed at first that the house would have to go too. For who was to run Battersea Rise? They—that is to say the two senior children, Marianne and Henry —had plenty to worry them and the exciting public events of the year seem to have passed unnoticed.

SISTER

1815-1852

At the time of their parents' death the ages of the Thornton children were:

Marianne	18
Henry	15
Lucy	13
Watson	12
Isabella	11
Sophia	9
Henrietta	7
Laura	6
Charles	5

ONE

The Reign of Sir Robert

SIR ROBERT INGLIS—as it is convenient to call him though
he had not yet inherited his baronetcy—was at this time only
twenty-nine, but endowed with gravity and benevolence beyond his years. It must have been these qualities that com-
mended him to Henry Thornton, for they had nothing in
common politically and little doctrinally. Sir Robert was an
unbending Tory, he dreaded not only revolution but reform,
and when he entered Parliament he opposed any measure
that promised social betterment or menaced the supremacy
of the Church of England. Weightily for twenty-five years
did he represent the University of Oxford. Two engravings
of him in his robes of a D.C.L. so oppressed my youth that
when they came into my possession I took one of them out
of its frame, tore it into small pieces, and burnt them in the
kitchen range. Duplicate Sir Roberts were too much. It has
taken me many years to realise that his dimensions were jus-
tified by his integrity. Here is a man of substance in every
sense. He had a town house at 6 Bedford Square, which he
quitted in order to take up the duties of his guardianship.
And he was also heir to a property with manorial rights in
Bedfordshire: Milton Bryan. When he died Milton passed
to his wife, and when she died it passed to their beloved
ward, Marianne Thornton.

Lady Inglis (Milady) was, and had need to be, of a different disposition—submissive, clinging, diffident. In all things she deferred to her husband's judgement, and "What will Sir Robert think?" echoes so much and so widely in the correspondence of the period that Battersea Rise begins to sound like Mansfield Park. Unlike Lady Bertram, though, Lady Inglis possessed an independent morality, and she could be distinctly severe if youths and maidens tried to sit up alone or rambled at night on the lawns. She was said to be a well-educated little woman, and at home in the world, but she was certainly less intellectual than her wards and less intelligent. How she must have dreaded the high-powered Marianne! And there were only nine years between their ages.

And Sir Robert's sisters must not be forgotten. The younger of them, Miss Louisa Inglis ("dear old Loo"), lived far into the century, and became a general pet. She was even more submissive than Milady, a Miss Matty of a woman, frightened of her ponderous brother, who treated her with the utmost respect but did not seek her company, and tending in later years to tuck herself away in Bedfordshire and repine. And finally there was, for a few years, old Sir Hugh. He seems to have been a more vital person than his son. He had spent his manhood in India as a midshipman and in other capacities, he had been secretary to the Governor of Bengal, Director and then Chairman of the East India Company. He returned to England at the close of the eighteenth century, inherited Milton from his first wife, and filled it with beautiful and strange objects. One of these—a Goa stone in a gold filagree case—was for a short time in my hands; it is now in the British Museum. His fine illustrated Rabelais is in the library of my cousin Ronald Southey. It was a grief to Sir Hugh that his only son was childless, he

Sir Robert Inglis, M.P., D.C.L., F.R.S.
by George Richmond (1850?)

was delighted with the guardianship, said he had nine new grandchildren and began to build extra rooms at Milton. He waited on Marianne in person, and made her feel "a little daughter-in-law like." He died in 1820, and in marble, and over life size, he lies in Milton Bryan church. Sir Robert lies there too, under a slab.

The Inglis irruption was ill received in Clapham circles. Little was known of the young couple who would now rule at Battersea Rise, and it was felt that the precious children and the sacred house ought to have been entrusted to some member of the family. Aunt Robert Thornton, whom her husband had deserted, was the obvious candidate—wronged Aunt Robert who thought almost everything wrong. And the children themselves were suspicious. They felt insecure, they were being put into the power of strangers whom they had but vaguely seen at their parents' deathbeds. Little Laura when told to put on clean shoes and stockings for the Inglises sat on the floor crying "Bother the Inglises, bother the Inglises." For which Nurse Hunter scolded her, said the Inglises were "very kind people," and anyhow she would not have such a word as Bother used in her nursery.

The estimable couple were kind, and they were considerate: that comes out in all they did. To have won the approval of Nurse Hunter was half their battle; by now she was deep in all family secrets and could have made trouble. With her collaboration they instituted a new economy which should resemble the old as much as possible. A high-minded governess, Miss Lamb, was engaged for the six younger children. Marianne, Henry, and Watson were accepted as adult. Much depended on Marianne. She instantly received her guardians into her affectionate heart. They became her friends for life—Sir Robert her counsellor as well as her friend; the Eighth Champion of Christendom she called him.

The reactions of Henry and Watson have not been recorded. Watson figures little in forthcoming events. Henry·figures. He was at fifteen self-contained and self-confident, he had inherited his father's ability; much was expected from him as his father's son, especially by Mrs. Hannah More. He was devoted to his sisters, particularly to Marianne, and he must already have been hoping for the time when he would be both director of the family bank and head of the family board.

In one respect the new dynasty was more liberal than its predecessor. It admitted art and science and it regarded foreign countries as interesting in themselves rather than as fields for missionary enterprise. Sir Robert adored travel—he was the typical tireless tourist—and he was to infect Marianne with his enthusiasm. There was something of the courteous dilettante about him; he was interested in Public Records, he founded a literary club, he was Antiquary to the Royal Academy, he encouraged young artists. One of these, George Richmond, requires particular notice. (What an excellent artist he was! When will a revival descend on him, and a monograph be written about him?) Sir Robert detected him when he was very young, encouraged his early marriage, and provided him with a sitter in William Wilberforce. The portrait brought him fame instantly: it was painted at Battersea Rise, and Wilberforce's chair is said to have perched for the occasion upon a table. He also painted Sir Robert himself, and sketched Thorntons and Forsters innumerable, and he became a close friend of the family: "I began with a Thornton and I shall end with a Thornton," he said, and he has expressed his surprise that he could be friends with a family so inartistic. Of the illustrations in this book no fewer than five are Richmond portraits.

With the death of her father Marianne's heroic period had ended. She was never again to be in the heart of affairs. No more parliamentary sessions or electoral struggles. No more danger to the tulip tree, except from rot. The past had been stormy and golden. The future was to be quieter and a little mediocre. The Inglises, though duly high-minded, had a stubborn inclination towards conformity, and she once said rather wryly, that she was the last representative of the Clapham Sect; all her brothers and sisters had followed Sir Robert elsewhere.

The most important events of her early orphanhood were her foreign visits—(to be described separately)—and the entry of her brother to the university.

Cambridge had been preferred to Oxford. It was supposed to be more in the Evangelical tradition: Wilberforce had been at John's, Simeon at King's, Isaac Milner at Queens'; Henry Thornton and Tom Macaulay were entered together at Trinity.

From Hannah More to Marianne (December 1818):

I pray God to preserve dear Henry from the contagious atmosphere of Cambridge. He carries with him Christian principles and ignorance of practised evil, he had a high call. He must never forget he is the eldest son of *Henry Thornton*. Much will be expected from him, his example must give the tone to the young men who have not had the advantage of such parents, nor the blessings of such friends as the Inglises. I am much changed with respect to the two universities. I used greatly to prefer Cambridge, but this Summer I have had so much intercourse with men of talents and piety from Oxford that I believe not only that the general discipline there is much stricter but in two or three Colleges religion is in more esteem. It behoves such youths as Henry Thornton and Tom Macaulay to raise the depressed standard of religion and morals by their exalted principles and exemplary conduct.

Every care was taken of the lads' moral welfare at Trinity, and out of thirty college washerwomen the most suitable to their character was picked by the tutor. They first shared lodgings in Jesus Lane. When they moved into college Macaulay had rooms in the Great Court between the entrance gate and the chapel, and I believe that my great-uncle's were near. They were both exemplary undergraduates, but Henry worked harder than Tom, with results that became evident in the Tripos.

Marianne to Hannah More (January 21, 1822):

The Cambridge battle has been fought under very trying circumstances. The bilious complaint which has hurt Henry's eyes and kept him half idle during all this term came on with much violence last week and he was confined to his bed, and then I think he must have stayed and have given up all thought of the Senate House but for the marvellous composure and equanimity which I am thankful he inherits,—so resigning his future honours quietly he gradually recovered, and he was persuaded by his friends, many of whom assured him he might be Senior Wrangler, to go into the Senate House on Monday, weak as he was according to his own account in mind as well as body. He was however able to go through Examination these four days, and on the 5th was declared 4th Wrangler and the first of Trinity College. . . . A happier house than this down to nurse and the coachman never was seen when the news that 'our Henry' had done well arrived. . . . We shall have him at home in a day or two to nurse and to pet. . . . Our pleasure in this event is much damped and Henry's still more so by the failure of his friend and companion Tom Macaulay whom it was found did not know mathematics enough to enable him to sit for the medal. Tho' his is not a mathematical head, they

say this little may be gained by almost any body who will read
with attention, and I am therefore doubly sorry, not on his
own account only, but on that of his sire, who has been so wise
and so wary in his management of his 'son of genius'. Perhaps
it may be of use to Tom in showing that there is no royal way
to Honours.

Fearful perhaps of having been priggish, she then becomes
more so:

These Cambridge Honours are fleeting things, and very different from those true joys which may await those that have
taken the better part. Still it is a pleasure to feel that Henry
has been doing his 'duty in that state of life unto which it has
pleased God to call him' according to the catechism account
of the matter, which some very excellent people in some respects
do not I think enough attend to.

Henry had certainly made a good start, nor had Tom
Macaulay made a bad one, for in a few years he was elected
Fellow. He was already deep in literature, politics, and eloquence. Henry, a steadier boy, settled down at once to the
study of banking. He was a terrific worker, and it is significant that he took no part in the foreign outings then in
progress. Watson was also developing satisfactorily—a dim,
prim, fussy, joking youth. He too went to Trinity, he read
for the Church, and after taking orders spent his life away
in Herefordshire. Little Charles—the baby of the family—
also entered the Church in due season.

When we pass from the boys to the girls we pass into a
world of whirl. Not that there was anything fast about the
six Miss Thorntons, but there were six of them and to disen-
tangle six maidens is never easy especially when the sound
of their laughter has gone. Unless a letter is signed I seldom
know which girl wrote it, and of four unlabelled drawings I

have no idea which represents whom; sloping shoulders, long necks, delicate features, abundant chignons give no help to the earnest researcher. Here is a little first aid: Marianne—she needs no introduction. Lucy—satirical, vivid, on the edge of first-class foolery; clever with pen and pencil; later on warped by ill health. Isabella and Sophia—both elegant and later on formidable, but not yet. Henrietta—very clever with her pencil: a most gifted domestic artist. Laura—very tall, tomboyish, shy-ish, animal lover; probably the least intelligent of the sisterhood.

Sir Robert held dinner parties in high esteem. Interesting conversation between important persons was his main objective, but he also appreciated the presence of youth, and as the girls matured they were encouraged, nay required, to take their turns as hostesses. These entertainments would have passed into oblivion, but for the chance survival of a shabby little dinner book. This gives a list of the formal dinners at Battersea Rise between 1826 and 1828, and of some breakfasts offered in London over the same period. Lists of the guests are appended, and they are interesting and significant: no one of immortal fame is present but nearly everyone has a brief notice in the *D.N.B.* Of still greater interest are the comments of the frivolous girls. They have avenged themselves on their boredom by scrawling down scraps of conversations overheard by them.

Let us with their help attend the dinner given on November 7, 1826. Lady Inglis sat at one end of the table, Sir Robert at the other. The company included: Mr. Grey, Mrs. Deacon, Mr. Colquhoun, Marianne, Mr. G. Eyre, Lucy, Henry, Mr. Deacon, Miss Calvert, Mr. Dunn, Isabella, Mr. Gorham, Miss Ward, Mr. Labouchere, Miss Emily Calvert. Seventeen in all, and Henrietta and Laura plus Mr. and

Mrs. Shaw, Aunt Robert, Mr. Thomason, Mrs. Stephen, and Mrs. W. Addington come in afterwards. Twenty-five total.

Caustic comments follow, and explain why people were sometimes afraid of the Miss Thorntons.

Miss Calvert: Who is the sweet looking lady in black?—Henry: Mrs Addington,—Is she a religious character?—Yes—Delightful! You have quite a delightful society of *friends*, quite evangelical, dear Mrs Shaw *and* Mrs Deacon, indeed Clapham is a favoured place and such a minister!

Mrs Stephen: La! do you walk in the rain? I never would like it—perhaps my plaid's too long but it dangles into every puddle and then bang it comes against *both* legs—such a state as my stockings are in—not fit to be seen. In short I feel like a drowned fowl or a damp Duck—Gorham! Mr Gorham! when you've quite *done* (he's doing nothing) just be so good as to hand me that paper,—I might as well have held my tongue, just wasting my sweetness on the desert air for any good it does talking to him. Is he *always* deaf?—1.2.3.4.5.6. All here. 3 brothers. 2 away. My brother is in India and I'm glad of it.—Henry: You must be *very* fond of him.—Oh *how* original you are! Fond of him—yes—I'm *fond* of him, but I'd much rather he was in India than here; *that* kind of fondness you know.—Mr Colquhoun: Had you a pleasant voyage from India?—I was so sick! Just that kind of thing I couldn't eat my dinner, you know. The sailors used sometimes to come to me with 'Your little Jemmy's climbing up the ropes ma'am, and swinging across the deck.'—Well let him swing. I'm so sick!

Mr Gorham to Sir Robert: Sir Robert are those mince pies?—Yes—I'll thank you for a pie sir!—Sir R:—Which wine will you take, Mr G?—Whatever's at hand, sir.

Mr Gorham to Sophia: Did you ever see Mr Thomason before?—I've seen him in the pulpit.—G: He has never been here before then?—He says he was here 20 or 30 years ago.—You weren't intimate *then!* Erhur erhur—Goodnight.

This nonsense sparkles, almost catches fire. And it is significant that the girls admired Jane Austen. The nonsense to follow suggests rather the comedy of Peacock. It is December 10, 1827. A grave company has partaken of nourishment, including Mr. Wolfe, a converted Jew, Edward Irving, the preacher, and the Rev. Charles Simeon, another preacher. They are concerned with the Jewish problem in some of its aspects. Scribbled round them and over them we decipher

Mr Wolfe:—I have a house in Jerusalem. The key is here and the door locked! It'll git damp! It'll git damp! I—I—I—I—I should like to know who's to air it (ring at the door—enter Miss Vansittart) 'Mr Wolfe—Miss Vansittart.'—Wolfe: What? 'Allow me to introduce you to Miss Vansittart.' W:—*What* is she? I—I—I—I—*What* is your name?

Mr Simeon (with his eyes shut) I'm delighted to see you. Peace be with you. May every blessing attend yer. Why does Mrs Thornton live here and her daughters at Sir Harry's? Is Sir Harry going to Jerusalem? Will he go in April? I can preach in 10 languages.

Marianne (eating her lunch): They are all full of the Jews. Mr Wolfe: Are *you* not full?

Miss Emilia Venn [on another occasion]: 'I am sure I have such a feel when I see a Jew. It gives me quite a shudder, they have such a hankering after money too.' Mrs Hankey:—'Yes Miss Venn that's a very natural feeling, but I think it is one of those we ought to strive to get the better of.' Harangue in favour of the Jew Society. When Mrs H. went away Emilia came up to her and told her she hoped she did not think she meant any disrespect to the Jews or the Society, or in short anything improper. Mrs H. said she hoped not, and they shook hands and parted.

Lizzie was not in good spirits, well dressed but very dirty. She told Mr Gorham she remembered he had once said he envied the Hankies their journey to Paris, to which he answered 'Do yer?'.

This slight humorous anti-Semitism is characteristic. Not until the present century did the British middle classes realise what jokes about Jews can lead to. Entirely inoffensive is this encounter between two elderly gentlemen, Sir Benjamin Hobhouse and Captain Willock.

Sir B. To Willock—Well General Wavell [*sic*] when were you last in Mexico?—W. with much indignation: 'Never Sir'.—Sir B. walking about leaning on Lady Inglis' arm: 'Did you ever see such a thing shameful abominable going away at half past 9, what's to be done, we'll lock the doors. . . . Captain Willock:—'I am of the opinion of the Persian poet who says a beautiful garden has no charms for me without an elegant and interesting companion'. Sir B:—Forgotten the place in 6 years? Oh impossible it seems to me as if I had left it but yesterday, how is the Tulip Tree?—Captain W. (looking at several Miss T's escaping through the library windows into the garden):—Pray is this the way in which the ladies of this family bolt out of a two pair of stair window whenever they have company?—Henry: No you see our windows go to the ground. —Captain W:—Oh very true. I once knew a young lady so shy that when we were a party of officers going to see her father she crawled under the sofa! We said we would wait in the room till her father came back, as he was out, we did wait some time and then we saw such a pretty little foot peeping out from under the sofa! yes such a pretty little foot . . .

At this point several pages have been cut out of the dinner book. The next entry is: "This book has been lost for two months."

In the dinner lists often occur the names of two Irish clergymen, the Rev. John Jebb, Bishop of Limerick, and

his chaplain, the Rev. Charles Forster. They did not belong
to the Clapham Circle; there is a reference to them in a
letter of Hannah More's, of 1818, when they were still in
the wilds of Ireland.

Mr Dunn is a creature of Etherial Mould. Apropos of *such*
beings I have a handful of letters *unanswered* from the two
Hermits of Abington Glebe, so elegant, so poetical, so romantic
in the best sense of the word, so unlike the creatures of 'this
dim spot called Earth' that they are perfectly amusing; pity
such a pair of affectionate heavenly-minded things should be
locked up in a dismal Irish parish with only forty Protestants.
If they had not caught a little tincture of Anti-Bible Society-
ism from dear Knox with a snatch of one or two other tinctures,
they would be perfect.

The pair became popular at Battersea Rise, and in the
'thirties the Reverend Charles Forster broke the charmed
circle of the sisterhood and became my grandfather. That is
a serious matter to be elsewhere treated. In the 'twenties he
was eager and charming and a little foolish. Lucy Thornton,
that sharp-tongued chatterbox, had some fun out of him:

In the evening the whole rabble of us were together and Mr
Forster. He was talking of 'comfortables' the flannelly things
to tie around the neck. Henry said 'O they're horrid I can't
abear them, they scrub so Mr Forster.' 'They're I-*rish* said F.
But they're nasty things said Henry, they remind one of the
wretchedness of one's bed sometimes Mr Forster, when the sheets
etc. drag and the blankets scrub so (a sigh) you may feel after
the sheet for ever with your feet but you can't find it, not till
the bed's made. Mr F. seemed to think this conversation was
not etiquette but he laughed so for some time he could not
speak. Henry was quite serious, Miss Louisa bit her lips and
looked down and all laughed so loud that Sir R's eyes at the
other table forsook his folio and gave an enquiring glance to-

Inside Holy Trinity Church, Clapham Common
by Lucy Thornton (about 1825)

wards ours. Henry did not at all understand our laughter—he said it was what we must all have felt.

This letter recalls the scribblings in the dinner book: perhaps Lucy was their authoress. She makes fun of the poetry of Robert Montgomery, whom Macaulay was to pillory:

Florence is reading to me the tenderest amorette between Javan and Zillah in the *World Before the Flood,* and now and then supplies a little explanation of their tenderness. 'You know Lucy they were *such* friends such *very* great friends, they thought of nobody but each other . . . and now don't look at the next page. Javan's going to have such a surprise. 'It was Zillah!'—his friend you know and now he's going to play to her on his pipe. . . . 'Then he woke her by his music', how lovely!

Alarmed she started from her lonely den
And blushing instantly retired again

How lovely! he played on a pipe you know, and had been hunting about for her and at last found her sleeping, and woke her gently on his pipe.

Lucy was clever with her pencil too. She did a laughable yet lovely water colour of the interior of Clapham Church. Perched high in the pulpit is a youthful preacher—Watson perhaps. Below is Anna, the schoolmistress, gesticulating wildly at her charges, who have escaped from her control and are fighting at the entrance to the vestry. Anna stands. The rest of the congregation sits, the backs of their heads visible over the pews. Each of them is numbered and named, and we can identify some lesser celebrities out of the dinner book. Here is Mr. Dunn of Etherial Mould. Here is Mr. Gorham, the curate, who troubled Sir Robert for a pie, and subsequently troubled church circles by the Gorham controversy.

About the same date is a charming volume labelled "Family Sketch Book." Henrietta was probably the artist. She has portrayed her sisters, her brother Charles, and again and again little Harry, the gardener's child, a pink and white and flaxen object, then in general demand. Loveliest of all is Sophia as a bridesmaid, in a delicate white net, saying, "It will be my turn next." There are several sketches of Marianne—already a little mature. A back view of her: solid olive-green costume, broad lace collar, combs in hair. Another back view, with Sir James Mackintosh, who has managed to turn his back on her. Sir James is saying: "It's an established fact that all ladies are deficient in geometry, grammar, and justice. Do you agree with me?" To which the spirited woman replies: "No. I should be deficient in the last quality if I did."

Still more important are Henrietta's large sketches showing all the brothers and sisters together in the library. They are memorial sketches—the family could never have been grouped just thus—and the standing central figure is in one version William Wilberforce, and in the version here reproduced Nurse Hunter. In each case the sketch is taken looking away from the window, towards the curved apse of books. Close on the left is the great green settee, with Marianne on it, working, and worried by a spaniel: she disliked dogs. From left to right follow: Henry, Sophia, Watson, Laura (my grandmother), Nurse Hunter (standing), Isabella, Henrietta, Charles, Lucy. The composition of the picture sets Marianne apart. She, who was to outlive her brothers and most of her sisters, looks tranquilly from her corner towards the garden and works, works, a beneficent Norn. Her father's portrait hangs above her. Her guardian is not present, but the group well symbolises his amiable reign.

The Library, Battersea Rise, with Nurse Hunter and the assembled family by Henrietta Thornton (about 1825)

At the opposite end of Clapham Common there was, it will be remembered, another large house, the home of her Uncle Sam. The relation between the two establishments was cousinly rather than intimate. The Battersea Rise party had inherited their father's critical outlook, and nothing that Uncle and Aunt Sam did roused their enthusiasm. Slight sniffs arise, mockery crackles. It is impossible to convey these subtle alienations without quotation, and a letter from Sophia to Laura comes in conveniently. It was written in 1827. Marianne had been stopping with the Sams at Chobham, in their country house. Sophia and Henry had gone down to pick her up.

We arrived at two. After lunch we all went out on the lawn before the house and played a game called 'One fool makes many'. It consists in throwing a large ring from one to another and catching it on the top of a stick. It is a truly juvenile amusement and we played at it for about an hour. Aunt Sam sat at the window and watched us. It is very much the fashion in that part of the world. Last week Mr. Fyler invited nine ladies of quality to his house who spent the afternoon at it. Uncle Sam has told us how many times the Duchess of Gloucester and Princess Sophia have called during the last fortnight and how many times they have dined there. In the evening Aunt Sam made us sit and talk to her about the maids' cloathes and about what they had for dinner on the wedding day, while Uncle Sam brought forth a string of anecdotes, very much resembling those which he produced at B. Rise one Sunday evening. He told us the words in which his father and his grandfather offered marriage to their wives. At 10 minutes before 10 he desired the prayer bell might be rung. Aunt Sam would have Quiz into prayers who did nothing but whine and howl, while Maria increased the noise by calling to him and patting him. We could not help smiling, which the maids seeing they all laughed.

After prayers Uncle Sam lighted our candles and saw us up to bed. We were off about 7.0 the next morning.

This tone is typical. And things got seriously wrong over the episode of the imbecile suitor. This gentleman (his name has not been preserved) was paying attentions to Laura. Her cousin Eliza (of the Samuel branch) warned her against him, and then encouraged him to transfer his attentions to her own daughter, for he was well-off as well as weak-minded. So far so good. Battersea Rise enjoyed its malicious laugh. But Henry in his merriment went too far. He wrote someone a letter in which he said that Eliza had been well advised to settle close to a lunatic asylum, for it would be needed. Which letter fell into Eliza's hands. She adopted a super-Christian attitude and thanked her cousin elaborately for his goodness to her in past years. If anyone else at Battersea Rise had written the letter about the asylum, she would have easily understood, she knew what the others were, but that Henry, that Henry the soul of Kindness . . . "Virago!" Henry growled.

Their slight disapproval of the Sams and their indifference towards dull Aunt Robert threw "the Battersea Risers" more and more into the arms of the Inglises. How excited they all were when their guardian bearded Queen Caroline! Writing to Hannah More at the time (August 1821) Marianne says:

Of one thing I am sure—that to our grand-children all our letters might be interesting, for new wonders arise every day with which to fill them, like the moving figures of a magic lanthorn on a white sheet. Your letter to me was full of the Coronation and Bonaparte's death. Since that another lofty spirit is laid low, as misdirected and consequently as mischievous as his but in her way as heroic. And *we*, English people that we were supposed to be, have proved the falsehood of that supposition by showing in fact we are semi barbarian savages who can quarrel and fight over a dead body like dogs growling over a bone, and can throw stones and tear our neighbours eyes out with the same sang froid of a Mohawk.

You know or perhaps you do not know the part Sir Robert had given him at the Coronation—to meet the Queen wherever she might present herself, and inform her that it was her husband's good pleasure that she should not see the show. She was so speedy in her movements that he had some difficulty in being ready for her, but when they did meet, we have heard in a round about way thro' Lady Anne Hamilton that the mingled gentleness and firmness of his manner induced her to give up the contest, and for the first time to behave in a feminine manner. And he in return was rather pleased with the submissive sort of way in which she spoke, and tho' I believe he has a worse opinion of her than almost anybody, he says had he known nothing of her but what he saw that day he should really have thought very well of her.

And when he was elected Member for Oxford University in 1829, how delighted they were, and how little did they realise that they had changed sides politically. For the election was fought on the issue of Catholic Emancipation, and their father had been in favour of it, whereas Sir Robert was against it. Peel, the sitting member, had been against it too, but had changed his opinion, and had resigned in consequence and stood for re-election. Sir Robert beat him. Wild was the enthusiasm at Battersea Rise, lengthy the letter to be despatched to Hannah More. "No Popery," all the ladies cried, forgetting that No Popery was what Mendoza the Boxer had cried at Henry Thornton.

On this happiest of happy days I must write one line to you dearest Mrs H. M. Many hearts are beating high with gladness, but none I do believe more than yours. It is such friends as you

that have done the deed—When people ask how the influence
of Whigs, Ministry, private friends—& (shame that it shd. be
so) many of the evangelicals have been overcome,—I know not
what answer to give, except that it has been the warmth & zeal
of a few individuals which have lighted the flame that has burst
out thro' England. Did you hear that a Dr. Cotton came from
Cashel in Ireland to vote for him, many from Guernsey—Yorkshire—& Lancashire—? * Most gallantly indeed have they
stood to their promises like true Men, for Sir R.ᵗ has already
polled *more* than had ever engaged to him while Peel's defec-
tions they say have been most numerous. Nothing else can account for such a *thorough defeat,* for when the battle begun
the promises to each were just even, & every body expected it
would have been a near run thing. Many people say this has
decided the R.C. question that after such a manifestation of
public opinion the Duke never will dare to press it.

Yesterday was a very nervous day. We had incessant accounts—some that the thing was running very near. Henry,
who has scarcely rested an hour for this last week, came down
to us at nine at night saying the next few hours must decide it
& that he should go back to the Committee when he had had some
Tea, & remain there till the Express arrived which had the
close of the poll. Of course none of us could go to Bed on such
an eventful night, so there we all sat over the Library fire with
poor dear Nurse, who reads Fox's Book of Martyrs all
day now, & fancied therefore that her only chance of not
being burnt is in Sir R.ˢ being returned—About three this
morn.ᵍ Henry returned, & the shouts of joy might have been
heard all thro' the House, when he called out 126 majority.

Sir Thomas's picture I think I told you we had cut down, &
have hung up y.ʳ Bedroom at Barley Wood in its place as our
Household God-dess—& really last night you looked quite as

* Voting in a university constituency was not by ballot: the voters
inscribed their names.

if you were one of us with your papers lying on the Table before you—like canvassing Letters for Sir Robert.*

You did quite right about y.ʳ poor Men, but yet you must
not say that Sir Rob.ᵗ will pay for them, (he will not) but that
a friend of his engages to do it. Hitherto no Oxford candidate
has ever paid any expences—but *then* there never has been any
thing like such a contest—we know that Peel has done it now—
but yet Sir R.ᵗ has not engaged to it, & it remains to be seen
whether his committee, or the D. of Newcastle may not pay the
large sums.—As for individuals like those you name, Henry has
told me from the very beginning of this contest that whenever
I liked I might make him responsible, for tho' he shd. think it a
very foolish thing to spend money on an election for himself,
yet in such a case as this he thought he could not do more good
with it—either in any public or private way. He desired Watson to send up any poor Men in his neighbourhood, on his account—Let us therefore know what yours will come to, & I
doubt not we shall gladly defray it. But remember this is quite
between ourselves, as Henry is anxious Sir R.ᵗ should never
know it.

We have crowds of friends around us today, so that I can
hardly write—The Bishop of Limerick is just come, *crying*
with joy—Charles Grant & W. Dealtry—the Mackintoshes—
all of all sides & sects seem to rejoice that such a victory over
dishonesty at all events is won.

Let us hear again from you soon—one line of rejoicing—
There is many a story of zeal & firmness which I could tell you
when I've time that would rejoice your heart—One poor Curate
had 7 official Men write to him 7 Letters most of them beginning *Dear Sir* to induce him to change his promise, but he stood
steady. All the influence of Government has proved nothing
against the conscience of the English clergy. Have you seen our
recreant Knight Sir Ac[land]? I'm in such good humour now

* I have inherited this little picture or one like it; it has been reproduced
in Dr. M. G. Jones's Life of Hannah More.

that we have won that I mean to forget & forgive all past of-
fences—Sir R.^t is better off, for he will not see or feel he has
any to forgive—he dined with Peel's Chairman the day before
the Election with many of Peel's Committee & said they were
all as friendly together as could be—I never saw anything so
perfectly unruffled as he has been all thro' the business—

Ever y^r affec.^e

MARIANNE THORNTON.

Party politics seldom induce wisdom; this letter is slightly
foolish in its tone, and its prophecies were quite off the mark.
Peel easily got a seat elsewhere, and he passed his Catholic
Emancipation Bill later in the year.

The Continent

In 1816, the year after her parents' death, Marianne was persuaded by the Inglises to go to Paris. To her biographer this comes as a delightful shock. She has been so unhappy, so overworked physically and emotionally, so voluble in describing symptoms and reactions and in replying to voluble condolences, and suddenly she is a girl again. The weight lifts, and her pen dances off as if held in another hand. Her ebullience proceeds from a rich nature. She was too big a person to be broken by a bereavement: her parents were never to be forgotten, but there's Paris too! Napoleon is in St. Helena, Louis XVIII ensures safety, and she has never been abroad.

She went with her Yorkshire uncle and aunt, the Dan Sykeses, and with two young people whom they had provided for her companionship. "It is very true, I am going abroad," she writes to Miss Patty Smith: "I thought of nothing less . . . I had been feverish and good for nothing . . . more as a medicine than a pleasure I consented, and now by talking about it and hearing everybody envy me so much, I have begun to think it will be a delightful thing. We go to Paris only." The letter, already rising in spirits, goes on to discuss *The Antiquary* and the possibility of a match between Edie Ochiltree and Meg Merrilies: "What a race of children we should have, we should burn all the Mendicity Reports!"

On her return she recounted her adventures to Miss Smith in a long and lively letter. Lively and loquacious. Her style has not yet matured, most of her sentences are a couple of clauses too long, and her observations lack the brilliance and precision she was able to give them in later years.

Their party crossed from Dover to Calais on May the 20th and "the sensation of first landing on a foreign shore was so strangely delightful that I am almost sorry it can never happen to me again." They took five days to get to Paris, so excited were the young people, who stopped at every town and most villages, and shrieked with laughter at everything French from a "set out of Postboys and Horns to a dinner being carried in." Paris reached, they were instantly admitted into aristocratic society, of a type they would scarcely have encountered in England, and Marianne also became "the intimate friend of all the filles-de-chambres, garçons, Frotteurs, Hôtes, Coutourières, and all the etc. etc. with which a Hotel abounds." The Dan Sykeses were quiet people, with commercial introductions, yet they attend "six or eight soirées of the old noblesse" and see something of the Duchesse d'Angoulême, the daughter of Louis XVI: "every washerwoman can make a better curtsey than the Duchess, and every Restaurateur has more to say to his customers than the King to his Court." And the Duchesse de Berri "has not mended matters, for she seems an awkward unformed modest little thing of seventeen, whom everyone pities when they see her joined to her coarse ugly husband, whose deréglements are the open conversation of all Paris." Marianne's conversation is getting open too, she "stares in at the pretty cafés in the evening, having no reputation to lose." And she summarises or rather expands her feelings about the French in some paragraphs which deserve quotation.

There is a sort of English way of considering the French as nothing more than monkeys, and saying one does not know why 'I hate the French nothing but old England for me' which nothing cures but seeing they really are human beings like oneself and in many ways much our superiors, though in the realities of life and in all its comforts we must hold our preeminence.

But pour s'amuser, pour le mouvement, pour l'interêt qui prenne chaqu'un de vous jours, sans vous en laisser beaucoup de fruits, mais aussi sans que jamais vous en sentissiez le poids, cette manière facile de conduire la vie, de la diversier, de la soustraire à la reflexion sans en écarter le charme de l'esprit, Paris is indeed 'la ville la plus sociale du monde', and at the risk of frightening all my steady aunts and all my sober friends, I must pronounce the French men handsome and the French women beautiful. They were uniformly kind to us too, 'voilà des Anglais bien gentils' was the only exclamation we ever heard about us, we were never called 'Messieurs Pommes de Terre', and all the Frotteurs, and Décrotteurs cried when we went away, and hoped the bon Dieu would send us back next year, though my uncle suffered himself to be cheated only in moderation, and though we persisted in having a fille to make our beds. I daresay they have almost forgotten by this time that we were ever there, but I was not the less obliged by their bienveillance whilst we were. It is always pleasant even to fancy oneself loved, and we certainly were a remarkably accessible and condescending Party and very thankful to anybody who would listen to our bad French.

This is a striking proclamation from a girl of nineteen, who had been brought up on Clapham Common and was visiting her hereditary enemies. It is educated, mature, gracious—all that John Bull (whom she attacks by name) so often wasn't. Gaiety and giggles, wisdom and warmth meet in it and reinforce each other. She is scribbling away to another girl without any thought of showing off, yet her remarks have a weight which men of the world might envy. She has fallen in love with the French, yet she can be shrewd about them. She can accept Duchesses and Filles de Chambre with equal ease. She can be friends with the "lower classes" and expect them to be her friends. Her love for France persisted throughout her life, and when she was too old to go there herself she would finance others. Her indifference to class barriers also persisted. She knew where she herself belonged if she thought about it, but she did not often think about it; what attracted her most was human beings, and she sailed through the nineteenth century without being suspicious of servants, shocked by social *mésalliances*, or scared by the poor. This is unusual. Battersea Rise taught her some of it, but some of it was learnt in France. In a strictly English sense, she was a Daughter of the Revolution.

But to revert to the Patty Smith letter, pages and pages in which remain untouched by me. Some of them are concerned with sight-seeing; the party "worked very hard, saw all the common sights once and most of them more than once," went to the Louvre almost daily, regretted the defacing of the public buildings by the restored monarchy, who were sticking up a fleur-de-lis wherever they pulled down an eagle: "it is very unfortunate that it does not look nearly as imposing." Uncle and Aunt Dan were definitely anti-Bourbon. They observe the inadequacy of Louis XVIII and are unaware of the vulgarity of Bonaparte, who appears to them as he would have wished to appear. Sentimental Imperialism flowers at Malmaison:

The melancholy magnificence of Chantilly delighted me the most; I mean that I should like to spend another day there, much more than at Versailles with all its pomp. Malmaison is very perfect too, and its good taste makes one an Imperialist at once, and the only thing I very much covet as I walk about our own garden is the hot-house, built round *each* separate tree every winter, that they may appear in summer as if they were in their native land, growing naturally.

The voyage back to England was a "woful passage of 40 hours, but I never believe anybody who told of 'dreadful storms' and 'narrow escapes', so I do not expect you would believe me." She finds Battersea Rise as usual, very much as usual: "I was half provoked with them for having done so little when I seemed to have done so much. But the quiet of this place is very nice now, and I find I *can* get through the day without a Cortège or a Fête." Finally: "France is a Fairy Tale kind of scene which we pied de lettre English people can neither describe nor understand." Land of magic and of grace; it had stopped her from thinking about the immediate past and her health is much improved. She only hopes that "Marianne's letters to her kinsfolk" will not get published in these publishing days and "add one to the innumerable number of stupid travels." She signs herself to Patty "Ever your affectionately," and she so signs herself to us, for we could not want a more heartening vindication of the importance of foreign travel.

Meanwhile Aunt Dan had not been idle, and had filled over a hundred pages of her journal with her neat sloping handwriting. Aunt Dan had a tolerant, trundling mind, she was well-educated and observant, but there is no vividness in her account of the tour: convents, churches, statuary, the ballet and the opera, hotel bedrooms, the uniform of the postilions, the marriage procession of the Duc de Berri all sound

alike. Her chief joy in Paris was the company of her husband, her chief anxiety his health. The channel crossing,
which Marianne had dismissed so lightly, becomes however
a serious affair. The sea had been calm as they left Dieppe,
but when they woke next morning Dieppe was still in sight
and the breeze freshening. They breakfasted pleasantly with
some gentlemen on deck, after which all drew up their chairs
round Mr. Dan Sykes, and he read one of Dr. Watts's sermons. Before he could finish it everyone began to feel sick.
"The storm kept increasing, the waves were dreadfully grand
& at last dashed over the deck & we were advised to go below." There Aunt Dan passed a terrible day and a still more
terrible second night, "every thing rolling about in the cabin,
candles with the rest." She could hear her husband and her
niece, "violently straining" in the distance without being
able to help them, and the sounds of the captain giving orders on deck, the heaving of the anchor and the rattling of
chains were dreadful. "Sick at heart as well as Stomach I
had no relief but in silent prayer." On the morning of the
second day the packet reached Brighton. Thereon by stages
to Battersea Rise, and she ends on a happier note:

We found all the children at the door to welcome M. who looked
well and happy to see her. The Inglis' were gone to town but
returned soon after and welcomed us. Many of M's friends
came this evening to tea:—Mrs Babington, the Grants, Mrs
Wm. Smith, & Lord Calthorpe all complimented her on the
improvement in her looks, affection and joy tinged her cheeks
with a bright glow, and she was delightfully animated.

The expedition was such a success that in 1817 Marianne
was off to the continent again. This time she was accompanied by the Inglises. Two lengthy letters describe their adventures. Her first, to Patty Smith, bears the postmark of

"Sept 2," and is written from Boulogne-sur-Mer where she has been "a peaceable and settled inhabitant" for several days. Boulogne is by no means the "French Wapping" she had been led to expect, and had she not known the grandeurs of Paris she would have thought it the "pleasantest thing in the world." Owing to "French faithlessness" their arrangements miscarried: they had to split up and sleep in three different parts of the town, foregathering during the day in a café. And the Dover-Calais crossing had not been "riante" —fourteen women and children able and willing to be helpful, but all sick. However all that is over, and they are now in the second-best hotel, most comfortable, six charming bedrooms, two superb sitting rooms, delicious food, all for the price of English lodgings.

She proceeds to some observations on Boulogne which may interest the social historian.

We see all the comers. I do not wonder at the number of starved looking English wretches, who are to be seen in the street from morning till night till I become quite ashamed of being one of that nation de vagabonds who infest this place. Yet the French are very civil to us and there is a general bienveillance about them. . . . They gave a Ball the other day to all the English with one of the politest little attentions belonging to it that I can remember—They hired four hackney coaches and sent round *gratis* to all the company. How I wish this were the way in our pays! A French Comte told a girl that we know that she danced like an eagle, and that is all I heard of its gaiety. . . .

There are multitudes of English here, but we luckily do not know one of them, except the Vice Consul and his lady by way of protection. I heard indeed this morning that a damsel who I had long admired on the sands for the stately stile with which she stepped out of her bathing machine into her splendid car-

riage, and the mock heroic tragedy manner of paying her sous
to the vielles who crowded round her and her vulgar companions, was votre actrice la plus célèbre de toute l'Angleterre:
Mlle O'Neill. Et c'est étonnant, as one of the Fish women said,
that personne de qualité ne la suivait, elle a seulement sa soeur
et son frère, pas un monsieur, un Milord Anglais dans le cortège . . . [here the letter is mutilated: was the writer becoming risqué or risky?] We run about the streets, learn the art of
rabattre in the market, bathe and hear all the Sand News of
which are women in men's clothes and which are escaping from
their creditors among the Heroes and Heroines who figure there,
and spend an immense time every day in our Abonnement de
Lecture, a species of amusement in which Boulogne certainly
excels. There are four or five really good libraries, not Caw-
thorne's quite, but they are full of books that one feels disposed
to read in such a place, and a frank a fortnight is all we pay,
so as we are very luxurious we belong to them all.

She then discusses what she has been reading while laid up
with a cold: French memoirs mostly: Madame de Motteville,
was on her list, but her preferred was "Mademoiselle, La
Grande Mademoiselle" *: "she is perfectly exquisite, I hope
you know her, if not let me have the honour of introducing
you—she is a most royal Boswell, but the worst or perhaps
the best is that she is Johnson to herself. During all the last
half I was afraid that I was taken in, for it seemed impossible
that a *woman* could have written it of herself."

And the letter continues to drift from bathing women to
priests "who have a sad idiotic look about them that one
quite pities," to Madame L'Hôte, "who fondes into Larmes
every Monday when her Bill is paid," to a local wedding, "a
fancifully pretty sight," and to plans. Her guardian, "notre
cher maitre," has already left, and he orders her and his sis-

* Mademoiselle de Montpensier, niece of Louis XIII.

ters to meet him in the Pays Bas, and visit the Field of
Waterloo. She does not want to leave "this quietly amusing
scene" and she is concerned at leaving little Milady alone in
Boulogne with some children. But her guardian knows what
is best and she must obey.

Next day she writes to Aunt Dan. She has already got to
Ath, in the Low Countries. In a short time many miles have
been traversed and much has happened, and we plunge into
a relatively wild scene: the nearest approach of the Clapham
Sect to Low Life.

My dearest Aunt,

Am I not a good Child to be writing to you, from a crowded
little inn, at wh. we are obliged to stop for the night instead of
reaching Nivelles near the Field of Waterloo, where we had
intended to sleep. You may be surprised at this movement as I
did not know when I wrote last, that my guardian intended a
Junction of the whole party at St. Omers, where an exchange
of Prisoners took place, & he is with his usual goodness letting
me go on with him and his Sisters to see Brussells, Antwerp,
etc. etc.—as it was all new to me. I only intend to make a beginning to-night, as I shall have so much to say from thence, &
I am very sleepy besides, the why & the wherefore you shall
hear, as it may amuse the Boys to see what we betake ourselves
to.

We found Lille gate shut last night to our utter disappointment, & were told we positively must be contented with the
Cahaut [?] till they were opened at 5 this Morn.ᵍ I descended
to reconnoitre, & found a chaumière—Eh bien avez-vous des
lits—Oui Oui, il y a le lit de Madame, & celle de Monsieur, c'est
assez—Elt ou sont-ils?—Par là.—I found with dismay they
were in the Kitchen in wh. I was standing, & alors vous pouvez
souper à une table d'Hôte—We had had no dîner so I anxiously
asked where. Par là encore, shewing me the Table at wh. two
Frotteurs were devouring some onions—Bon! that decided me

it w.^d do, so with many a hearty laugh the Miss Inglises joined me, but their brother looked a little grave when he heard our doom. Some Souper I w.^d have Frotteur or not, so they brought us some cochon à la huile, some choux bouilli dans l'huile & 'au naturel', some Navets in the same stile soi disant à l'Anglais, & in walked the Hair dresser & Shoe Maker of the Place as we think them—The first thing we saw of our future companions was marching in to Madame L'Hôte who was sitting in the Scullery out of respect to us, & giving her a baiser à la Française. 'Finissez donc she said, voilà des dames comme il faut, qui doivent souper ici, allez comportez-vous comme il faut.' And so they did for since the days of the flood, never did I hear so many pretty things said to 3 demoiselles in the same time, we c.^d eat nothing & they were desolé they w.^d cook themselves for us, w.^d we honour an omelette with gouté-ing it. I tho.^t the fun compensated for the Supper, & was great friends with them. The Miss Inglises laughed, & so did my guardian too at last, when he got over his first panic at seeing us in such company. They have promised to come to England, & I shall give them a supper at the little 'Plough' if they do. At last we exterminated our companions, & even the last lingering Frotteur was sent off that we might go to Bed, but we found that tho' we had the State Bedroom, the sheets &c. were not inviting enough to persuade us to come very near them, so we got all the pelisses & shawls, & again my only consolation was repeating to my fellow sufferers that we were warriors taking our rest with our martial cloaks around us, not rest indeed for me, for I was so much more inclined to laugh than to sleep, that nothing but the orders of my companions c.^d have prevented my adjourning to Frotteur Hall, where our late society at Supper had retired for a little chat, & where during the whole night we were waked with 'encore de l'eau de Vie', 'de bonne bierre vite vite'. Once when I called our waiting Maid an English Officer appeared instead, & seemed inclined to send me for his Supper, but as I was not caparisoned for such a service, I told him our case, &

he was very polite to us, thro' the door. So we went on, I laughing & talking with every living thing that came near us, since
sleep was out of the question, till poor Miss Inglises were
obliged often to repeat je n'ai pas besoin de—you know the
rest. At last came the morning. My guardian's adventures I
never ventured to inquire into, I suppose he shared the Frotteurs nest, & forgot to wake them for he & I had to load the
carriage & mend a wheel, but we made up in our morn.ᵍ magnificence for our nights amusement, for they brought us four
Horses instead of three, & as we have shafts to the carriage
they yoked them *abreast*. To be sure one of them went for two
miles with its leg over the Trace, but n'importe said the Post
Boy, tenez-vous tranquille & j'irai au plus vite nonobstant & so
indeed we did.

Oh I have quite forgotten our old Brussels adventures now
for all Yesterday was spent on the Field of Waterloo & tho' I
went there as cooly & as Imperialist as cᵈ be, tell my Uncle I
came away Ultra-Royalist. We arrived at Hougomount about
three Oclock, I was surprised to find it a very pretty Chateau
with beautiful Gardens, tho' now all in Ruins except the chapel
wh. they spared. The Trees are even yet covered with holes, &
every thing appears as if the enemy had left it only yesterday,
excepting indeed that the mounds of earth now cover what
wᵈ have been a Soldiers Body. While I was sketching & Miss
I———s relic gathering an English Gentleman & an old
Farmer passed by, & the former on seeing us said Faites-moi
l'honneur de me permettre de vous presenter Monsʳ La Coste,
le Guide de Bonaparte. The English Man turned out to be
Professor Monk whom we met at Scarbro', he persisted in taking us for French to my great amusement, for my Uncles
French is beautiful to his.

Whether this is the real La Coste, I am such a heretic on
these matters I chose to doubt, however if not he does as well,
as he knows the Ground perfectly, & has either heard or seen a
good deal of the Emperor, he assures us that one of the Mar-

[*103*]

shalls *himself* at Buonaparte's own desire tied his (La Costes)
legs under the Horse, his arms behind him, & his Bridle was
held by an Adjutant. Sauve qui peut, is *not* true; Buonaparte
on seeing the Prussians come up, said voilà les maudits Prusses,
tout est donc fini, il faut nous sauver, but in a calm manner, &
not as if panic struck as our books describe him. We walked
with him (*not* the Emperor but La Coste) over some fields
to La Belle Alliance where as not even the enthusiasm of Waterloo c^d. prevent our feeling famished, they gave us some cochon
& eggs, all they had, & I sat in the Dukes Chair, & drank the
Dukes Wine (it is capital & only 2 francs a bottle even now)
& flirted with La Coste who shewed me the place where the Duke
met Blucher & begged I w^d. take a sketch from thence. We then
took him upon the Coach Box to La Haie Sainte, & the village
where there was that dreadful carnage as the Houses plainly
shew, the Sun was just setting as we got to a beautiful Pillar
in memory of Sir Alex. Gordon close to l'Arbre de Vellington
as they call it, & when we arrived at Waterloo Church it was
so dark that we were obliged to have it illuminated as if the
Priests were going to say Mass that we might see the eight
monuments wh. are there. I was almost sick with Le Coste's
description of the horrors, wherever the Corn was very green
there had been beaucoup, beaucoup de morts, & down one little
ridge there had been buried 7 thousand frenchmen. The horror
of horrors however is the sort of shew that the People make of
it. Boys were continually offering us bones, pieces of hair, buttons, Bullets etc. etc. wh. they declared they had picked up
for a few Sous. There are quite a collection of these curiosities
at the Farm, but I am a bad Catholic & have no faith in them,
tho' when I accused the people of manufacturing them as they
were wanted, they answered truly enough that it was easier for
them to pick them from a Field where 150,000 Men had been
engaged than to go to Brussels for new ones.—You will believe how often I thought of poor John * during the day, I

* Cornet J. C. Sykes, a cousin, killed.

asked La Coste where the 1ˢᵗ Dragoons were & he shewed me the place, waving now with such beautiful corn.—

At eight oclock we came on thro' the Forest of Soignies here, & of course did not arrive till very late, especially as one of our Horses came down three times, owing to the bon vin de Vellinton as I rather suspect, wh. we had given to our Postillion, desiring him to drink to the Health of our Duke & his Prince, I told him not to forget *poor* Louis dixhuit, he laughed & said il ne vaut pas la peine, so he had another Glass to encourage him in such good sentiments.—Tell the Boys to mind not to mention our Visit to Waterloo to any of the Cottingham party, I am sadly afraid Watson will forget, but if he does he shall not have a little Bullet I have got for him. Your letter & his have been the only ones I have received since I left England my dear Aunt, you have now recᵈ another of mine from Boulogne I hope.—My Paper is almost done, & they are calling me to come to look at this beautiful City as it appears from our Windows, but I have not yet been out, it is 8 O'clock, & I have written all this, am I not a good Girl. Oh you *must* come to Brussels next year.

As we were streaming thro' the Streets led by our Laquais this mornᵍ we met, streaming another way led by his Laquais Mr. Brougham. I longed to ask him about the recorder, [?] but tho' he bowed, I suppose because he found out I was like my Uncle, I did not venture.

The People here seem much more daring in expressing their Imperialism than they were in Paris. A man at Lille in ansʳ to some good royalist sentiment of mine said C'est très vraisemblable que nos voisins n'aimaient pas notre Empereur comme nous mêmes.—And then he added mais votre guerre étoit très genereuse aussi, car s'il avoit été votre ami au lieu de votre ennemi, vous auriez été le second Peuple de l'Univers. I told him we were now the first & so we ended.

I don't like le Pays Bas as a Country so well as our dear merry France, tho' the People are very nice. The Scotch are their highest admiration, & my plaid Gown has more than once got me thro' a Crowd. 'C'est une dame Ecossaise laissez-elle passer donc.' They say the Scotch made themselves *friends* in the families where they were billeted, the English were only very quiet & respectable Lodgers.

So successful was the Waterloo expedition that in 1818 Marianne was off yet again. This was too much for Hannah More, who thus disburdens herself to Zachary Macaulay:

Poor dear Marianne! I believe her conscience is tender for she was guilty of a little disingenuousness. She never wrote me a syllable of her plans till the very day before she set out, and then told me it would be too late for me to answer her as she would be gone the next day, but begged me to write her some warnings while she was abroad. I would speak with all due tenderness but I must say that three visits to France within two years of the death of her excellent mother is not a good example for Henry Thornton's daughter. I am sure it would be painful to her incomparable friends and protectors, the Inglises.

But it was the Inglises who accompanied her. From France they went to Switzerland. And there were further Swiss visits in the 'twenties, in which others of the Thornton sisters took part. The entertaining water colour reproduced facing page 106 bears the following label

Travelling in Switzerland in 1825 before Railways. Sir Robert Inglis, Lady Inglis, Dowager Lady Inglis, Miss Inglis. Miss L. Inglis, Marianne Thornton, Lucy, Sophia, Henrietta, Charles, Mrs Green, Mrs Draper, Bairr courier, Schmidt avant-courier.

Henrietta pinxit.

Some of the people mentioned and some unmentioned occur in the delightful composition. The main object is Sir Robert's family coach, drawn by four spirited horses. The young lady already on the box, looking very happy and pretty,

Travelling in Switzerland
by Henrietta Thornton (about 1825)

wields a pale blue parasol. Bairr courier advances with a blue band box in one hand, a black bag in the other, and under his arm a brown wooden box bound in brass, containing the cash. Close to him is a confused crowd of passengers and well-wishers, for the coach is just leaving a Swiss hotel. Perched high on a wooden balcony is the landlady or she may be a chambermaid, and the fine Englishman standing on the ground beneath her is Sir Robert Inglis himself: amply built but of a fresh complexion, garbed in grey. He has tilted his top hat as he leans against the hotel to watch the coach fill up.

It must not do that yet, for I have only dealt with the right side of the composition. Let me attempt the left. Two postilions in blue and red uniform and plaided top boots control the four horses. One of them is in the saddle and a youth of such beauty and grace that Henrietta pinxit has paid special attention to him. Ahead of the horses is a kicking little pony with Schmidt avant-courier seated on it: he has very short legs: it is held by a stable boy who prevents it from galloping into the view. For observe Switzerland arising—not majestically but sufficiently steeply. A round grassy hill is spiralled by a road and two chaises rush furiously upward towards a village and a windmill. How I wish that I could paint a picture like that! Or indeed that anyone now alive could! It breathes the spirit of cheerful cumbrous travel and of a sure return to a well-equipped home.

Swiss journeys included the Hospice of St. Bernard. The Brother in charge of visitors, Chanoine Barras, became attached to Marianne. There are four letters from him to her (1821-1827) enquiring after *le chevalier* Inglis *et les chères demoiselles*, giving her news about the exploits of his dog Jupiter, the weather, etc., and enclosing on one occasion a gentian, the colours of which are still blue. His kindness

[*107*]

and the obvious goodness of the monks made a strong impression, and there were moments when she felt her Protestantism melting.

They received us as if we had parted yesterday. Their lives are spent in such active benevolence amongst the weary and frozen travellers who cross their fearful mountains, the music in the chapel is so sweet, the black robes look so graceful amidst the eternal snows of their heights, that I am always a less good Protestant there than any where, and even Sir R. cannot resist their kindness and hospitality—but he only wishes there were any Protestants like them.

It is impossible to keep track of all the continental visits. They were mostly to France and the Low Countries, and were fortified by historical reading. She went to Rome, and Naples is suggested by a piece of lava into which a ten Tornesi coin of 1825 has been thrown. Once Sir Robert took young Charles to Vienna, and once he went alone to Jerusalem, and brought back my grandfather a piece of the Mount of Olives. Thanks to him his wards became mildly Europeanised, and his influence persisted into the next generation, and softened the raucousness and the contemptuousness that sometimes attend stay-at-homes.

THREE

The Birchin Lane Bank

MIDWAY IN THIS amiable decade of the 'twenties there was an appalling financial crisis. It exploded suddenly.

The Bank which provided most of the family fortune had had a fairly prosperous career since its establishment in 1773. It had first functioned as Marlar, Lascelles, Pell and Down. When Marianne's father entered it in 1784 it changed its name to Down, Thornton and Free. At his death in 1815 it had passed out of Thornton control. Young Henry longed to join it, but he was only fifteen and nothing could be done.

By the time he was twenty-five the situation had altered. His claims were now considerable. He had had a successful career at Cambridge, he had served three years to learn his job, he was well thought of by his Uncle Samuel Thornton, by his Thornton cousins, by his Melville cousins, and by others connected with the profession of his choice, he had the integrity, the intelligence, the industry, the business acumen that might be expected from his father's son. Early in 1825 he became an active partner.

The Bank had again changed its name. It was now styled Pole, Thornton, Free, Down and Scott, or, more compendiously, Pole, Thornton and Co. It was said to be yielding £40,000 a year, and was regarded as one of the most stable and most extensive banking houses in London. Sir Peter Pole was the leading partner; an elderly gentleman who lived in the country. The active partner was Peter Free, and it was his incompetence—according to Marianne—which had been responsible for worries and shortages at the time of her father's death. On the surface all was now serene. Young Henry must have stepped aboard the family ship with confidence and pride, and with the expectation of a calm voyage. He never suspected that before the end of the year the ship would founder, and nearly wreck Battersea Rise too.

The letters from Marianne to Hannah More, describing the catastrophe, are the most considerable she ever wrote. Besides being vivid and documentary, they show financial insight. The causes of the disaster may have lain deeper than she or even her brother realised, but she thoroughly grasped such facts as she knew. The fruits of her early education become evident. The little girl who had been talked to by her papa about paper credit and had helped him to do his accounts reveals herself at twenty-eight as a woman of business.

I will print the letters in full from my own copies of them. They have already been published in a shortened form in the *Three Banks Review* for June 1951.

Battersea Rise,
7th December 1825

Private and Confidential

Dearest Mrs. H. M.,

I am so delighted that Henry has desired me to tell you some late events which have occupied all my thoughts and time, and which I know will interest you almost as much. He thinks that you may have heard some rumours which he knows are flying about Bristol and many other places, that Pole Thornton & Co. are about to break, and as it may be some pleasure to you to be able to say on the contrary they are in higher credit than ever I am to tell you all the story, only if you please it is all in confidence—for where no report has reached people, it is much better they should hear no contradiction.

Well then I am afraid I must begin with the beginning of the story, tho' I don't like going so far back. Ten years ago I think you knew that Peter Free contrived by his speculations nearly to ruin us, Down and himself. Sir P. Pole, however, an immensely rich man, came in, and since then the profits have been immense, and the House going on apparently most prosperously. Three years ago Henry began to serve his time there, merely to *learn the trade*, under the understanding that when the Partnership dissolved, which it did last Midsummer, he was to come in. He met with some opposition from Pole—who is a mere sleeping partner and did not like his share being diminished by Henry receiving some of the profits—and from Free who did not like being watched. However, for very shame's sake they admitted him. As soon as he was there, and let into their secrets, he found that Down and Scott were perfect cyphers, Pole never came near them, Free governed supremely, and he was not satisfied with many parts of his proceedings. There was a spirit of speculation, a love of concealing what he did, *making the best* of a story, which to Henry was intolerable, and they have had some lively disputes about things; on one occasion Henry set off in the night, and brought up Pole from Hampshire, to interfere by nine the next morning, because he could not make Free give up a plan which he did not think strictly honourable and *therefore* not prudent.

That there were these disputes was rather known, and made people think Free had been worse than he really was. There is just now a great pressure in the mercantile world, in consequence of the breaking of so many of these scheming Stock Company Bubbles, and Free had been inexcusably imprudent in not keeping more cash in the House, but relying on that credit in them which never had been shaken, and which would enable them to borrow whenever they pleased; he had really run things so near, that Henry had often remonstrated, especially as Pole's property is much of it in land, and cannot be turned into money the minute it is wanted. He was not however particularly uneasy till last Thursday and Friday, when there seemed to be something like a run upon them, and a difficulty in borrowing money which they had never felt before.

On Saturday however—that dreadful Saturday I shall never forget—the run increased to a frightful degree, everybody came in to take *out* their balance, no one brought any in; one old steady customer, who had usually £30,000 there, drew it out without, as is usual, giving any warning, and in order to pay it the House was left literally empty. Henry went out to endeavour to borrow but people made shuffling excuses—some said they would go and fetch some, and never returned—in short both he and Mr Free returned unsuccessful. Such a moment of peril completely turned Free's head; he insisted on proclaiming themselves Bankrupts at once, and raved and self-accused himself, and in short quite lost his powers of action.

Old Scott cried like a child of five years old, but could suggest nothing, Pole and Down were both out of Town. Henry saw it all lay upon him. Had he believed the House was really insolvent he said he would have stopped instantly sooner than have involved a human being any farther, but he was sure the money was theirs only they could not get at it, and he resolved to fight it out to the last minute, tho' what he endured, knowing that if any *large* Bill was presented they *must* stop—he says he never shall forget.

They shut up always at five. At four, he ordered the balance for the day to be struck, and found that during the next hour they would have to pay thirty-three thousand, and they should receive only twelve thousand. This was certain destruction, and he walked out, resolved to try one last resource.

There had always been such a jealousy between their House and Smith's (the Carrington Smiths I mean) that Free had often observed that morning how pleased they would be to hear they had broken, but John Smith had been an early friend of the Sykes', and particularly kind to Henry, and to him he resolved to go—but not according to Banker's etiquette, as if he did not care whether he gave it him or not—but he told him honestly he believed they must break, and he could hardly expect him to lend it, but yet if he could get them on till five, it would be an inexpressible relief. John Smith asked if he could give his word of honour that all was safe, that is, that the House was solvent, Henry said he could. Well! then he said they should have everything they could spare, which was not quite enough tho', for they had been hard-pressed themselves that day, but he went back with Henry to watch the event.

Two people had chanced to pay *in* some money whilst Henry had been absent, this, with what he had borrowed exactly met the demand upon them—but never, he says shall he forget watching the clock to see when five would strike, and end their immediate terror—or whether any one would come in for any more payments. The clock did strike at last, and they were safe for the moment, but as Henry heard the door locked, and the shutters put up, he felt they would not open again at that dear House, which every association led him to love so dearly.

I suppose there was something in the sight of so youthful a pilot weathering such a storm, which interested John Smith and one or two old-stagers, who had seen his father act just like him in olden time, and they told him that the openness and the firmness with which he had acted, made them very desirous to see whether nothing could be done. No private assistance could save them, for in proportion to their immense credit in general would be the run now, but John Smith declared if Henry would make a statement of the accounts and prove their solvency, he would apply to the Bank of England for them. Henry had little hope from this, for the Bank had never been known to do such a thing in the annals of Banking, but willing to save them if possible, he proceeded, with as much composure as he would open my work-box this moment, to break open Free's, Pole's and Down's desks to procure the books. He told them afterwards, they had left him alone in extreme danger, and he must resort to extreme measures; he next sent off expresses for his Uncle Thornton and Sir P. Pole, and put four confidential clerks to a thorough examination of the state of their affairs. In the meantime the Smiths worked for him like post horses in running after all the Bank of England Directors, and appointing a meeting the next morning at 8 o'clock.

Near one in the morning Henry returned home. I had been a little anxious about him, and had been sitting up for him, but, hearing his usual calm voice tell Nurse to get him some tea, I was just getting into bed when she came to say he wanted me to make it for him. I ran to him, and found him perfectly white and bloodless with the anxiety and the exertion he had gone through, but so quiet and composed, I could scarcely believe it when he told me they must be proclaimed Bankrupts Monday morning, but not to mind it for no one would lose anything by it; but he was certain the House was solvent, and he had rather break at once than go through such another day. He said they were very kind to him in the City, but here *could* be no hope from the Bank; he was more sorry for the ruin it would occasion, as they reckoned that thirty-eight country Banks would fail in consequence. That it was owing partly to Free's folly in locking up the money partly to the pressure of the times, but help or hope he thought there was none. He next proceeded to do two or three things which almost broke my heart. He paid me and Nurse two or three pounds he owed us, for he said he shouldn't feel any was his own by Monday.

He then told me that one of his young Cambridge friends came to open an account with them that day; he dared not tell him they should stop by night, he *could* not take the money, and feel it would be impossible to get it again in three hours, so he put it into his purse instead of into the account, and brought it home. He and I sat up most of the remainder of the

[*114*]

night, for sleep was out of the question. I am sorry to say I behaved much the worst of the two, for the thought of their breaking was very intolerable to me. I had indeed suffered much greater trials, but they seemed to come direct from Heaven and *must* be borne; this, being through more second causes, I could not make up my mind, as he did, to the disgrace and the confusion which it would occasion. At six when we, that is Nurse and I (for we never can help telling Nurse anything), saw him off again, he desired me to say nothing to my sisters, or any one else of their difficulties, and I had to get through Sunday as well as I might.

Fortunately ours is rather an active Sunday, and what with schools and Church, tho' very miserable, I had not time to realise it to my mind till the quiet of the evening. My sisters in high spirits were preparing a good scold for Henry when he came in for being out all Sunday for the first time in his life, and I felt he would return to say all was over. But when he did come, and I opened the Hall door for him, he whispered to me 'we are all afloat again', ran up to his room, tired out, and threw himself on the bed; he then told me the marvellous tale of their preservation, but wishing to keep himself out of the foreground, I never rightly understood it, till I heard it from a friend of his who was with him. It seems he first got the accounts from the Banking House, made poor Scott wipe his eyes sufficiently to go with him, wrote to advise Free to keep quiet, and went off to John Smith's where he met all the Bank of England Directors who were in Town, and some of the principal Bankers in the City. John Smith began by saying that the failure of this House would occasion so much ruin that he should really regard it as a national misfortune, and also that what he had seen of the conduct of one of the Partners at a crisis of extreme peril, had convinced him that, could it be saved for the moment, it might be well managed in future; he then turned to Henry and said, 'I think you give your word the House is solvent?' Henry said he could. 'Then,' says John Smith to the

Directors, 'your money is safe.' Henry then proceeded to tell
them he had brought the Books, those precious things which no
Banker will ever let another catch a glimpse of, and which he
begged they would examine thoroughly; he trusted Sir Peter
Pole would soon be there, who could give him an exact statement of his property—but he believed the House not only to
be *sound* but after paying everything to be worth a good deal
of money. 'Well then,' said the Governor and Deputy Governor
of the Bank, 'you shall have four hundred thousand pounds by
eight tomorrow morning, which will I think float you.' Henry
said he could scarcely believe what he heard.

Then Sir P. Pole, Uncle Sam, and Free came in, the former
in a dreadful fright, Uncle Sam ditto, Free with an affectation
of carelessness and unconcern. They had a most thorough examination of the affairs, during which the Governor said he saw
the business had been a most profitable one. 'Yes,' says Henry,
'but', looking at Free, 'it has been grossly mismanaged.' 'That
shall be provided for' and they proceeded to arrange that this
enormous sum which they lent was to be watched by three of
their number from accounts sent in not by Pole, Free, Scott or
Down, the Partners who have been there for twenty years, but
by 'Mr. Henry Thornton', who entered it five months ago. Can
you believe it? I really hardly can. They were all to give the
most ample security for the money, and it was settled that
Free should go out, and Henry choose another Partner who
should work with him. But Sir P. Pole's nerves have been so
shaken that he seems anxious to be off, as he has now a very
handsome fortune left, tho' Free has wickedly injured the enormous one with which he came in. So Henry begs he will decamp
and means to get a fresh Partner, just as rich and rather more
wise. So Down and Scott are left, one of them foolish, the other
old and failing, and these Bank of England Directors advised
Henry to give them both an annuity to keep away, rather than
to come there, and to be content with one working, and one
paying Partner—both of his own choosing.

It still appears to me magic that when we only looked forward to his rising in years to come, he is at once placed at the head of one of the first, in some respects the very first, Banking House in Town. He was off again in the dark on Monday morning to the Bank of England, where he found the Governor and Deputy Governor who for the sake of secrecy had no clerks there, and they began counting out the Bills for him. 'I hope this won't overset you my young man', said one of them, 'to see the Governor and Deputy Governor of the Bank acting as your two clerks.' He went back to the Banking House £400,000 richer than he left it on Saturday. For the first hour there was a little run, but the rumours that the Bank of England had taken them under its Wing soon spread, and people brought back money as fast as they had taken it out on Saturday, and by night they were so full of cash that they might have done without assistance.

On Wednesday, the Country Banks who had only then heard of it, made a little breeze, but so slight Henry said he 'rather liked it', and from being near stopping, no House in the City is considered so safe, and indeed it never really was so safe as now that it is backed by the Bank of England itself.

So ends this fearful tale, and from the deepest sorrow, we are all at once the happiest of the happy. To me a special Providence seems to watch over those walls. Those same qualities of high honour, strict principle, and fearless integrity which once built it up, have now saved it from falling, and may they ever do so.

Sir Robert exclaimed to Henry 'I only trust you will have grace to keep you humble, for indeed it is enough to spoil you.' I am not so much afraid of that, he takes it so quietly, and says that his character could have done nothing, if it had not been for Pole's money, and assures me the Bank *must* have assisted them, because it knew that some of their late arrangements had increased the present pressure. But that he may now have his head so filled with business as to have time for nothing else is very possible, and I trust that he may remember 'this is not our rest'.

> Ever, my dearest Mrs. H.M.,
> Your affectionate,
> MARIANNE THORNTON

The opening of the next letter is puzzling. The "worst anticipations" had not been realised and this is admitted as the letter proceeds.

> Battersea Rise.
> 12th December 1825 (Monday)

Dearest Mrs. H. M.,

I little thought when I closed my last happy letter to you how soon it would all be reversed—and that a few hours would realize our worst anticipations. On Thursday and Friday the new Partnership was all but formed, they had one man of great property in it, but it was necessary to have another who had ready money at command, and at such a time of commercial distress this was not easy to discover. I believe however that one day more would have accomplished it, when on Saturday morning there was another tremendous crash among the Country Banks which produced such a sensation that Henry said whoever else entered the new Partnership, he would not, for he foresaw only ruin on all sides from the general want of confidence which ensued; this of course produced another run upon them, but of a very different nature to the one before. Then Henry had been all alone and unfriended till he went to John Smith uncertain of his reception—now he was surrounded by Bank of England Directors, and all the principal Bankers of London, whose magnificent offers of support are hardly to be credited, but Henry calmly settled that on the whole it would be best to stop payment.

If he had borrowed more money it would have only been to lend to Country Banks, who might all have stopped tomorrow. He felt sure that the House was solvent. This too was the only

[*118*]

way of getting rid of Free's old embarrassments, and tho' it is
hard upon Pole, since he chose to come into the House on those
terms, he *must* now pay them all, and in short they went on till
the usual hour of shutting up, and then wrote round to their
Country Banks that they meant to stop payment on Monday
morning—this notice being considered a handsome thing.

I was dining out, quite unconscious of the events of the morning, at a large dinner party, when I received a note, which tho'
very guarded convinced me of what had happened, and said
that Henry wished me to come to him at his cousins, the
Melvilles, in that street, so I persuaded Sir Robert directly to
let me go there. I found John and Eliza Thornton in loud distress about it, the Melvilles almost as bad, Henry exactly as
calm as usual, assuring us it was the best ending if we would
but think so; he said that a new Partnership formed in such
haste might have led to great inconveniences, that he could not
feel responsible for mismanagement in this concern, in which he
has only had any power for the last five months, and that the
kindness he had met with during the short and stormy part of
his reign was enough to keep up his spirits. He drove me home
in his gig that night, and almost talked me over to his belief till
I found the poor girls at home waiting in high spirits to know
who was to be the new Partner, and when they heard the termi-
nation of it all they were miserable indeed.

However, by today we are beginning to look up again. That
Henry's career in the City is but just beginning I firmly believe, and whatever may be the close, he will be a greater and a
better man as long as he lives for these events. The marvellous
way in which the City grandees speak of him, and the unmeas-
ured confidence they have reposed in him, proves it; indeed he
said in his quiet way yesterday, 'You have no idea, Marianne,
what a great man breaking makes of me, I have had all these
first-rate people trailing after me as if I had been Secretary of
State. I always loved the character of a City Merchant and
Banker, and it is delightful to see how they unite the powers

of a man of business with the romantic effects of the heroes of
fairy tales. I said the other day John Smith appeared to me
like a beneficent genius in a fairy tale, he not only promised
impossibilities, but he was always performing them.' If any
exertion of money, of talent, of time could have saved that
House, it would have been done, but Free's mismanagement ex-
tends through a long series of years, during which he had been
left to his own speculations, first and last. Henry says he thinks
he must have run through nearly half a million. He would however have gone on much longer if this state of things in the City
had not brought things to a point. The examination last week
shewed the House was solvent, but had no large surplus, and
therefore if their Country Banks broke, it might, had they continued, have all dwindled away. The accounts are so enormous
and so complicated, that it will be difficult for the present to
be quite sure how matters will turn out, it will partly depend on
how the Country Bankers stand it—but at present Henry
seems quite satisfied that every one will be paid in full, and Sir
Peter have a wreck left, 'enough to make a man happy'.

Henry we think must be safe, while any of Sir P.'s remains.
We are quite safe, I mean we Girls, you will be pleased to hear,
and many other little things which might have plagued him are
nicely settled. The Bible Society and Missionary Society money
which was kept there was all drawn out, and indeed owing to the
immense assistance of the Bank they have scarcely a London
creditor to whom they owe £1,000, except that same wealthy
personage, the Bank, who may afford to wait for her money and
has good security for every farthing of it. The Governor of
the Bank was standing by Henry during the run on Saturday,
and said 'if you had brought this all on yourself I should say I
was sorry for you, but that you were behaving very well now;
but since none of it is your doing, I can only tell you this is
just the scene to make a man of you, and I can't be sorry for
you after all.'

The young Smiths have been working for Henry like so many

clerks—more than one night last week they sent Henry home to bed, and long after he was asleep, John Abel, his Cambridge friend, was sitting up, and running over London for him, resolved to save his House if it were possible. Another man, in spite of Henry's warning, would leave his balance in to shew the world what confidence he had that the House was solvent. One thing pleased me much, that Henry walked off on Saturday to call upon poor disgraced Free, because he thought it kinder than letting him hear it through a clerk, and to enquire how Mrs. F. bore it. Free only told him 'it was a confounded bore' that the House had stopped, but seemed very little touched with the recollection that it was his own performance. As to the other Partners they were inconceivably supine, and I hear they mean to give poor Henry the winding up of the affairs. They say this is a good thing for him, for that it keeps him in the way of advancement; but still it might be a pleasanter employment.

We find it quite impossible however to be very unhappy whilst he is amongst us—he says 'if I had behaved like a rogue and ruined myself besides, you could but be so miserable; *now* I do think my character is rather the higher, and I believe the money is safe, so where is the use of being unhappy?'

Ever, dearest Mrs. H. M.,
Your affectionate,
MARIANNE THORNTON

In spite of the good will and help offered by other bankers, winding up the affairs of Pole, Thornton & Co. was not easy. In the meantime Henry Thornton was asked to join the banking house of Williams & Co.

[Fragment]

December 29, 1825

. . . There have been ten thousand difficulties in the way, his capital locked up in Pole's House, his name can't appear now for some weeks, as he is not clear of his old affairs, but his

City friends have one and all come forward to help him in every possible way. Alexander Baring says there are two things he hates—an abolitionist and a saint—and yet he can't help liking that young Thornton, in proof of which he very carelessly yesterday offered him £200,000 to begin with, if they were likely to want it. Henry says he never had so much command of money as since he has not been worth a shilling, and wonders how it happens. Pole's affairs are decided: they will pay everybody, and have a hundred thousand left, but Henry is obliged to let his capital go in the first instance to be repaid hereafter.

In the midst of these anxieties, we have had some of a different kind, in hearing Watson read prayers for the first time in Clapham Church on Xmas Day; and he preached on Monday a little quiet sermon when there was no one but his sisters and cousins to hear him. There was something fearfully nervous in seeing him in *that* pulpit, but he was so composed himself, and though I say it that should not say it preached so well that I could not feel anxious to the end. Gibbs, our clerk, said as he came down 'he has done excellently well, but then I take the greatest delight in him because I saw him christened, and have seen him at church most Sundays since'. Nurse said she turned so red she was sure everybody would know she was his Nurse, 'but to be sure he did read so beautiful!' We don't mean him to preach on a Sunday for a year at least, but he is doing the occasional and reading prayers duty for Dr Dealtry for a week or two, which is a great pleasure to us. Goodbye, dearest Mrs H. M. for I have many letters to write.

Ever your affectionate
MARIANNE THORNTON

The old *Times* has announced that one of Pole's partners is to join Williams, a young man who is supposed to have strong connections in the dissenting interest! This, Henry says, is very hard when he has generally found time to slip off to prayers at St. Paul's on Wednesdays and Fridays during all these troubles: it is so quiet and refreshing there.

Battersea Rise, January [1st or 2nd]
1826

Already my dearest Mrs H. More I believe we may congratulate ourselves on Henry being again afloat, and on Monday next his new Bank opens, with every prospect of being as like the old House as possible in the days of its glory. I can hardly yet believe that so few days should elapse between the downfall and the rising, but I feel so convinced now that he is a *cork*, that the deeper he is plunged into the water the more quickly he reappears, or to speak more like a Christian, that gracious Providence which we know always watches over us, has in this instance made plain those ways which are sometimes hid in darkness for years.

You will be surprised when you hear that it is perfectly obvious that even the stoppage of the old affair was the greatest blessing that could have happened to us—had it gone on we might have been *all* involved in the ruin and a hundred others. But as you tell me you like my long stories, you shall hear this one, for it is curious to trace the little causes from which come great events.

You perhaps saw the failure of Williams Bank, a very large one, the day after ours. It fell in our train for the Houses had always been much connected in the habit of lending each other assistance, but though the property in it was enormous it had been badly managed and they could not get at it when they wanted it. There was a young man in the House much in Henry's case, on whom the chief labour had devolved, while the rich sleeper kept out of the way. On the House stopping they went immediately to Henry to say they meant to go on again, for they were still worth enormous sums, and to ask if he would join them and become their managing Partner—he rather laughed at it, and said he supposed as two negatives made an affirmative, two deficiencies made a surplus, as the only explanation of their asking a *failed* man to join them.

However, about ten days ago, Cunningham who is their

[*123*]

brother-in-law came down with a proposal to Henry to unite the ruins of his House with theirs, the old Partners of Williams going out, and leaving it to him and to his young friend Charles Williams to manage it, if they could find another monied man to join them, which would be needful to give the thing stability, and this he hoped he had done. It seemed all delightful when their *rich man* proved to be not worth as much as was expected, and Cunningham and Charles Williams arrived here one eventful Monday night to say their wits were exhausted to find a Partner, and they feared they must the next day give themselves in as Bankrupts, twenty four hours only remained in which to discover a man worth £300,000 and willing to risk it in these troublous times at a day's notice with two young men who had nothing to offer but the ruins of their respective Houses.

The case seemed desperate—so much so that even Ladies were allowed to meddle in it. Long shall I remember the anxious faces round the fire during the many hours of the night we spent in discussing every person likely and unlikely who could be applied to. Mr. Williams with a large sheet of paper taking down the names which our ready wit supplied by hundreds— but some were fools, some were knaves, some worth nothing, some speculative, and the prudent Henry sat there, as we said, to object to every being who was named, but as the burnt child dreads the fire, he said he had rather be reduced to want at once than connect himself with people on whom he could not rely. But people had been so terrified with the late events, that to find one of sufficiently strong nerves who was yet a prudent man seemed impossible. 'We won't give it up tho',' said Mr. Cunningham, 'Henry reminds me of the Man in the Parable who fell among thieves who wounded him leaving him half dead —if we behave like Priests and Levites, we shall bitterly repent it one day. It is the difference between ten thousand a year to him or nothing, for if he does not set up directly, people's sympathies will be over, and it will be useless to attempt it six months hence.'

Among the last resources somebody mentioned our neighbour at Broomfield, Mr. Deacon, late Partner of the Barings, who made £19,000 a year, and retired from business some years—and it was thought he might know of some one—and to pursue the same connection two of my sisters were to be off as soon as it was light to besiege the bedside of Mrs Staniforth, a sister of the Barings to know whether her brothers would take it in hand. So when we met at breakfast, a disconsolate, pale-faced lot—things already looked better. Mrs. Staniforth thought of an excellent young Baring who she thought would do, and had sent off to her brother. Mr. Williams had routed out Deacon, who to our amaze confessed that time had been very heavy on his hands ever since he had quitted business—that he had a large family growing up, he had a regard for Henry, and in short that he thought he should like it. They gave him 24 hours, by which time he consented if the accounts proved as satisfactory as was stated. He and Henry have rummaged over them like two cats after mice, and being thoroughly satisfied, it was yesterday settled that young Williams, Deacon and Henry and John Melville, whom Henry has brought in, start on Monday—and the young Baring who is now in Hope's House in Amsterdam comes in after a few weeks.

Henry has slipped in Melville, who was to have been one of his Partners if he had raised his old House, because he had been a thoroughly good man of business for some years, and has behaved to Henry lately with all the affection and zeal of the most anxious brother. It is the greatest comfort to know that these are all *good* men, so whatever else happens there will be no iniquity to mourn over as in the last case, and they are such a prudent lot that I was telling Nurse I don't think a Bill will ever get signed, they will look it over so long first. Such the end of a Drama, that in the 5th Act is a marriage—and so the end of ours is a resuming of payments, which has indeed taken

place today, and a happier person I have seldom seen than
Henry, after fourteen hours of intense work, but so pleasant
he says, people pouring in with all their congratulations and
their accounts—so that in spite of the numbers, who having
wanted to pay their Christmas bills drew out of the House small
sums—the number of new friends who paid in left them with
a much larger sum than they had in the morning when they
opened. Sir Peter Pole who has behaved very well up to this
day, was at last touched with a little human feeling of envy
at seeing Henry so soon afloat, and showed it by going into
a violent passion at some of the Clerks following Henry to his
new House. Henry says he let him rave on till he was quite
tired, and then asked him whether the Clerks were not free
agents, and might not choose what master they would serve,
etc. etc. and would you believe it! the old man at length came
round, and ended in giving him leave to take the remaining ones.

Old Scott, tho' rather late, is turning out a Christian and
is exerting himself in Henry's favour to obtain his old customers; Henry said to one of the principal ones who had followed
him, 'And, Sir, and if you do not see that we do business in an
exactly opposite way to the old House I hope you will leave
us immediately.' Deacon, who is one of the best of men and
a strongish Calvinist, says that there must be some mysterious
leading of Providence that induced him to enter business when
he had so long left it; and I for my part do not go far to find
it, for I think the setting up Henry again one of the most provi-
dential events that ever fell to the lot of Man. That he should
have had the power of choosing four Partners out of six and
be set afloat so instantly is so remarkable that I can only compare it to your 'turn' of the carpet; we really saw the wrong
side only for one minute, and before we could begin to wonder
what it meant, we saw the reverse.

It is very naughty of me to tell you Banking events, and
this is one which if you please you must keep quiet, for it is
very important that it should not be known. But two days

before they opened, they discovered that it was absolutely necessary they should have a very large supply of sovereigns in their House for their Country Banks, but such is the scarcity of gold now in London that they could not by any means obtain as much as they wished. The Partners were in despair, and separated in the evening, fearing this difficulty would prevent their opening on Monday: but Henry called Melville aside and told him he saw one resource, to get into a post chaise instantly, go during the night to Brighton where John Smith was, knock him up, persuade him to return to town with him, go with Alexander Baring to Rothschild, and these two Princes of the City might, they thought, induce the Jew King of City, Rothschild, to give them the money, for he, probably, was the only man in England who *could* help them having it is suspected, been hoarding up sovereigns for exportation for some time.

Henry did the deed, found Mr J. Smith, whose kindness is beyond all praise, quite willing to return with him, and by dint of a little persuasion and exhortation the Jew was induced to bring out his gold, first charging 2½ commission, then saying he did it out of public spirit, and lastly begging they would never tell it or he would be besieged night and day. However Henry and the sovereigns were in William's House before hardly any one knew he had been further than home during the night.

In the midst of all this our thoughts have been differently occupied by a very different theme. Dearest Mrs Grant was attacked by an illness yesterday from which Pennington does not give any hope that she will recover. She has been in Charles' arms ever since, surrounded by her other children. She the only calm and collected one of the group, aware and almost rejoicing in her danger, and still—even to the last—retaining her accustomed character of comforter to the mourners and the weeping. Nothing can be more sweet and serene than this almost translation to a better world—for indeed she seemed to cling to this only by her affections, and they are chiefly centred in those who have gone before her. It reminds me only of that expression 'the peace that passeth understanding' and that is surely hers, and will continue hers now for ever.

I must conclude with once more thanking you for your delightful little bit today. I wish you and Nurse could talk over Free, she says 'mere hanging is too good for him'. Perhaps it is, but poor creature, he is suffering far more from the loss of everything, and no domestic happiness or peace of conscience to support him with it.

Ever your affect. MARIANNE THORNTON.

I forgot to say that Henry's new partners told him in the handsomest way that though his name could not appear as yet, they considered his share as beginning from today.

It will be noticed that Sir Robert Inglis scarcely comes into the exciting story. It is the triumph of youth. Henry Sykes Thornton, at the age of twenty-five, stands forth as the head of the family, surrounded by his rejoicing and adoring sisters. It was a great moment, the greatest in their combined lives. He must have felt that he was master at last in the house of his father, and that though the girls might be technically Inglis's wards they would look to him and take their orders from him in future. At the moment of his triumph perhaps was born to him the wish, the hope, that none of them would ever marry. And perhaps from this moment his nose—the prominent rather predatory nose that turns portraits of him into caricatures—began to assert itself at the expense of his softer features.

A cheerful letter from Lucy to Marianne shows him and his partners happily enthroned at Birchin Lane, and dispensing hospitality to their womenfolk.

We spent a pleasant day at the Banking House, and the Partners who were present did all in their power to make up for the absent. Mrs C. Williams and Harriet with 2 children were there when we arrived. Harriet enjoyed herself extremely. . . . The upstairs room was so cool and fresh that we quite enjoyed it after the drive; the luncheon was rather like a Harrow one, only so orderly and gentleman like and the ice was much praised. They have no man-servants to wait, but the maids brought the dishes into the room, and Henry and Charles Williams carved, talked, carried spoons, ice, plates &ct to their company. Melville sat at one end of the table. C. Williams regretted Labouchere's absence every 10 minutes and said how angry he would be at this taking place in his absence. Harriet kept looking at the maid's dress as they appeared at the door, laughing and whispering across the table—wondering which of the partners had told them to trim up their caps. They were very nice looking. She also told us that before we came one of them had offered to show her to the W.C. and wondered whether it was her own idea: she was very Harriet Melvillish indeed. Then we went all over the premises and saw their underground fireproof place &ct &ct. Henry went with us to see the Monument, but I had 'Emma' with me in the carriage and sat with her. They went to the top.

The Bank that underwent these vicissitudes still flourishes on its original site: Williams Deacon's Bank Limited, 20 Birchin Lane, E.C.3.

FOUR

May Meetings and William Wilberforce

ANOTHER ASPECT of the decade now requires examination. Like her parents, Marianne was but little concerned with ritual or dogma. "I was brought up not to think H. and L. Church of *very* great importance, and for the life of me I can't now dwell much on it," she wrote in later years, and she spent no time in worrying what the clergyman wore or didn't wear or what stood upon the Communion table. When the Tractarian Movement developed she was puzzled by its antics and blind to its colourfulness. What she cared for was the Christian life, rooted in the family and flowering in action, and she desired to see that life growing all over the world. The example of Christ was present in her prayers, but for practical purposes there was a convenient exemplar in her parents; they had been good Christians and she had known them well. She would be as like them as she could. She did not imitate them idolatrously: the world was moving and she with it, and she abandoned their elaborate examinations of self and of others, and adopted a lighter psychological touch.

They had left twin comforters behind them in the persons of William Wilberforce and Hannah More. From 1815 to 1833, when they both died, she had these two precious relicts to guide her spiritually. The guidance was implicit: no let-

ters have survived which ask for their advice, and she sometimes did things which they disapproved. It was their continual presence that helped her. She could always think,
"There they still are." Hannah More had to be written to—
she was getting too old to come up from Somersetshire and
had to be kept in touch with the religious gossip of the capital. Wilberforce had to be watched and followed and adored
and if possible tended; he was all over the place—fragile,
whimsical, inspired, and would wear himself to death. The
"May Meetings" ("notre Sainte Semaine")—so important
to her during the early 'twenties of the century—were dominated by him even when he was too unwell to attend.

These meetings were held every spring in Exeter Hall, in
the Freemasons Hall, in the Offices of the Hibernian Society,
etc. They originated in the British and Foreign Bible Society which had been founded back in 1804, and annually
presented a report. To the Bible Society were added other
organisations, all of them founded by or supported by members of the Clapham Sect: such as the Church Missionary
Society, the Anti-Slavery League, the African Society, the
Society for the Conversion of the Jews. Pious people, many
of whom were also lively and intelligent, came up for the
meetings from all over England, followed the reports and
discussions, took part in the voting and contributed to the
collections. For some, the Week also acquired the aspect of a
dramatic festival: they loved the crowds, the scenes on the
platform and in the audience. Hannah More herself had
written plays in her day, and must have enjoyed Marianne's
vivid reports on the proceedings.

Let us begin with the C.M.S. meeting of 1820. "Every
year the meetings increase in seriousness and talent," the girl
remarks; also such a crowd, exceeding she should think "the
crush room of an opera in spight of tickets and barriers,"

[*131*]

Grants and Noels and Babingtons and multitudes of the excellent of the earth around her, Mr. Wilberforce perched on
a chair with Lord Calthorpe, the Bishop of Gloucester clinging to Lord Jocelyn on another, Sir Robert Inglis and Mr.
Cunningham sharing a third. The report was however "very
long," and Zachary Macaulay did not think it very judicious; he sat on some steps.

One instance of the monstrous depravity of the African
negroes was their having boiled 9 little pigs alive and eaten
them skin and all. As we have nearly murdered 9 cabinet ministers [in the Cato Street Conspiracy] I thought the poor
Blacks might have retaliated.

After the report had been read a Mr. Harrington who had
spent many years in India warned the audience not to expect
too much success there; upon which up leapt Mr. Wilberforce to counteract him crying, "We know nothing of despondency here, we proceed as the word of God directs us,
we must, we can, we will, we ought, we shall prosper." There
was wild enthusiasm, indeed the whole meeting took the form
of a personal tribute to the great abolitionist. Bishop Jebb
of Limerick spoke—he was increasingly drawn into Clapham
concerns—also Lords Calthorpe and Jocelyn, and a wild
Irishman, "too light but very entertaining," and a gentlemanly speaker who "seemed almost too much elevated to be
able to say much." Finally Admiral Lord Gambier, G.C.B.,
rose to close the proceedings, and he is one of her chief comic
characters:

Lord Gambier, who is the best friend in the world, is for that
reason the worst Chairman. His friendly feelings so got the
better of his decorum that he took to tacking the oddest resolutions together, such as that Missions should be sent to Otheite
and that the Meeting returned their warmest thanks to his

[*132*]

very dear very much esteemed very excellent much beloved friend William Wilberforce; the next time he stuck the poor Bishop to some other, and so he went on to the no small annoyance of the poor suffering praiseds. The going out was nearly equal to the coming in, and Miss Grant and I got crushed against a young man whom we thought we had destroyed, but it turned out to be her tall brother Robert.

In the 1822 Week "many good *May* faces" were to be seen at the C.M.S. Would that some spirit of the air could have wafted Mrs. Hannah More to them on his wings! And there was a "beautiful story" in the report of a slave ship landed again in Africa, and the reunion of relatives and friends who thought they were parted for ever: "Oh Massa! my brother —my sister—my wife—my countryman . . ." and Mr. Wilberforce, improving on this, built such a picture of the Celestial City where reunion shall be general and eternal that the audience was tranced and could not return to the world. They were recalled by Mr. Fowell Buxton's "rattling peal of thunder": he reminded subscribers that they gave "at the utmost two and forty shillings a year amongst a hundred thousand heathens. The end of this reasoning appeared to be that one half of us should leave our bonnets and pelisses on the plate and the other half go out as Missionaries. However it took the taste of the Meeting." Pious, but as always observant, she went on to a soirée at Lady Teignmouth's, "called by the prophane All Saints Day." Later in the week she attended "the Jews on the Friday, where as usual the bit is wanted more than the spur. I really think Lewis Way will go mad." She could not stand or understand emotionalism. But she enjoyed the singing by converted Jewish children of "Unto us a Son is born." And she intended to go to the "African": otherwise "I don't think I shall leave our sweet roses and nightingales, which are now delicious."

After that the tempo increases. It was at the 1824 meeting that Tom Macaulay leapt into fame. It was convened by the Anti-Slavery Society, whose President, the Duke of Gloucester, was in the chair, and the platform was full of notables. The occasion was of national importance. A Methodist missionary in Demarara, a Mr. Smith, had been wrongfully accused of causing disaffection among the Negroes, he had been convicted of sedition by a court-martial, and he had died in prison of ill treatment. Wilberforce had raised the disgraceful case in the House of Commons, where no one had attempted to justify the trial, but it had been argued that Mr. Smith would have fared even worse if he had been tried by a jury of planters. The argument is disquietingly modern. One can hear it being employed today wherever racial liberty is in retreat. Young Macaulay made hay of it, with a pitchfork already substantial, and, not averse to the arts of rhetoric, he referred to Mr. Smith's widow, who was present, and brought the house down by his pathos:

'Mrs Hannah More must be written to, for they will never tell her about it. Oh! how I wish she had been there' was repeatedly said to me by Henry as we left the Freemason's Hall today, where to use Mr Wilberforce's expression 'Tom Macaulay has most nobly won his spurs on that hard-fought field —the anti-slavery', when he made a speech of which I feel it is perfectly impossible to say too much. I was so delighted with it that I should hardly have trusted my own feelings about it, but when I saw the grave old steady senators all so carried away by the eloquence of the youthful orator, that even the decorum of the platform were forgotten, and the dignity of the Royal Duke compromised, by Mr Wilberforce and Mr Stephen catching hold of him as he was going back to his place, and keeping him there, each shaking a hand, while the very walls seemed to be coming down with the thunders of applause.

The argumentative parts reminded me of Brougham, and the eloquence of Charles Grant—but really in sober earnest he has exceeded *anything* I have heard of either.

Throughout Tom Macaulay's speech, exclamations of "capital" and "wonderful" had proceeded from Wilberforce, and when it was over he addressed himself with his usual felicity to Zachary Macaulay, "who may be called away like Philip before the battle is won, but he has left an Alexander who will triumph." The whole meeting was profoundly moved; the aging heroes who had fought the long war for abolition saw their labours crowned and conserved by the boy who had been bred among them, and as for poor Mrs. Smith—if anything could console her for the loss of a husband it must be this.

I am writing in haste, hoping this may go today, for you have always felt so much interest in Tom Macaulay that I was sure you would be delighted to hear he had succeeded so splendidly, and yet you see all his own family will take it so quietly, so I must now conclude, ever dearest Mrs Hannah More

Yours affect. MARIANNE THORNTON

The friendship of the Thorntons with their brilliant contemporary endured, but did not mature. He moved into bigger, busier circles. The following letter shows him getting a bit above himself.

The Macaulays dined here a little while ago—Seven of them to meet we nine—& nobody else, & the effect of this junction of two such Clouds was a thunder clap of course, for I seldom saw a merrier, or a noisier party, Tom as usual reigning King of the Mob, & amusing the young ones as much with his fun, as he might have delighted elders with his eloquence—I wish his manner were quieter however, for entre nous, tho' I think in reality he is remarkable for being easily pleased, & wishing

to be civil & to oblige every one—his first manner certainly has
too much of the pedagogue about it—It will wear off—& no
one who knows him can dislike him I think—but such a very
authoritative way of speaking frightens so many people from
entering into any discussion with him.

She remained intimate with two of the Macaulay girls,
Fanny and Hannah (afterwards Lady Trevelyan); and
through the Trevelyans a family friendship has persisted,
much to my own advantage.

Of the May Meetings of 1825 she has much to say. The
movement was now moving into troubled waters; Wilberforce was too frail to attend, and the news of his abstention
flung the Anti-Slavery Society into hysterical grief. Uncle
Dan Sykes wept so much that he had to leave the platform
and hide behind it, stern Mr. Stephen collapsed, young William Wilberforce, when invited to say a few words on behalf
of his father, burst into tears. The old man was however
well enough to call down at Battersea Rise and to derive
pensive pleasure from the haunts of his youth.

I determined as usual to write you an account of the merry
makings last Week (what a name to give them, I am quite
shocked) but one of them knocked me so completely up that
I took some time to recover for the African, where dead or
alive I determined to go; & where I did go yesterday—but before I tell you any thing about the meeting I must tell you
that its patron Saint—Mr Wilberforce himself surprised us
beyond measure by appearing on our Lawn on Monday to pay
us a morning Visit, & he was strong enough to spend almost
the whole of it in walking upon the Grass inhaling as he said
the Gales of Roses & listening to concerts of Nightingales. He
looks very very thin & reduced, & walks feebly but really he
is almost a proof already of the immortality of the Soul—for
I never saw him in such spirits—or appear so keenly *alive*

[*136*]

upon all subjects. He explained it by saying they had begun to feed him with roast beef again & that he was so highly *animalised* & exhilarated he hardly knew how to keep within due bounds; & perhaps the degree of comparative quiet in which they now keep him makes him enter with more spirit & soul on the subjects on which he *does* dwell—I wish you could have seen him as he stood under the Tulip Tree talking of you & many more whom he had seen pass & repass amongst our Shades —& they are gone—& here am I—he said, a wreck left for the next tide—but yet a-bounding in blessings & enjoyments—

Up in London pandemonium developed. The meetings had become fashionable and were attended by persons who were trying to advertise themselves. Edward Irving the preacher talked constantly. And there were religious polemics. There was trouble over the Apocrypha. And foolish Protestants would attack the Catholics, and the Catholics went for them hammer and tongs, and in came all the griefs of Ireland. Marianne was distressed but entertained, and gives a gay account of the trials of Lord Gambier in the Hibernian Hall: there had been rows other years but never as noisy as this.

Poor dear Lord Gambier was never intended for a conflict of words, whatever he may be in time of battles, or at least he moves so slow like the heavy artillery, that there is no bringing him up to action in time.

He allowed the meeting to run on unchecked, and some imprudent Protestant clergy to become abusive; "if he does not stop this we shall have a breeze," remarked Marianne to the Dean of Salisbury, and how right she was. A buzz from the back, and a little man screamed that he "*would* be heard," upon which the walls nearly came down, most of the audience bellowing, "Chair, chair," but a few shouted,

"Fair play, let the Catholic have his turn, let Ireland be heard." Amidst loud encouragement Lord Gambier managed to get his motion passed, but was then so ill advised as to call upon a Mr. Pope to address the company.

You would have thought that this row would have taught Mr Pope that he had better have kept on safe grounds, but actually the man was foolish enough to begin a number of stories about priests and idolatry till the Catholic party again began their uproar and Lord Gosforth got up to beg that Mr Pope would desist from this line of argument. He did it rather too violently perhaps, for the poor Pope (in name not in nature for he was extremely fallible) stood up, cried, wiped his eyes, cried again, said he had a good deal more to say but he supposed he had better stop, was cheered, went on—got into mire again and finally ceased.

Mr. Pope was followed by Edward Irving, who shook his staff at both parties, scolded them right and left, and was so violent and incoherent that nobody had any idea what he was saying; "after this most parties seemed to think the meeting had better be dissolved, and so it was." But it was not the end of Irving. At another meeting of the season he managed to involve Lord Gambier in play-acting on the platform. Irving had been intoxicated by praise ("brother beloved in the Lord") and by indiscriminate head shaking, and ended his rambling speech by declaring that silver and gold had he none, not a farthing belonged to him, but he would present the Society with a treasure given him by his brother—his watch.

Accordingly he pulled out a large warming pan watch with chain and seals, pressed them to his heart and then presented them to Lord Gambier. Lord Gambier, delighted at the deed, ran after him across the platform to induce him to take it back.

Irving declared that all the power of Earth and Heaven united should not make him take it back. 'Well then said Lord G if you wont take that take *that*' and he stretched out his hand, and now, said he, your left hand *does* know what your right hand has done.

The excitement over the admiral's epigram was terrific, the collection plates were full of the rings and brooches of "silly women" (it is interesting to find the expression in such early use), Irving's watch was put up for auction and redeemed at a tremendous price. "The genius of Merry Andrewism" pervaded most of the week, she thought. And as for "The Jews on the Friday," they surpassed themselves. They were the climax. Mr. Lewis Way "ranted and raved." Mr. Cunningham disputed with Sir Thomas Baring, and then apologised and told the audience that Sir Thomas was so good-natured that he was called in India good-natured Tom. Mr. Lewis Way then rose again holding a manuscript in his hand. He had intended to publish it, but the Bishop of Lichfield had so taken the gall out of his heart, that instead of publishing it he meant to tear it, "and so on the platform he tore it leaf from leaf and stamped and danced upon it." Lord Gambier was dazed. Then Irving functioned, and the meeting was closed by a famous Calvinist, Mr. Macneil. He said "he hoped everyone would go home and forget all that had passed, for it has not pleased the Lord to vouchsafe to any of his servants to speak that which was suitable on that day." Sir Robert Inglis agreed with Mr. Macneil, and vowed it was "the last exposé of the kind he would ever witness." Sir Thomas Acland said, "Man will be a charlatan to the end of time." Marianne trusted he would lose it in eternity: the scene had been "very amusing to we good people who do not go to plays but seriously speaking it is said to see such tricks played before high Heaven." There were further May

Meetings but the Jews on that Friday were the last that she records. She, or her advisers, had been shocked.

But she had not done with Edward Irving. That strange personality fascinated her. She had to admit his charm and originality and sporadic sincerity. Later on (1832), when he had founded the Irvingite church, she went to one of its services and reported to Miss Louisa Inglis on the disquieting phenomenon of the Tongues.

It's so evident there is nothing supernatural, or what any human being who had strong lungs enough to make the dreadful noise may not do, and the way in which Irving's prayer winds them up and excites them to expect a message from Heaven only makes me surprised that the whole congregation do not catch the infection and begin when you consider what excitable and impressionable beings we are—specially we women who form the chief of the congregation. I feel however equally sure that they are not impostors. If it was a trick it would be pleasing instead of disgusting, and there would be more meaning in what they say: for it consisted entirely of little short words such as cry, cry, cry, repeated: and which reminded me of Wolfe, who used to go on just the same way: build, build build build thou the walls of Jerusalem.

It was such a relief after these unconnected exclamations to hear Irving read a few verses out of the Bible, the contrast never struck me so strongly before between real inspiration & these violent and unmeaning cries. After the calm and 'reasonable service' of our church it is amazing how people can find much comfort in such prayers as Irving's, which were wholly for averting the coming judgments upon the blinded National Church (which sounded so like pique for turning him out) or for the immediate & visible descent of the spirit, which was to be manifested not by the fruits of the spirit, love joy and peace, but by the cries & shrieks which reminded one only of agony and despair.

[*140*]

The letter then takes an unexpected turn, and Harriet Melville—her pleasant cousin whom we met at lunch at the Bank—comes painfully into the picture.

It is odd that the sounds I heard there I had heard once and only once before, as I was telling Harriet when I came home, and one thing that made it so very painful was that I could have fancied myself in this very room the day her operation was performed 3 years ago by Brodie, those awful screams which sent Lucy into hysterics and drove Melville out of the house as they penetrated even into his room. I never believed before that the human voice had such strength.

Operation for cancer without an anaesthetic? It sounds like it. The surgical sufferings of those days are unthinkable. Shortly after the above letter was written Harriet Melville died.

To revert to the subject of meetings: "A very nice meeting for Baby Schools" falls into a pleasanter category and reminds us of her constant interest in infant education. Under the influence of her parents and of Hannah More, she had tried to teach poor children while she herself was only a child, she had gone into primitive schools of the early century and helped. It was her duty and it was also a pleasure. She had never been afraid of the poor, and she had too much faith in human nature to foresee that education might be a hindrance to happiness.

> Unto this truth I set my hand
> Learning is better than house or land
> When house is gone and money spent
> Then learning is most excellent.*

was her unalterable belief.

* Quoted from Arthur Bryant, *The Age of Elegance.*

This particular meeting was what is called an "important one," and was expected by its organisers to usher in the millennium. Statesmen, men of business, of money, and of war were all in conclave, trying to make "the lives of these little animalculae a little happier." Wilberforce was there, speaking about babies exquisitely. Irving was of course there; in the course of his eloquence he turned to Lord Brougham and said, "Except you become as a little child you shall in no wise enter into the Kingdom of Heaven," which caused that dubious statesman to draw back his chair and look uncomfortable. The meeting was amusing, it was even impressive, but Marianne's thoughts strayed from it to the children themselves: how were they going to benefit when these important persons had dispersed? What in particular about the "under fives"? And her letter ends with a touching reference—more touching than she realises—to her own "babyising" in Clapham parish, to the two "settlements" she and her sisters have organised, to the "mattress at one corner" when the very little ones rest in the middle of the day while the bigger ones sing them to sleep, to the "self-supporting school," where sixty babies at $2d$. a head a week paid the mistress's salary, to the school treat where a little boy broke his arm, "but he had better keep on at school," said his mother, "if he stays at home he may break the other one." It was to realities and simplicities like these that her mind reverted; she enjoyed meeting eminent people, she accepted the structure of society, but she concentrated on the individual Clapham babies whom she hoped to help.

To Hannah More, July 24, 1824:

The young Macaulays were here a few days ago to assist at a Baby School feast on the Lawn—which tho' it concluded with a tremendous thunderstorm began very gaily—the company consisting of nearly Seventy Little Beings under Six years old were *carted* up and *shot* out on the lawn, where rocking horses, Swings, baby Houses, Sugar Plumbs formed the delights of the scene—and a moderate quantity of Gooseberry pie and Cake according to the capabilities of the little recipients concluded the day.—Many were too young to feed themselves—and these the young Macaulays took to cramming within an inch of their lives.—Mr Dealtry was of course, the greatest Baby there.

She kept in touch with Wilberforce behind the scenes, and has described visits which she paid him in his retirement. The date of her first visit is not recorded: about 1820. He is at Tonbridge, *i.e.*, Tunbridge Wells.

He has withdrawn from the world with a vengeance, for he is in so little a bit of a House or rather Hutch, that some of his servants and most of his guests are sent off to the Inn, a mile away from the house, to sleep. Mrs Wilberforce seems to like this hugger mugger way of going on, but I am right glad they are to move to Hendon, where he has bought a large place as far as grounds are concerned, but the House I believe is still a bad one. There is something melancholy to me in all these changes at his advanced age, 'the rolling stone gathers no moss', and it seems as if 'moss' means those thousand little associations of habits and ways that you feel in a place that years have endeared, and it was as unnatural to see a person of Mr Wilberforce's standing always on the move as it would be to see a little child still. . . .

Things go on in the old way the house thronged with servants who are all lame or impotent or blind, or kept from charity; an ex-secretary kept because he is grateful, and his wife because she nursed poor Barbara, and an old butler who they wish would not stay but then he is so attached, and his wife who was a cook but now she is so infirm. All this is rather as it should be however for one rather likes to see him so completely in character and would willingly sit in despair of getting one's plate changed at dinner and hear a chorus of Bells all day which nobody answers for the sake of seeing Mr Wilberforce in his element.

She and Wilberforce proceeded to deplore "this Apocrypha business in the Bible Society." It was one of the many controversies which disturbed and enlivened the May Meetings, and the facts about it are not easy to convey. In its simplest form it concerned the insertion (or the omission) of the Apocrypha in Bibles issued by societies on the continent which were affiliated to the parent society in London. But one must go further than that. It linked on to a regrettable case known as the "Strasburg Preface," when the Strasburg Committee had tacked an introduction of their own on to a Bible for which the London committee had paid, and had thus laid themselves open to charges of popery, infidelity, and rationalism. Might not similar charges be brought or be more readily brought if the Apocrypha was included? Some thought so, others thought not. No one came to a conclusion more sensible than Marianne's:

We all thought that the Bible Society was so simple in its form and its object that none of the frailties of mortality could touch it, and that, whereas in all other Societies there might be some chance of jarring discords, this alone was secure from all the conflicts which belong to human undertakings: but it was conducted by men, and so there must be imperfections, and the only possible rock on which they could split, the Apocrypha, has crashed them to pieces.

She goes on to suggest—and not humorously—that "all ladies should side with the gentlemen among whom they live": this would reduce public controversy, which is seldom vital, and avoid domestic controversy, and she is relieved that all the gentlemen she knows (except Zachary Macaulay) are on the same side over the Apocrypha; *i.e.*, put the Apocrypha in.

Presently the Wilberforces made their move to Highwood and to "a state more faintly resembling repose," though in 1826 she found the traditional confusion there—many dinner bells ringing but no dinner, dissenting ministers ringing the door bell because they heard the dinner bells, the house a collection of rabbit hutches containing two married sons and their families, the blind secretary and his family, the deaf butler and his, and the secretary who could see could not find a book which was required or even feel that it was his duty to find it. In the fields attached to the property the eldest son was trying to become a dairy farmer: "I wish William would keep company with his father instead of his cows. It would be quite as profitable and much more agreeable."

To her sister Henrietta (1828):

The scene at prayers is a most curious one. There is a bell which rings when Mr W begins to dress; another when he finishes dressing; upon which Mr Barningham begins to play a hymn upon the organ and to sing a solo, and by degrees the family come down to the entrance hall where the psalmody goes on; first one joins in and then another; Lizzy calling out 'Don't go near dear Mama, she sings so dreadfully out of tune, dear', and William, 'Don't look at Papa, he does make such dreadful faces.' So he does, waving his arms about, and occasionally pulling the leaves off the geraniums and smelling them, singing out louder and louder in a tone of hilarity: 'Trust Him, praise Him, trust Him, praise Him ever more.' Sometimes he exclaims 'Astonishing! How very affecting! Only think of Abraham, a fine old man, just a kind of man one should naturally pull off one's hat to, with long grey hairs, and looking like

an old aloe—but you don't know what an aloe is perhaps: its
a tree—no a plant which flowers . . .' and he wanders off into
a dissertation about plants and flowers.

In a passage of her "Recollections" which refers to this
period, she comments on the family with some bitterness: she
had never liked Mrs. Wilberforce, and perhaps she was jealous of her:

Most of the sons were pleasant and distinguished themselves
in after life, all except the eldest who never was endurable.
I have often wondered what could be the fault in their education which has occasioned them to miss the positions that such
children of such a father ought to have held. He loved them
so much and was so anxious for their real welfare, and much
as he was occupied with public business he really never neglected them. They were proud of belonging to him, but on that
account rated themselves too highly, thinking everyone should
be at their disposal because their names were Wilberforce. This
idea they got from their mother as well as many penurious ways
which I fancy came from the Spooners being of Jewish extrac-
tion. Mrs Wilberforce was a religious woman but lived much
with a lower set of people 'professors' as they would have called
themselves—who had a great deal of pious phraseology, and
some of them not a very high standard of morality. I think
that these sort of people unjustly disgusted her sons with
'evangelicals' and made them turn to a more gentlemanly school
in the Tractarians at Oxford who were just rising into notice
when the three younger Wilberforces went there. In his old
age they tried to make their good father a High Churchman,
but beyond admiring The Christian Year I do not think they
succeeded.

And how right she proved about the cows. "You have
heard of Mr Wilberforce's losses through William's cow-
keeping," she remarks in 1831, "and that he is obliged to

leave Highwood. He is behaving beautifully on it they all say, as one might be so certain he would. He comes to us with his train next week." He died two years later. In 1835 his son Robert began to write his life, aided by his son Samuel.

We have had Robert Wilberforce 'dull Robert' as he is called here since last I saw you [she writes to Patty Smith], and verily I wish you and I were rich enough to buy up his father's life and burn it, out of love for the great old Man. It is pitiable to hear the measured calculating un-Wilberforced like tone of the man. He is not to be blamed though, nature has made him a thorough Spooner from Birmingham and this is where his blameless useful existence should have passed. I wish there were a law obliging men to take their mother's names when so utterly unlike their fathers. But as to thinking such a creature as that can appreciate or describe that winged being and all his airy flight—why you might as well put a mole to talk about an eagle.

But I agree with you about Bozzy—long life to him! for there will be 50 Johnsons before there will be such another biographer. I once, like you, wrote down a whole summer morning talk between Mr Wilberforce and Sir James Mackintoch, and two better talkers or more disposed to talk their best never were, but I burnt it the next day out of pure humanity to their memories.

"Dull Robert" and "Soapy Sam" (as he was called when he became Bishop of Oxford) would no doubt do their best, and she tries not to blame them:

I am not afraid it will be anything worse than rather dull and heavy, but the two most concerned in it are very good natured, and are I think anxious to conciliate all sorts and conditions of men. They are absurd high churchmen, but seem

quite aware their father was no such thing, and will I believe
do it fairly enough. . . . Mr Wilberforce's letters were like his
talk with one foot on the step of the carriage and one off,
desultory thoughtless, loving, and often nearly unintelligible.
It is a sad loss that he never, or rarely at least, gave his mind
to a letter, for I know not how else he is to be described, and
as when I saw Joseph's horrid statue I longed to break it, so
I am afraid when I read his life I shall want to burn it.

She has refused to help the sons with any reminiscence, for
"those rapid turns in conversation which seemed so exquisite
would evaporate if they were written down! Only Boswell
has preserved them—perhaps because he places the whole
picture before us instead of an insulated sentence. . . .
Have you looked at Coleridge' Table Talks? How wretch-
edly he reads! . . . Robert Hall's 'on dits' are equally
poor." But will not Patty Smith look through her own
papers and contribute something? "I should feel then as
if I had thrown my stone upon the heap that will be his
monument."

Her beloved Hannah More was threatened by a similar
fate. She too had had to leave her home in old age—the
reason in her case being dishonest servants. She too was
menaced by one of those Lives that might be called Deaths.

She calls Sir Thomas Acland in one of her notes to me 'the
recreant knight of Devonshire' * which Roberts thinking un-
civil I suppose, has altered into 'the excellent and estimable
Sir T. Acland'—two words that playful woman never used in
her life. Somewhere else she began to me 'When I think of you
I am gladerer and gladerer and gladerer', which he, thinking
bad English has done into 'I am very glad'. Now if such an
oaf as that will write a book at least he should be honest.

* P. 86.

She had lost her two best friends, and she felt they would also be lost to posterity through incompetent recording and stupid bowdlerizing. Anyone who has known and loved a public figure privately will understand her feeling of helplessness.

FIVE

The Marriages

1833 BROUGHT CHANGES even more important than the deaths of William Wilberforce and Hannah More. The marrying started.

It started with the strange affair between my grandfather and my grandmother. He had long frequented the house and been universally liked, and when Bishop Jebb's health declined they both quitted Ireland and settled at Wandsworth to be near their good friends. All went well until he wanted to marry Laura. There was instantly terrible trouble. Henry was shattered at the prospect of a change in the domestic economy; moreover as a man of substance he disapproved of this particular match; Mr. Forster might be pious and personable, but he was poor. Money must marry money, as it had always done hitherto. He put every obstacle in their way, subjected them to interference, curtailed their correspondence, and managed to persuade himself that Mr. Forster was persecuting his sister and snubbed him as follows:

> Battersea Rise
> April 12, 1832.

My dear Mr Forster

I shall be out today from very early in the morning till late at night & it will therefore be out of my power to see you. If you still wish it I will see you on Friday but as I have talked the matter over very fully with Laura & entirely coincide in the view she has taken of the subject & in the motives which have led her to give a negative—I feel that any conversation on the subject would be most painful & could not be attended with a good result—I cannot describe to you what distress this business has given me as affecting the happiness of one whom I cannot cease to love & value—Do let me advise (as the Bishop tells me he has done) quiescence on the subject as the present system of continual discussion & intercourse on the subject is most harassing to all parties concerned. I again repeat that if you wish it I will see you, but with my view of the subject I am sure it must give us both pain.

Believe me
affectionately yours
H. S. THORNTON.

This brought down upon him a counter-rebuke from the Bishop, which it is a pleasure to quote.

April 12, 1832

My dear Mr Thornton,

I am extremely sorry that you have written a note, and permit me to add such a note to Mr Forster, without having previously conferred with your sisters. He requested an interview with you, in full concurrence with all the members of your family: I had, at her own desire, a long conversation yesterday with your sister Laura; and am obliged to say that I believe, and even know, you have conceived an erroneous impression of her real sentiments. In fact everything but a formal acquiescence was pronounced yesterday to me, in this room, by your sisters; and it was not without the knowledge, nor against the approbation of those most concerned, that Mr Forster requested an interview this morning with you. I perceive this letter is as incoherent in composition, as it is abominable in penmanship. But you will excuse the necessary result of extreme agitation. Enquire of your sister Etta all that has passed.

[151]

You will I think find, if you enquire calmly, and listen patiently, that Mr Forster has, throughout the whole business, been any thing but harassing—he would rather die, than force himself on the acceptance of your sister. And I hope and believe, that I am as unlikely a person as exists, to abet any unreasonable, or indelicate procedure. I must have expressed myself very unfortunately in conversing with you, to be so wholly misapprehended. I never could have advised, for I never, since I knew how matters stood, wished or even dreamed of Mr Forster's quiescence.

> Believe me,
> Your very affectionate friend,
> JOHN LIMERICK.

Meanwhile the Thornton sisters—that is to say Henrietta, Isabella, and Sophia—Marianne and Lucy took no part—formed themselves into a committee and wrote constantly to their future brother-in-law, informing him of Laura's state of mind and of his own prospects, warning him, encouraging him, giving him cause for caution or hope, transmitting messages provided they thought the messages suitable. He replied as constantly to them, he enjoyed their palpitating missives, and an atmosphere of transferred amorousness sprang up which I find inelegant. When Laura was away from them all on a visit, she found it possible to communicate directly with her lover, but her sisters and her brother and the Bishop and Nurse Hunter and the Inglises had between them got her so confused that what she wrote cannot have given him much comfort. She tells him she adores Battersea Rise and unless he gives her time the wrench at parting will be unbearable. "I know full well that I love this home too much. I fear that I idolise it, and I doubt not that infinite Wisdom has for this reason ordered that I should not spend the rest of my life in it." After this backhander

The Rev. Charles Forster
by George Richmond (1833)

she assures him that he has done all a man could towards convincing her that she might be happy elsewhere. It is a snubby letter, and the irreverent outsider may wonder why he did not defeat the intentions of Infinite Wisdom by breaking off the engagement. However lovers have warmth and tendernesses which do not go into words and are often the contrary of words, and the two were assuredly in love.

When the reluctant Henry consented, settlements were drawn up by him with foresight. My grandfather only possessed £1,000, though he had reasonable expectations of a legacy from the Bishop. Henry compelled him to insure his life for £5,000, the annual payments on which were made out of my grandmother's income of £300 a year.

They were married on August 31, 1833, in the church on Clapham Common and Henry was married at the same time and in the same place, as will be presently related. Most of the family were present at the double event; not Charles Thornton, who was on holiday abroad and did not choose to return. He wrote Laura a significant letter:

One cannot look back on the years past without a longing look, feeling as one must that all is breaking up and no more to be what it has been. I agree with you in hoping that we shall have no more quarrels, 'common' or 'family', henceforward for ever more. I am sure that old feuds would never have occurred if we had all done our best to promote to the contrary feeling.

After the ceremony Laura and her husband went off to live with the Bishop, who had had a paralytic stroke and required nursing. What a honeymoon! He died later in the year, and was buried in the Thornton family vault at the other Clapham church—St. Paul's. Amongst the bearers were the three Thornton brothers—Henry, Watson, and

Charles—and Sir Robert Inglis. Whether the Bishop deserved posthumous honour is doubtful, for he left a most
disappointing will: he bequeathed my grandfather a pair
of knee-buckles, and they were the very pair that my grandfather had previously given to him. Laura burst into laughter at the news and the more she looked at her brother's face
the more she laughed. The buckles lie beside me as I sit
chronicling the disaster—an unobtrusive pair in a wooden
case. They are said to be of gold but do not look it, and to
have been worn by the Duke of York but do not show it.
With them came one hundred volumes from the Bishop's
library.*

The dismay of the prudent and honourable Thorntons
may be imagined. This is what came of quitting the family
circle and marrying an Irishman! Poor Laura already on
the rocks! The Bishop had never paid his chaplain one penny
of salary throughout his years of service: they were soul-
mates with a single purse, and it might have been supposed
that the equivalent of the salary would have been bequeathed.
But the Bishop's mind did not work that way. Nor indeed
did my grandfather's. He felt not the slightest rancour for
the shabby way he had been treated and was sure that things
would turn out all right. They did, more or less. His friend
the Archbishop of Canterbury (Howley) appointed him to
Ash, a living in Kent worth £150 a year, and there one of
his earliest problems was the insertion of a full-length statue
of his friend into the parish church. The churchwardens objected—what was a Bishop of Limerick to them?—but my

* This is our traditional account. I must add that the Bishop's will (as
cited in my grandfather's life of him) lists other items besides the buckles
—e.g., some pebble buttons, and a tortoiseshell-and-silver penholder—the
number of the books is two hundred not one, and there is a pecuniary
legacy of £100. To my mind these additions make the Bishop's behaviour
odder, not less odd. He left the rest of his fortune to his family.

Laura Thornton (Mrs. Charles Forster)
by George Richmond (1833)

grandfather had an iron will and carried all before him. It was not until thirty years later, when he was rector elsewhere, that the statue, which was of plaster, came to roost. The then incumbent of Ash wanted to remove it, to make room for the organ. This threw my grandfather into a sacred fury. He appealed to the Archbishop of Canterbury, high heavens rang, and he would not be appeased by the offer of the statue to his present church. "They are all combined against me," he cried. Marianne pointed out that his only real enemy was the Rector of Ash, which caused him to thunder, "You are right, Marianne, he is alone in his iniquity." The statue finally found a resting place in the Crystal Palace, and there an irreverent nephew encountered it and flung up his cap with cries of "Cheers for the Blessed Bishop."

The new living was at Stisted in Essex (£900 a year) and there my grandparents spent the rest of their lives. They produced ten children: John Jebb (called after the Bishop), Charley, Henry, Laura (who did much to preserve the Thornton tradition), Doanie, Ella, Edith, Eddie (my father), Arthur, and Willie. There too my grandfather produced ten books: a *Life of Bishop Jebb*, the *Letters of Bishop Jebb*, a *Historical Geography of Arabia*, *Discourses on Scripture History*, *Mohammedanism Unveiled*, *One Primaeval Language*, *The Three Heavenly Witnesses*, *Six Preacher Sermons*, a *Commentary on the Epistle to the Hebrews*, and another on the Rosetta Stone which remains in manuscript. The Forsters were naturally not well off. Marianne became their chief financial supporter and Laura's confidante. The sisters wrote to each other continually during the next thirty years: babies, illnesses, church repairs, illnesses, babies, parcels, when can you all come, when shall I come. The Forsters came often to Battersea Rise and

Laura adored it, but my grandfather never went down there as well as he had in his bachelorhood, and as the years passed he became less charming and more excitable.

To return to Henry, the same day that Laura married, and in the same church, he was united to Harriet Dealtry, the rector's eldest daughter.

Dr. Dealtry, a mathematician of distinction, had succeeded the beloved John Venn at Clapham in 1813. It was he who had prayed by the deathbed of Henry Thornton the elder, and he was much esteemed for his piety and sound doctrine, his parish work, his activity at May Meetings and School Feasts, and he and his wife frequently figure in Sir Robert's dinner lists. But he does not occur in Marianne's "Recollections" and the references to him in her letters are incidental. It does not seem as if the two families were intimate. Harriet Dealtry's arrival brought intimacy of a sort, and for seven years she and her sisters-in-law lived under the same roof. But here again references are infrequent— until indeed Harriet became ill, when there is affectionate concern. She was a gentle, friendly creature, ill suited to be mistress of a large household; she bore her husband two daughters and a son, and having fulfilled her duties to that extent she died—died in a little upstairs dressing room which was always associated with her quiet sojourn. Henry bore her decease phlegmatically; it was observed that he interrupted his usual routine as little as possible. His marriage may also have been phlegmatic; he may have taken her to wife because he felt that the charmed circle of his youth had been broken by the defection of Laura.

The three children certainly brought changes, and pleasant ones. Marianne and Isabella enjoyed being aunts, Nurse

[*156*]

Hunter, still in action, welcomed the arrival of a new generation in her nursery.

Another consequence of Henry's marriage had been the withdrawal of the Inglises. It was thought that they might have stayed on if pressed, but he made no attempt to press them and they moved off to their Milton Bryan estate and to their Bedford Square house. They had reigned at Battersea Rise for twenty years. If the rule of her parents had been Marianne's golden age, the Inglises represented the silver age for her. The Age of Iron had not yet revealed its contours.

Sophia was the next to go. She married in 1834. Hers was the grand match, for her husband, John Melville, had the prospect of a title. Later in the century he became Earl of Leven and Melville, and Aunt Sophy, whom I can just remember, died every inch a countess. He had further qualification. He was well off, and had been a staunch friend to Henry in the great financial crisis. He was one of the young partners who had given the pleasant luncheon party at Birchin Lane. Who could have been more suitable! Yet Henry resented Sophia's marriage far more than Laura's. I have never found out why. Perhaps he disliked the consanguinity: John and Sophia were first cousins. Perhaps he disliked the cousinship between Sophia and John's first wife, Harriet, who had been one of the Samuel Thorntons. Perhaps—and this is the official version—he was so fond of his sisters that he was always upset when they quitted his roof. He certainly made it difficult for Sophia to return to it. So preposterous was his behaviour that he alienated her.

Henrietta was the next to go. Her choice was Richard Synnot, the son of an Irish Knight. Henry was grumpy as usual, and Marianne thus expressed herself to Patty Smith:

Etta says she feels in a cage with the door wide open, and I am anxious that *she* and no one else should close that door, and then she will not feel a prisoner. What a thousand mixed feelings the marriage of a sister calls up. Nobody seems good enough or nice enough or rich enough. At first it is such a wrench, and then *all* women are so much better than men— then it seems so impossible that the girl should like him well enough for *that*. It's the first time all one's feelings have not gone along with her, and to find her ready to entrust her fate to someone whom you can yourself only *like very much*, seems strange. But by degrees I have happily always contrived to fall in love with my brothers-in-law myself, and then all goes on well. While the girls have been deliberating it has always been my fate to be courted by them, & this has been my occupation lately, till I tell Etta to come back soon or I will have him myself. . . . You remember Lady Synnot at Rome probably, a kind generous old lady she is, and you will think of Richard as I often do now—a curly haired flaxen headed Raphael-looking child who was called Cupid when the children were all playing together at the Palazzo Schiarra.

They married in 1836, and judging by a watercolour Henrietta made of Richard, he retained all his beauty. But his health deteriorated and five years later he died. Shortly before that event Marianne visited them, and took part in an ominous discussion on the subject of the guardianship of the two children. Their Uncle Henry—the obvious person—was rejected by the Synnots as unsuitable. The dying man thought that Henry would just do, that he had improved, that there was just sufficient agreement in religious outlook, but Henrietta, her baby girl in her lap, cried, "No! Think of this poor little thing in a love affair, how he will use her!!"

I don't so much look to *that* [Marianne writes to Louisa Inglis] as to the general fact of what he says of himself, that

'nobody minds him any more than if he were a child', he has
no influence with any human being, just because he is so uncertain and inconsistent, and you would not want to put a
child under the care of one who behaves like a child himself.

So, as regards Henrietta also, Henry proved inadequate.
There was no open break, and she rented a small house at
Clapham so that her children might enjoy Battersea Rise.
The boy, Inglis, took his first name from Sir Robert Inglis,
his godfather. The girl was called Henrietta after her
mother. They were charming and unusual children, and
much will be heard of them in the future.

After Henrietta, Charles. In 1837—in orders himself—
he married a Miss Harrison whose brother was a clergyman.
All was appropriate here, but in less than two years he and
his wife both died.

Watson married Miss Frances Webb in 1842.

That almost concludes the marriages. The library of Henrietta's picture has been rapidly depopulated.

Why did Marianne herself not marry? In all the letters
and documents I have examined there is not one hint of an
affair, not the shadow of a name. When her parents died
she was young, good-looking, good-natured, amusing, intelligent and practical, she enjoyed the company of men and
frequented suitable society, she had some money, and she
was under no obligation to stay at home, for her brothers
and sisters were in the competent hands of the Inglises. One
would have expected her to find a husband during the next
ten years, or at any rate after her brother's marriage, but
she passes into spinsterhood without regret. She was certainly in love with the house, like them all, and she was devoted to Henry, particularly since the Bank crisis which he
had allowed her to share with him, and she was deeply devoted to Wilberforce, her father's friend. Here is acceptable

explanation of the sublimated type. Still I'm puzzled and my frustration would amuse her, for she did not approve of inquisitiveness, and enjoyed thwarting it.

After the death of Henry's wife in 1840, life went on quietly. The widower drove up in his gig every morning to the Bank, wearing his stovepipe hat, returned in the evening tired, and disinclined for company. He adored his children, and his sisters did what they could to make the house comfortable for him. Marianne was technically in charge, but she had a rival in the authoritative Isabella. (Lucy died in 1844.) Isabella annexed Harti, the eldest girl, and the little son, as the more important infants; Marianne adopted the frail Emmy. A mild schism arose which was observed by the sharp eyes of another little girl, the younger Laura Forster, and recorded in later years by her pleasant pen. Copying Marianne (Laura was rather a copycat), she too wrote her "Recollections," and the comedy of the two rival aunts has been preserved. They used the lawn as a drawing room when the weather was fine and held their respective courts there: carpet and table and sofa and easy chairs were placed under the shade of the tulip tree. Further off was a chestnut tree and a hammock. Next door were the Trevelyans, who came clambering over the wall as the Macaulays had before them. Early morning was Aunt Marianne's hour: at 7:30 all the children converged on her large and sunny bedroom, over the library, and there she spun them stories about "a wonderful and wicked Mother Bell on the spur of the moment," and if she showed a tendency to go to sleep they punched her. Mother Bell stole children, robbed churches, went down coal mines and among gipsies and to the holds of ships and grew so exhausting to her creator that she had to be killed.

When the children descended to morning prayers there

were other pleasures. For Henry Thornton (contrary to one's expectations) was most enlightened on the subject of fire. Before prayers began he would burn a lump of sugar for each child with a red-hot poker, burn it exactly as much as the child directed and no more, and leave it to cool while devotions proceeded. If the child fidgeted during prayers it was supposed not to get its sugar. He would also sit upon a burning newspaper—an accomplishment he retained till the end of his life:

One morning he discussed the danger of fire and said that when he was little he was told he must never play with it or he should get burnt, but now he was a man he knew better, and would show us he could play with fire quite nicely and not get burnt at all. He lit a good sized piece of newspaper at the fire, put it all blazing on his leather chair, and sat down on it to our delight and horror.

The vision of that substantial extinguisher descending cheers me, the sun comes into the library again, the trees wave freshly on the lawn, tiny cousins collide and jump. . . .

We wandered where we liked, or played hide and seek in the large shrubberies and outhouses [Laura's "Recollections" continue], but my general impression is of liking to keep my aunt within sight, confident that if no tiresome grown-up person called us we could run up to her for advice or sympathy if our amusements flagged—Lady Trevelyan would be no impediment to this, only we should feel we ought not to stop longer than to ask a question or two, but we never interrupted when strangers were in possession. My aunt also liked to have children within reach, and we were pleased whenever she called one of us to go on a message for her or trusted us to fetch a book or some work from the house. This mutual desire to share unobtrusively the life on the lawn then seemed to me a common and almost inevitable state of things, but later life has shown me how much tact and sympathy my aunt must have had to make us feel her going into the house brought a blank into whatever we were doing. She never interrupted us without cause and I think it was partly to this respectful attitude to children that the Thornton sisters owed their charm.

Then there was a Christmas party, recalling the philosophic fête given nearly half a century earlier. Though this time it was an artistic fête. Mr. Richmond came and arranged tableaux. Isabella had organised a tub and a tree and threw cold water on the tableaux, said they would bore the children and suggested acting instead. Acting! the sinful word sent Marianne flying over the wall to consult Lady Trevelyan, who was duly horrified. Acting was prevented and tableaux went forward—Red Ridinghood with and without the Wolf, the Little Princes in the Tower, etc. An upstairs door was taken off its hinges by clever Mr. Richmond and Mr. Severne, a dining-room picture frame nailed over the aperture, black gauze stretched over it, eighteen wax candles and three lamps fixed behind, "and blue calico beyond all for the sky." The audience filed past the entrance— over a hundred of them. "Some of the children screamed and some of them sobbed, but they would have looked at it all night." Marianne had "never supposed Tableaux would be so lovely." I remember thinking them lovely half a century later, in my own childhood. What trouble must have been expended in draping and posing the loveliness! And how irrevocably it disappeared.

This pleasant show was soon followed by another: by the marriage of Isabella Thornton to Archdeacon Harrison. "And were you ever so amused, and were you ever so pleased. Ben and Bella at last!" The Archdeacon was a dear little man with a squint, who had been hanging around for some time, but no one was sure whether he would come to the point

Battersea Rise from the garden
by Lucy Thornton (about 1825)

or whether Isabella would accept anyone so small. All the day he had been particularly uproarious, had mimicked a canon singing, had ventured on giving an opinion, which he was not prone to do, and at night when Marianne's hair was being brushed and her feet were already in hot water for bed the news arrived and she had to go down. Nurse Hunter was called down too. "What, for our precious Miss Isabella, Oh thank God what a blessing," she cried. "Why its just what we've all been longing for, he's got a beautiful bit of money, and he's a kind master, and Miss Isabella she'll have children of her own and how happy she'll be." Henry said, "Yes Nurse, if I could but take four years off her age and add four inches to his height there would be nothing further to be done.—What does that matter he's got plenty to keep her. . . ."

Isabella exulted. At the age of forty-five she was leaving a dubious and divided empire to queen it in The Precincts, Canterbury. In a rather skittish letter she exposed her joy to Laura:

Ben was very much delighted with Mr F's notes. How strange it all seems to me. I feel in a complete dream. How in the world I am to be uprooted from here I cannot imagine but I suppose people do live thro' such things. I have not long to think about it as they talk now of the 18th July. I care mighty little about my garments which I suppose is generally the case, and not much about any of the arrangements.

You would be amused to see my incumbrance and myself in our new relationship. He is much the most épris of the 2, but very proper in his behaviour as you may suppose. Complained much to the others because I would not let him walk down to Lady Synnot's with me yesterday even by daylight. I let him fetch me away. I told him I did not like to disgrace myself so far—the news being just now divulged. He has got to give up his Oxford Studentship. He said they wanted him to take his Dr's degree but he would not because he knew he should be called the little Dr. I suppose by that he knows of a less Archdeacon.

I have never got intimate enough to ask about his money matters nor do I ever profess to him that he is on anything but approbation. Now and then he gets impudent and asks what kind of travelling carriage I should like and yesterday even enquired whether I would let him send my books to Canterbury. I pretended not to hear as I do not want him to be uppish. The Bp. of S. & M. has offered to perform the ceremony but I am obliged to decline as the Bp. of Lond. has been fixed on by Ben.

For outfit I have as yet purchased only 2 dressing gowns and a pair of wh.sat.shoes which last are very slack as I intend to wear them as dressing slippers after their first appearance. What shall I be m^d in? Hakewell says white glacé flounced with silk or lace or white brocaded silk plain with tulle and rib. trimgs. I fancy this last the most. Drawn tulle bonnet and lace or mus. mantilla. I mean to get next to no clothes. . . .

I was taken to visit Aunt Isabella once when she was a very old lady. She had outlived the Archdeacon and had left Canterbury, and was living in the Bedford Square house the Inglises left her. She had never "taken me on"—there was still this partitioning of nephews and nieces amongst the aunts, and I "belonged" to Marianne. So the visit was a formal one. I remember the elegant room and the fire between the extending fire-screens and my mother saying afterwards that all had gone well.

Isabella's marriage was followed by a melancholy event—the death of beloved Nurse Hunter. Earlier in this biography I undertook not to describe illness and death at any length, and I have kept my promise in the cases of Mari-

anne's mother, William Wilberforce, Hannah More, Bishop
Jebb, Harriet Melville, Charles Thornton, Mrs. Charles
Thornton, Richard Synnot, Harriet Thornton, and Lucy
Thornton. In the case of Nurse Hunter I shall break my
promise, and quote what Marianne has to say. She has more
to say than we may care to hear, but Nurse's case is special
and her relation to her employers interesting. Only now do
we learn that she had a son or that she was married, for
presumably she was married. Hitherto she has appeared as
a sexless emanation of Battersea Rise with no existence outside it.

The letter describing her collapse was written to Henrietta Synnot, immediately after it occurred. It runs to eighteen pages. Similar letters went to Sophia, Laura, and Miss
Louisa Inglis. Henry more briefly informed Watson, Sir
Robert, and Mr. Harrison, the butler. It is addressed from
Regency House, Brighton, where they had taken lodgings
for a holiday.

I hardly know how to begin to tell you of a sorrow which
has come upon us all, that we knew could not be very long
delayed, but yet now it is come it seems as bitter as if it had
happened years ago—worse indeed in some ways. Our dear
dear Nurse was taken to her rest without illness or suffering
this evening about 9 o'clock, after a particularly cheerful,
comfortable day, she had been out in her carriage for an hour
in the morning & when I told her it was cold said she did not
find it so, she had been driving in the sun. She had read her
Bible as usual after breakfast, & Henry had read several stories
to her out of the newspaper. Mrs Cripps called while we were
out & had a long talk with her, & Mrs C. said afterwards how
much sensible advice she had given her about housekeeping.
In the afternoon she & I had a long talk about the children
in which she showed all her usual acuteness. I thought she

made but a bad dinner (she always dined with us at a little table of her own), & told her she should have early tea, which she had. I came in rather late before dinner & asked her whether the children had been good with their governess, for they always had their lessons in the room with her. 'Very good today' she said, 'much better than Saturday, I shall quite learn my french again by their lessons.' At dinner I offered her some duck, but she said she would rather have it at supper, & Henry sent it out of the room that there might be plenty left for her. The children & their Papa took to playing at dominoes, & I went up stairs to write a letter, & saw her no more till after Tea, Henry being gone out, & the children to bed.

Louisa called me down saying she was not well. I found her in her own bed-room adjoining the dining room, in her arm chair, partly undressed, & at first thought she was only fainting from the heat of the room, which was very warm, & desired them to open the window; the expression of her face was perfect calmness & placidity not a feature was altered, & yet I felt it was not sleep which was pressing down her eyelids so heavily or made her head so weighty as she leaned it against me, taking my hand in hers, which was quite warm & soft, I could only think of 'that ever deepening repose' wh. made me dread that there was a stillness in the countenance that would never be removed. Sage & Louisa were already in the room, she had rung for Sage, having walked into the bedroom, & on her proposing her supper, she said she did not feel well, & would have none, only some brandy and water, & would take a pill. Sage fancied there was something unusual about her, & instead of going for the brandy & water, called Louisa & sent her for the pills, but Nurse said 'there's no occasion to tell Miss Thornton, I shall be better soon', & these were her last words, for she didn't speak after I came to her. They thought she had better go to bed, & had taken off her cap & began to unfasten her gown, when seeing she was worse they sent for me, & yet I almost wonder they did for I could not realize the idea of illness when there was not a trace of suffering or even discomfort.

We sent instantly for Henry, Mr Hunter, & any medical men near, & till any of them came, feeling her head grow heavier, & the pulse more indistinct, it did seem such a dreadfully long interval, she was yet breathing when Henry returned, but he set off at once for Dr Dill, who lives very near, & when they both returned, Dr D. said it was all over. I still would not believe him, & hoped he would try some remedies, but he said it was disease of the heart, that all the Physicians in London could have done nothing, the machine was worn out, & it was the easiest & most painless death there was. He & Henry moved her from the chair to the bed, & we put on her cap, and she looked so exactly like herself I still thought something might be done, but he felt her heart again & again, & assured me it would beat no more.

Her poor son soon came, & was in dreadful distress at first, kissed her over & over again & would not believe she was gone, but he soon grew calm, & he, & Henry & I sate in the room for an hour or two. You know how soon all men begin to arrange about funerals, & I was almost as bad as they for I so disliked the plan H. & Mr Hunter had of her being buried here, that I begged of Henry to please me to let it be at Clapham. I know it is all imagination, but I could not endure the idea of seeming to leave her behind us, & that all of you should never see her earthly resting place. She belonged much more to us than to her Tom even, & tho' at first he had wished her to be laid by his wife & child, he soon said he really had rather, if I wished it, that she should be moved to Clapham, and I think in the end really preferred it, as a greater mark of respect. Henry was very good-natured in giving in to me, & there are other advantages in the arrangements, as now she will be moved up in a day or two to B. Rise, & the funeral will not take place till we are returned on Friday week.

There is something incongruous with merry children around

in such 'emblems of mortality' in a house in this gay place,
& yet one would not like to hurry it, or to have her moved
anywhere but to her own home, & then instead of Henry hurrying up & down to it, we shall all be quietly at home, & all
the servants may be present.

I can hardly believe that I can be writing on, on such a
subject, when six hours ago I was with her, as well—indeed
better than she has been for months, for Mary, who has just
been talking to me says that after the first two or three days
down here, she has been much better than usual—not stronger
—but more cheerful, & enjoying herself. I think that at first
finding herself living with *us*, and not the servants, rather depressed her, but afterwards she found what was the fact that
she was much fitter company for us than for them, & liked it.
The only thing that use to upset her, and make her cry was
when Henry waited on her as he sometimes did, buttered her
toast, or carried her her tea, she did not mind me, & the children used to fight who should do it. On Sunday I read her a
bit of the Bishop of Oxford's All Saints Sermon, which I had
received that day from Lady I. and I left it with her to read
while I went to Church,—she seemed really to have read it, &
said Sam was grown a great preacher. It seems such a mercy
to me to have witnessed such an easy dismission, such a happy
death after such a useful & happy life—that I long to give you
the same impression. With tomorrow's light and tomorrow's
truth I shall begin really to feel her loss, I was thinking only
yesterday that in no part of her existence was she of more use
& pleasure to me than during the last few weeks—I have never
once seen her worried or put out unless when she found the
children were hurting themselves, she was constantly at hand
to see who came in & out, to be present with the governess, &
knew all that went on, & gave me as good advice about the
servants as she could have done 10 years ago. There is nobody
to whom I could, & did, tell everything as I did to her, & there
was no one who could give me such good advice.

I have after all cut several pages out of the above, and there may even be further pages of it, for it ends without signature. The energy expended in writing it is amazing, and she was writing letters of similar diffuseness throughout her life.

With Nurse's death, the last of the ancient pillars falls, the house garnishes itself ominously for change, and Marianne's sisterhood nears its final chapter. 1815-1852 has been a long period and a rich one, and as I look back on it I see many odds and ends that I have omitted. For instance, I have never described the visit she and Lady Inglis paid to the exiled Queen of Hayti: the queen and her daughters all so black and in such deep mourning that it was difficult to distinguish anyone from anything, but Mlle. Améthyste spoke excellent French. I have never described how she stumbled upon Olney and upon Cowper's barber, who burst into tears because her grandfather, John Thornton, had preserved him from starvation in the winter of 1782; or how, proceeding from Olney to Weston Underwood, she wandered about and read the poet's letters until she felt he was with her. Or the mad dog on Clapham Common that bit a Thornton—though perhaps it was not really mad. Or her attempt —finally successful—at planting a Miss Martin's book, *Three Years' Residence in Italy*, on a publisher. Nor have I quoted—where could I have worked them in?—fascinating scraps such as: "Mr Arkwright has left Mrs Eden £14,000. The moment Mr Eden heard it he rushed to town and bought her a little brougham with the ugliest horse in England for £150."

She is so lively and so sociable that one is in danger of becoming desultory about her, and losing the main stream of her domestic life. I will return to it in a moment. Before I do so, there are two episodes which merit special mention.

They are the Guildhall Banquet and the Hereford Tea. They took place in the same year—1842.

The Banquet will not detain us long. She went to it with the Macaulays. Her reactions were mainly frivolous, though she was overwhelmed by the artificial lighting.

I think the first entrance into the Hall the finest thing of that sort I ever saw. No chandeliers, but the Gothic lines of the architecture all traced in thousands of gas lamps against the wall and the roof which made it seem like a hall of fires. It had a curious effect as there were no shadows and it seemed like daylight only much lighter, and with the flags and the armour and the gold and silver plate and the antique dresses it was like some old chronicle.

The company were inferior to the decorations:

A man near me eat pineapple with his fingers, rind and all, and a woman near Fanny Macaulay [Tom's sister] after picking her bones said 'Last Sunday I went to Greenwich and I said if I do but meet Mr. Bryan please the pigs I'll get him to walk with me and I *did* meet him the first thing.' One of our Common Council men offered to help us to coffee: 'But how shall I manage about clean cups? 2000 persons to be served, no difficulty about the gentlemen, they *prefer* a cup that has been used by a lady' . . . I begged for some sugar: 'Here's a piece as long as the Commercial Road.' Another Lady complained she was as cold as a five shilling piece. And their speeches sounded so much more ridiculous from people covered with jewels and feathers and satin. Fanny Macaulay laughed so I was afraid she would get into a scrape. Altogether it is a sight to see, tho' I still think the Hereford Tea the more interesting of the two—inasmuch as John Venn is really a greater personage than the fat rosy vulgar Lord Mayor with all his chains and ribbands.

The Hereford Tea letter once had much family prestige.
It was read aloud to me as a boy and I was told that it was
the amusingest letter Marianne ever wrote. I would not advance that claim for it. It suffers from volubility, like much
of her earlier writing. Later on her style strengthened. Still
it manages to give a picture of a society which was new to
her and would have remained unknown to us. It plunges us
for a day into the company of lower-middle-class youths in
Hereford. Where else could we take such a plunge?

She was staying with the Venns there, having come on to
them from her brother Watson's. They were the son and
the daughter of the former rector of Clapham. John Venn
had taken orders like his father, had become vicar of St.
Peter's, Hereford, and was a great success there, as the letter will evince. He had worked for and with the townspeople,
and, by founding the Hereford Society for Aiding the Industrious, had enabled the poor to get their corn ground
cheaply, to rent allotments, to buy coal at 6d. a cwt. He had
warmth and charm and personality, and, though now quite
bald, had been very good-looking in his youth. His sister
Emilia kept house for him. She was a talkative and tirelessly
amusing spinster, also popular: we have met her in passing
at Battersea Rise. The pair had managed to combine their
peculiarly virulent Evangelicalism with jollification and
joy; this Tea was their annual apotheosis.

From Marianne to Louisa Inglis and to her sister Henrietta, who are together at Milton:

I will proceed to tell you about the young man's tea, of which
you are pleased to enquire, but I feel rather as we did after
seeing Chatsworth, that it's no use to talk about it, for nobody will believe it. And yet you will think it must have been
something, that, with a short interval for dinner, could keep
me down at that room from eleven in the morning till near ten

at night, not helping or being of the smallest use, but amusing myself by seeing all the various witty devices, and hearing the curious sayings of the Hereford people. It is etiquette for the Venns to have nothing to do with it till tea time, but I wanted to see all the proceedings, so Emilia went with me and left me there, whilst she went on into the town.

The preparations were more like those for chairing our M.P. for a county than anything else. Such burthens, as they called them, of flowers and greens sent in for the room. The whole town of Hereford seems to have been wailing at the early frost which cut off the dahlias, that used to be their chief ornament; so to make up they had sent not only mountain ash berries in haycocks, and branches of rosy apples, but forests of laurels, and in every leaf a gold cross, a V, and a crown stuck on, and baskets of paper Dahlias, with gold eyes and wire legs, and China roses in such abundance that I'm sure there can't be one left standing in the county. Either you have seen the room, or at least a bit of it I think; it was all put into one, and pieces of rope had flowers tied onto them so as to make long festoons dangling at intervals all along the roof above the gallery, and very frightful it was to see the number of young men's legs, dangling also amongst the beams, nailing them up. The youths were working like dragons, each having some pet idea of his own. One asked me if I had ever been abroad, and on my saying I had, asked me whether what he was making was not like an Indian Palm, for which he intended it. It was the leaves of laurels threaded and tied round a pillar, and branches of fern at the top, so I couldn't own to having been to India, but was sure it was very like a palm. Some others were nailing green baize all along the gallery, and sticking on it the most unutterable pictures which had been used at the lectures, large idols, and mummies, and beasts and leaves, and starfish, and bones and pyramids. You who know Emilia's pictures can guess. Next came two ships whirling up in the air, manned and rigged, and then an enormous oil picture was reared at one end, and

[*172*]

a bible and I don't know what, and in gold letters 'Let not the wise man glory in his wisdom, but let him glory in this, that he knoweth me, saith the Lord . . .' and beside the picture were two globes, and beside them two short plaister figures in militaires, one looking up and one with a book, 'reading and praying', as Yapp called them, and then a pedestal covered with pink calico, on which were perched an electric machine, chymist looking glasses, models of churches, and a dreadful little beheaded head, with streaming hair, which the men put up with perfect gravity, tho' Emilia and I were half killed with laughing at it. They use it at their electricity, or something it seems with which they make that hair stand on end.

I was rather impressed suddenly to see the Colosseum of Rome whirled along on a youth's shoulder and then perched aloft, and the Temple of Concord followed, all made in cork. Then a stuffed owl was knocked up against a pillar, with such a bush of ivy, and even an unremarkable looking little rabbit, that might have been one of Harti's, was stuck against the wall. But these things they said were 'a nothing' compaired to a device of Prout, the schoolmaster, who had been labouring for months I believe, on a scenic representation of a shipwreck, which Yapp didn't seem entirely to approve of, as being worldly, and I think savouring of stage plays, till I suggested calling it a missionary enterprise. It's wood and pasteboard, which by some contrivance represents the sea in a storm, and the waves roll and a ship dances to the sound of a fiddle, and then the ship is wrecked, and a life boat goes out and saves the men, who did once crawl up and work but afterwards stuck. But next year they will go better, and the ship is to be loaded with Bibles, and little blacks appear to take them. These waves and the ship were worked by one devoted youth, who laid on his back on the floor, and moved the machinery above. John had a raised table with a dais, and these palms and paper dahlias over him, and all the rest were cross tables.

About 5 it was finished, and a little plaisterer, who had been breathless with exertion all the morning, said to Emilia 'Well, if this is so beautiful, what can 'eaven be—that must be so much more beautiful—and what must that crown of glory be that Mr Venn talks to us about so nicely!' He certainly thought this the nearest approach to Heaven. Yapp walked about in a grey dressing gown in a fatherly manner amongst all his youths, and when Emilia proposed to pay some workmen to help, he exclaimed 'What! pay for the Lord's work!' so his family baked the bread, and made the cakes and tea, and he ordered everything with the cleverness of a general, as Emilia said, and the liberality of a prince. At 6 they lit the gas which made it as light as day, and Emilia and I took refuge in the class room, where, observe, we had private tea, coffee and cake, while the youths were all admitted to the gallery, to look down on the 400 cups, saucers and spoons, that were shining on the table below. When at last John arrived, and they rushed down, there were between 3 and 400 females, mostly ladies, struggling outside the door for admission into the gallery, which was soon crowded almost to suffocation. Many were foolish enough to bring children, who are, as Emilia says, very noxious things in such places, specially when they insist on being lifted up to see Mr Venn, one perched itself on my back for the purpose. John looked excessively happy and unconcerned too, and soon left his elevated place and walked about talking to one and another. There wasn't the least noise or confusion, and not so much scrambling as when we've a dozen children to tea, but when it was over they got rather uproarious to see the shew of the shipwreck, which so excited them, that I don't know how they would have been quieted if John hadn't set them to singing 'God save the Queen'. Then a very witty report of their proceedings was read, with an honourable mention of Watson's lectures, and then John addressed them as only he could, so full of gaiety and of goodness too, telling them stories of Arkwright having been a barber &c and urging the young shopmen to patience and civility, when tried by ladies giving them

[*174*]

trouble and not buying in their shops, and such like advice,
ending with a bit of a sermon, a hymn and a prayer, and then,
hotter than ever people were before, we departed. It's the sort
of thing one never could see anywhere else. With any one else
it would degenerate into a mere mechanic's institute, or else
dwindle into a small prayer meeting, but as it now unites the
two it does give John great influence with a class that he never
could meet in any other way, and they are so fond of him.
Emilia says that when he is absent, a party amongst them met
together privately, to pray for his safety and welfare. Well,
I should think you were tired of my young man's tea, but
you'll never have to read another account of it you know and
so must have patience now.

To return to the main stream.

I have said scarcely anything yet about Stisted. Marianne was constantly staying at the rectory. Both Isabella
and Sophia were generous over money matters, but it was
she who worked for the Forsters with her hands and tried
to tidy up the confusion into which they were sinking. Sometimes she is ashamed of her "single blessedness" when she
thinks of "poor dear Laura 20 times iller than I am rushing about after her 10 children and her groaning husband
and crying maids and low-sperritted governesses." At other
times she can do nothing but laugh.

It was a strange establishment. My Forster grandparents
died long before I was born, and—perhaps because I never
knew them—I find them unsympathetic. Immersed in the
country, and deprived of the Bishop's companionship, the
Reverend Charles soon degenerated into a Hebrew Prophet
who has nothing to prophesy about. He denounced, he ex-
horted, he pardoned. His sermon on the Fall of Paris was
impressive rather than appropriate, and on other occasions
he preached on the Errors of the Pelagians and on the Sin-

fulness of Hurrying from one Dissipation to Another. He was attentive to his flock, he alleviated suffering, and for this, and for the combating of Dissent and Popery, he had the full support of the Squire. Stisted was remote and rural. Parson and Squire ruled unchallenged, tenants who did not vote Tory were turned out, no policeman was ever seen, and my grandfather got a Sunday delivery of letters stopped. The official communication from the Post Office acceding to his request has been preserved; it is signed "Anthony Trollope," and reminds us that we are by now not a thousand miles from Barsetshire.

He performed his duties conscientiously, but he had plenty of spare time, which he spent up in his study writing his books. They are worthless. He was not in touch with such Oriental scholarship as existed and his method was to accumulate such scraps of erudition as fitted in with his convictions, and to commend them forcefully. When, in his later life, breaths of the broader theology touched him he went nearly frantic: his pencil annotations on the margins of *Essays and Reviews* must be read to be believed. My grandmother was a very different character. She had a reputation amongst her sisters for unconventionality, but it was unconventionality of the helter-skelter type that flaps about in bonnet strings, puts babies to sleep in the bath, and forgets where they are. Her mind was completely conventional. Her letters are as long as Marianne's and as unforced, but naturalness is not enough, and they are seldom worth reading. Poor woman; it is surprising that she had a mind at all, for most of her life was spent in bearing children, nursing them, and burying them. Seven out of the ten died. The rectory was—and still is—an attractive house. It stands on the higher ground, overlooking the valley of the Blackwater. Lower down is the Hall, its grounds now derelict. It is a gentle Tennysonian scene, entirely of the nineteenth century, for thanks to my grandfather's zeal the church has been mercilessly restored. His family vault can be found in the churchyard, surrounded by a rusty railing, and a list of young names can still be deciphered on the covering slab. Otherwise

> our memory fades
> From all the circle of the hills.

To reach this questionable paradise, Marianne had to take a train to Braintree, where she was met for the eight-mile drive by an excited waggonette-load of children. The letter I have chosen for quotation was written by her in 1843. On arriving at the rectory she found Laura recovering from the birth of her sixth child, and expecting at any moment a visit from Mr. Jebb (the Bishop's nephew) and his wife.

I chanced to ask Laura where Mr J. was to dress. Why says she in the shower bathroom. I told her I'd passed it ¼ an hour ago and saw it full of dirty cloathes for the wash. She begged I would go and look at it and sure enough its furniture consisted of 4 dirty cloathes bags all overflowing, the shower bath full of ditto—a band box of old shoes—and a heap of cast off cloaks of the maids. On investigating further I found every drawer in the Jebb's bedroom crammed with odds and ends of Laura's, which as last time Mrs J. brought 14 gowns and a trim maid did not seem suitable, so I screeched till I got everybody I could collect and piled all their aprons with the contents which were haycocked in Laura's room for the present. Where the dirty things went I never asked. The tub I should hope. With great good nature I emptied my only chest of drawers next, and shoved them into the Jebb's room, made the maids give up a looking glass and Maber a table, and was in the midst of the mess when Laura sent to say I *must* come to her. Old Sibley begged I'd make haste for 'it's to make Missis's bed and she will make it yourself if you don't speed'. So I rushed

to her and found her sure enough out of bed and threatening
to put on the clean sheets. She said No harm either for she'd
made it the last time it was made—that is in her labour! Sibley
is old and decrepit, she can hardly do anything unless it is to
hold the child, but amongst us we sheeted the bed and I persuaded Laura to get *in*—not on—as being more confidential
to see Mrs Jebb *in*.

They came before we had finished. I thought they both seemed
excessively nervous—Mr Forster happily hobbled down to
them, at first I really believe they thought neither intended
to see them. I like her. After all she brought no maid and very
plain cloathes.

At night as I was just going to bed I found I had been
grossly deceived, and that Henry [aged 5] was *in* my bed
instead of being laid on the ottoman as they'd promised. To
be sure the ottoman was covered with my cloathes with the
want of the drawers, but such a night as I had with the dear
child, who with true Forster sociability *would* be so close to
me and then kick so stoutly sleep was out of the question. At
last I got up my pillow to put it between us, on which he sat
upright: 'Aunt Marianne will you be so good as to take this
thing away, I want to be near you'—'No dear you make me
so hot.'—'But I'll promise not to make you hot if you'll let
me come near to you.'—'But you keep me awake.' 'Then if you
are awake would you be so good as to tell me a story.' All
this was going on at 3 in the morning. I very nearly bestowed
myself on Laura but it's lucky I didn't as she says Mr Forster
found J. J. [eldest son] so restless in his little dressing room
that he came to her.

Sibley Laura has found out is an encumbrance, and says
she shall pay her 7/6d tomorrow and send her away. I've never
said a word against her and mind you don't or she'll keep her
—and she has done nothing I see except shell pease—Susan
has drest the baby.

The letter ends with the attempts of Miss Maber to act as Missis and Hostess in Laura's absence—attempts which Marianne thwarts, "and I think she has seen through me."

The children were happy enough in this country chaos and Laura the younger has written rose-coloured accounts of it in her "Recollections." Since babies are in the air I shall permit myself to quote a pre-Raphaelite passage decribing the goffering of the baby's caps.

The goffering of the frills so fascinated me I shall describe it, as I always watched the process from beginning to end, and longed to assist in it. The long piece of lace to be quilted was produced, together with a bundle of straws and a board about fourteen inches by ten. The lace was put on the board and a straw placed under it and over it in close succession till the row of alternating straws was long enough to go round the baby's cap, then the lace was turned, and a second and third row of straws was built on the lower one. Then came the delightful climax; the straws were tied firmly to the board, the kettle was made to boil its hardest, and the board was moved slowly backwards and forwards near the spout, till the steam had penetrated to the very lowest layer of the lace. After that the board was put aside till the lace had dried and stiffened into shape, then each straw was drawn out carefully, and the quilting of delicate lace was left in perfect order for that most sacred part of a baby's wardrobe, its best cap.

On one occasion there was a Forster-Thornton reunion at Cambridge—that academic stronghold of Evangelicalism. It was the parliamentary election of July 1847. Henry and Watson came up to record their university votes. Henry brought his two daughters, also Marianne, and he invited the Forsters from Stisted to be his guests. As parents of large families will, they brought an uninvited boy with them, and the party of eight had some difficulty in cramming itself into the Bull. All went well. My grandfather did not get too frantic when people differed from him politically, Henry was not too much irritated by my grandfather, and Marianne reports to Miss Louisa Inglis in the highest spirits.

When we arrived after a thoro' wash and dressing, for we were pillars of dust as Watson said, we had such a dinner! as might have fed all the Senate house almost, concluding with ice à discretion, and then we went into the College Gardens which were very near, and sate there or in King's Coll Chapel till it grew cool. In the latter Mr F and Laura read the Psalms for the day which L. said they had not yet had time to do! Then we went to the Senate house, at which I was rather shy, it seemed so thronged with men, but they let us into the place where the voters go up, and where there was no crowd, and where we saw our friends as they went in or out, the Forsters knew great numbers of people, and Laura's eagerness when 'Mr. Wigson of Coggeshall, or Mr. Smith of Bocking' appeared, was not to be told, they came and sate with us afterwards, and the place is so large that we could talk without being called to order. Mr. Forster came there full of wrath against that 'weak misguided Peel ridden creature Goulburn' * but no sooner had he seen and talked with him, and heard him say with what pleasure he recollected his intercourse with *the* Bishop than he found out he has a heart full of affection and in the right place, and I believe nearly persuaded himself that if the blessed Bishop had lived Mr. Goulburn would have voted rightly. We came back to tea, sate down on the grass in Kings Coll. for a rest and went back to the Senate Ho from 8 to 9 to hear the closing cheers and yells of the undergraduates, they made up in noise what they wanted in numbers.

Yesterday I told H there were only two things I was anxious to see, the rooms in which Dean Milner and old Mr Simeon lived, and he goodnaturedly managed both, I remembered as a child staying a week at the Queens' Lodge with the Dean,

* One of the two successful candidates; Ewan Law was the other.

and on going there was telling the others that I recollected his
shewing me a trick with a card, and in throwing it up it stuck
to the ceiling in his room whether by design or not I didn't
know, but he said it should stay there, but as it was above 30
nearly 40 years ago of course it was long since gone. The maid
overheard me, and said Oh the card is there now, and no one
knows how or why it was kept, and opening a door into his
private room there it was! the room when whitewashed is always
watched that that card may not be displaced. It was very odd
that I should have recollected it, for I do not think I had ever
thought of it since. We went over Mr Simeon's rooms [H stair-
case, Kings] and talked to his bedmaker, who said he was a
very particular old gentleman, but everybody loved him for all
that, he died in such a beautiful french polished bedstead in
his dining-room, and dear old gentleman it made him so unhappy if they weren't careful of it; there are scrapers on every
landing for the shoes, and many little relics of him that interested me very much. In the evening we got into a boat, Emmy
steered and J J rowed with another boy his own age, but as
Henry said, nothing but a strong design to murder could get
us into the water there, it reminded me of Venice gliding up
and down at the backs of all the Colleges they looked so still
and peaceful, and unlike the row and bustle of the Election
which was so near. Cambridge has a most vivifying effect on
Henry and Watson, particularly the latter, who was more
amusing and ridiculous than I have seen him for years, Laura
never fails in that way, and I don't think a merrier party ever
filled the parlour of the Bull! with throngs of people we knew
going in and out all day. During the heat Henry and I established ourselves in the University Library where it was quite
cool and I found every sort of book, even Gammer Grethel for
Emmy.

We had lovely rooms, but J J not being expected there was
none for him except a little bed in his father's, and Laura said
she should dress and wash with me and Emmy, and leave the

2 men (Mr F and J J) to do for themselves. As far as I could
see she was never out of our room, dabbling in the water and
making haycocks of her cloathes on the floor, and of course
tho' I lent her a dressing gown, she left it always in Mr F's
room, and when Henry came in to us last night she was in her
day chemise, and told him, he must wait till she could put on
her black silk mantilla, the only 2 garments she had on from
head to foot. Henry was excessively amused at her, and said
having the F's had thoroughly answered. It was difficult to
conceive that J J. enjoyed it as much as they said he did, but
yet he seemed to know all the names of the Colleges better than
I did and always knew the numbers of the Electors but hardly
spoke ten words the whole time!

By the late 'forties the Forster boys had begun to go to
school at the Charterhouse. It was then in its original quar-
ters, only a few miles from Clapham, so they sometimes spent
a week end with their aunt. Marianne wrote Laura a nice
rollicking report on young Charley who is "ten years older
all at once, something so manly and bold and decided about
him." A dialogue is contrived: Marianne asks, Charley answers, and much pleasure must have been given at the rectory. Everything capital at school, strong tea like Mama's,
excellent puddings and tarts, no need to spend money on
grub and tuck, but 10/- for the library such a capital library, Papa would like it, yes Sunday books here, and they
are some of the nicest, the monitors know which they are,
and would not let us have any other on Sunday. Graver
matters are then approached. Marianne: "Amongst so many
I should fear there must be a good many bad boys." Charley:
"Oh yes there are some very bad little fellows—I heard of
one very shocking thing, that 2 boys made an agreement to
smoke and drink."—"Where? At School?"—"Oh no it would
be impossible there, but as they went home at the holidays

they settled it—but they were found out." "Don't you ever hear bad words?"—"Oh they wouldn't like *me* to hear them for fear I should tell the monitors, but the new fellows do sometimes till they have been thrashed for it."—"Dont the big boys sometimes teach the little ones bad words?"—"Oh no they darent, you don't know old Saunders, he'd flog a boy oh how he would flog them if he found it out, and through these monitors you see almost everything is found out." Etc.

The boys were always welcome at Battersea Rise. On one occasion the pious and silent J. J. was the innocent cause of much trouble. It was a children's Christmas party and "I had already told Laura that I really could not promise there might not be a little dancing," she tells Miss Inglis. J. J. was allowed by his father to come, but arrived accompanied by a prohibition against dancing—or rather by something far more tiresome than a prohibition: by a request that the matter should be discussed in full conclave, children as well as adults being present, and the sinfulness or non-sinfulness of dancing determined accordingly.

Tho' no advocate for balls I had much rather the children danced than that they were set to canvas their father's opinion in the matter. I gave Henry Mr. F's letter when they were all gone to bed. He said he respected Mr. F's scruples and would not hurt them for the world, but he had told Harti that this year they might dance while we dined if they wished, and he could not conscientiously say he thought that a very wrong way of amusing themselves for half an hour. He instantly got the Sermon on the Mount, but declares there's nothing in what Mr. F. refers to against dancing.

The more Marianne thinks about dancing the less harmful it seems; moreover Tom Macaulay has reminded her that when Lord Teignmouth gave the Twelfth Night party in

their childhood * "Aunt Robert danced with old Mr. Lut-
trell," and if Aunt Robert, who thought nearly everything
wrong, had danced, how could it be wrong? Besides—what
was one to do when the children wanted it so much?

Last year there were the Villiers, Jenkinsons, and Forsters,
who all objected—at least so we thought, and Laura herself
staid up to prevent it, & we had the piano locked & every pre-
caution taken, & yet once or twice the children began jumping
about in a gallopade & nothing could stop them—& this year
as everyone who is coming is taught to dance, it's pretty nearly
impossible to prevent it. And of all the temptation likely to
beset poor dear J. J. I am sure that of figuring at a Ball is
one of the last.

How it ended I do not know, but they certainly danced.

She was excellent with boys, and maintained that nice
balance between equality and inequality which is so necessary for grown-ups who would stand well with them. She
was excellent with girls also—not one of the spinsters who
concentrate on a single sex. She enjoyed youth, and never
forgot that she and her brothers and sisters had once all
been young.

By the middle of the century she possessed about twenty
nephews and nieces. It was for them that she was to compose
her "Recollections," and in August of 1851 she took her
first consignment of them abroad. Travel was part of the
family tradition: her father had stood close to Marie Antoinette, she had gone to France after the fall of Napoleon,
and now it was the turn of the younger generation.

Sir Robert and Lady Inglis should have led the expedition, but got no further than Boulogne, because a stone had
been thrown through the window of the train and injured

* P. 50.

Lady Inglis's eye. Marianne went on with Henrietta and four children—the two Synnots, and J. J. and Laura Forster the younger. Amiens was their first stop: in the Cathedral was a military band, an immense and frightful golden statue of the Virgin, and a dressed-up lamb with which made everyone laugh. "I was glad the children were there," she tells Sir Robert, "for they could not have had a better display both of the splendour and the absurdity of the Roman Catholic religion." An old French woman who was kissing a relic of John the Baptist was asked by the party who he was: "Je ne saurais vous dire Madame, mais je crois il était un des pères de l'église" was her reply. Night brought further excitement, for a house close to the hotel caught fire, pails of water were passed, hundreds of soldiers rushed by screaming, and little Inglis Synnot dressed in a sheet harangued the French from the balcony in his personal French. "It was such a curious sight, I am glad if it were to be that I saw it."

Paris was reached next day. A hotel in the Rue St. Honoré provided vast apartments but no hot water and only pie dishes to wash in. Pleasure persisted, and they sat out till 9:00 in the Tuileries Gardens, the two sisters moralising on the changes that had happened since last they were there, "and the children chasing each other like butterflies." Next day they went to St. Denis and saw its tombs under the guidance of an old Bourbonist who hoped that Louis Napoleon (then President) would soon be sent packing. The church was "as good as pages of French history for the children, and the liberté and égalité which meets them at every turn is a proof, as we told Inglis, of the necessity of some rule and order amongst boys and men." Moreover the French were discovered, or rather rediscovered, to be untruthful, and not to mind being found out. Still the food was delicious,

good dinners, ices and coffee, *beignets de pêches*, interesting
and amusing sights everywhere. All her old love rushes back.
"I am much struck with Paris and I suppose I had forgotten
what an interesting city it is. It is not the fine buildings,
though the Place de la Concorde which is new is splendid,
but the picturesque air of the old houses and the incessant
variety in their forms and in the shadows that slant across
the high roofs, make the mere driving through the streets
a pleasure to me." And although their visit was so short she
had the energy to shift from their gloomy hotel into the very
hotel where she had been with the Dan Sykeses in 1816, she
got the very same room and slept in the same bed and established the continuity she longed for. The past of thirty-five
years ago had been linked to the present, and the present
would be linked to the future through the four children on
whose account the outing had been devised.

To conclude this period, I must refer to her philanthropic
activities—the full development of which comes later. Since
Isabella's marriage she was the only sister living at Battersea
Rise. Nurse Hunter was no more, and much as she loved her
widowed brother and her nieces, she was beginning to find
certain aspects of the old home unsatisfactory. She looked
outside it more—helped people, was interested in them, enjoyed herself with them and through them—and perhaps it
is at this time that the seeds of interference (that besetting
Thorntonian fault) were sown. The seeds germinated slowly
and they never produced a Upas Tree.

I will paraphrase a typical letter of the period: to Lady
Inglis in 1851.

It is largely occupied with the problem of Mrs. Elwes.
Lady Ellis, a very good woman with a Wesleyan twang,
kept an authorised establishment for the mentally unsound,
and maintained that one of her inmates, Mrs. Elwes, was

perfectly fit to be at large. Marianne herself was not so sanguine: still she had given Lady Ellis an "enormous load of documents" on the case, together with much advice: Mr. Barnard, concerned with lunatics, was to be avoided; Lady Parke was to be written to and consulted whether Mrs. Elwes should write to the Chancellor. Could Sir Robert Inglis help? Could, as Lady Ellis hoped, a lady and gentleman be found who would take Mrs. Elwes for three months to Italy on payment of their expenses, together with a good courier and a confidential maid? "I would almost answer for it— as far as I can answer for anything in this world—that she would return completely recovered" had been Lady Ellis's opinion.

The subject of Lady Ellis and Mrs. Elwes then disappears into the darkness with Carlylean completeness though without Carlylean crackle, and the letter goes on to the subject of Willingale. This was simpler. Willingale, an excellent woman with an imperfect character, had been successfully placed as housekeeper to the Governor of the new prison on Brixton Common: £30 a year, all found, and no untruths told about her; "I advised her not to send anyone to me as I must tell all I knew, and though I did not think the worse of her other people would."

Willingale follows Lady Ellis and Mrs. Elwes into oblivion, and now we spend "a very pleasant day at the Crystal Palace" with the Venns, the Richmonds, and my grandfather. All is animation. The Venns wanted to take everything back from the Exhibition to their parishioners at Hereford: "the hollow bricks first of course, and the dancing balls in the fountain would amuse very old people more than a cat and be less trouble, and the jumping bed would be good for heavy young sleepers, and bonnets made of strings should be wonderfully cool for Sierra Leone." While

[*187*]

George Richmond "was in an ecstasy of delight at the beautiful lights and shadows, and at the graceful forms of so many objects, was worth more than a guinea an hour guide for pointing out beauties and said he should not sleep for a week." The letter then discusses the chance of visiting the Exhibition at its "final close." Special tickets would be required: once more could Sir Robert Inglis help?

In the midst of her activities my grandfather would moan and groan to her about his own. To Miss Louisa Inglis:

Mr. F. came on Monday, most amusingly like himself—quite weak and delicate—'he had been so *hunted* and harried on Sunday, he'd had no rest—7 fellows had actually *bearded* him for their registers, that is 2 had come for their own and 5 others, they were going to emigrate but what was that to him—said they must have them, they'd pay, but what pay made up to him for being hunted in that manner—had to have the Parish Register brought up all the way from the Church, and then he and Beckwith had to hunt it—and then he had to transcribe them—and he'd been too tired to sleep—the clergy ought to be protected against such inroads.'

Laura however cut him short by saying she hoped they w^d never cease coming, the 2/6s were a treasure, and I ventured to hint what sleepless nights *I* might have, for my district people never are at rest now emigration is so common, but come to see me 'at all hours' and 'beard me' to write to all sorts of country Parishes for their registers, and I had one such a pretty answer from a Welsh clergyman who refused to take anything on account of my name.

Thus cheerfully, thus usefully, did she fill up her time. I have however mentioned that Battersea Rise was becoming less satisfactory, and this statement must now be expanded.

SIX

Deceased Wife's Sister

THE GENERATION to which Marianne belonged had now completed half a century without undergoing any special stress. There had been the ordinary stresses of illness and death, and there had been the Bank crisis which nearly ruined them. But the illnesses had been treated with affection and competence, the deaths signified no eternal separation, and as for poverty—had it come it would have found them cheerful, united and resourceful. One would have supposed that Fate could have no special trick in store for such a family. Yet a fantastic mishap was awaiting them, a contretemps which they could only regard as tragic, and it was consequently a tragedy.

After the death of Henry's wife, Harriet, her younger sister Emily Dealtry (sometimes nicknamed Di) continued to frequent the house, and it was natural that she should do so for she helped to look after her nephew and her nieces, and Marianne or Isabella was there to chaperon her. She was willing to come, for her own home life was not comfortable since Dr. Dealtry had died. Sometimes another sister came with her—Ba, a lively lass who made apple-pie beds and got smacked. The house became more cheerful, and Henry, who had always liked young people, found it pleasant to return to girlish chatter after a day's work at the

Bank. Only gradually did his sisters realise that Miss Dealtry was there permanently and that gossip had started.
They did not know what to do. Passion and intrigue were
no part of their tradition. Marianne behaved civilly to the
girl indoors and did not answer her back when she was
cheeky, which she now tended to be, but refused to accompany her into society. Isabella took a stronger line and refused to see her anywhere. On the rare occasions she came
to Battersea Rise she announced her arrival beforehand and
Emily had to hide. The situation became very awkward. The
Dealtrys disliked it too, and mutterings were heard from
Emily's brother. Then the scandal exploded. Henry announced that he intended to marry Emily although she was
his deceased wife's sister, that he was going to get the law
altered in Parliament, and that until it was altered he and
she would live abroad.

Much occurred that has not been recorded. The first news
I can find is in a letter from Marianne to Patty Smith. It
is probably written in 1850.

My dear Patty

Your kindest of Letters shall not remain unanswered another day, and I will begin by replying to the last page of it.
I am surprised that the news came upon you so suddenly, for
I always think that in whatever nook you hide yourself, you
always know more than those that are in the midst of things.
It is years now since the tidings first came upon me, and much
that was very painful at first has worn away from that universal healer of all woes time—and use—but there are other
feelings that I fear nothing can eradicate—for they seem like
an instinct planted in ones very nature—that in this generation
cannot be worn out. Should the law be altered, probably the
next will wonder at our scruples. I have never thought as alas
all my family do that it is very wrong—only that it is an *im-*

[*190*]

possible sort of idea—in short it seems not a sin—but a shame
—if indeed those two can be unconnected—a loss of taste and
consideration and a want of refinement on the lady's side—
nothing more. This arose from nothing but amiable feelings
on his side. Compassion for her whose home was very unhappy
—and then a desire to remove her from that home—has led
to a state of things that now one can scarcely see thro'. Should
the Bill not pass he talks of becoming an Alien and a foreigner
—and what such a separation involves to me and the poor
Children you may guess. However as the Irish proverb says
'there is a silver lining to every cloud', and so I can see here
distinctly more of the Child^{ns} affection for me, and more of
their real character than years of common life would have given
me. Henry and I never mention the subject, but live on together
tête a tête, comfortably and almost cheerfully, with all this
load of thought between us, but it is a mercy that the close
of our companionship of half a century—if it is the close—
should be unembittered by any reproaches on my side—or irritation on his—and I have a dim sort of foreboding that some
chance or change may waft him back to me to finish our journey together at last. He has been a victim of a power under
which we know the wisest and the best have fallen—and no
doubt he will awake from it and wonder at the enormous sacrifices he has made.

What a lovely letter! Marianne is a sincere Christian with
high moral principles, she has suffered from Miss Dealtry
personally. Yet she can write "not a sin but a shame," and
"should the law be altered probably the next generation will
wonder at our scruples." We do wonder at them, but we
wonder much more at the greatness of her character and the
goodness of her heart. The rest of her family were ready to
be hostile but she, with the most to bear, pardons and hopes
to endure. I will quote the next paragraph of the letter—
not because it is relevant but because it is not relevant: she

turns at once from her domestic tragedy to her charitable schemes.

But I will turn to the other bits of yᵣ letter, tho' I fear there are few of your questions that I can answer. *Our industrial home in London for needlewomen has gone to pieces.* They got 40 into it, promising them work to the amount of 7ˢ a week which was to pay for their board. The work was very bad— and would not sell. The women quarrelled with each other and with the matron. They are deep in debt, and can neither pay nor get rid of their inmates who complain they have been duped.

The bill to which she refers is the Marriage Bill of 1850, the second reading of which was introduced on February 7th, by Mr. Wortly, the Member for Bute. It sought to modify the Marriage Act of 1835, under which marriage with a deceased wife's sister carried civil as well as canonical disability. Henry Thornton spent vast sums in trying to get the 1850 bill passed. Bitter must it have been to him to realise that Sir Robert Inglis was its leading opponent. Sir Robert, it is true, opposed everything except science and art: he was against the Jews, the Catholics, the Dissenters, and now he denounced the Deceased Wife's Sister Bill as "an alteration of the Law of the Land, an alteration of the Law of the Church, and an alteration if man could make it, of the Law of God." He also asserted that it was against "the unanimous feeling of *one* sex in this country," blandly ignoring the feelings of poor Miss Dealtry. The debates were solemn rather than acrimonious in tone: members quoted Latin to each other, even Greek, and the meaning of Leviticus XVIII: 18 was deeply pondered. Some feared the bill would break up the home by transforming "beneficent aunts into hostile and partial stepmothers." Others quoted petitions from clergymen who implored that the bill might be passed, since many of their parishioners had already married their sisters-in-law, under the belief that this was the best thing for the children—and of course it was the best thing for the children. Such an argument did not convince the Bishops in the House of Lords, who denounced thunderously: indeed the Lords were far more passionate than the Commons, as sometimes happens when the subject is sexual.

Far milder, much more tentative, were the painful proceedings at Battersea Rise. With what delicacy does Marianne open her mind to her brother.

My dear H.—I must send you a line to tell you that my disinclination to hear you talk over your future intentions tonight did not arise from any want of affection for you, or of interest in all that concerns you and yours. You have been too kind to me during the many years that we have lived under the same roof, and your children seem to me too much like my very own, not to ensure my sympathising deeply in all that concerns you and them. But in the present case it has been my most anxious wish to avoid discussion with you. . . . I do not see the sinfulness of an alteration of the Law in the strong light that many people do—still I feel so differently about it from what you do that it would only be painful to both of us to enter upon it. My own brothers- and sisters-in-Law have always appeared to me so exactly like real brothers and sisters that any other connection seems an impossibility. I cannot realise a different state of feeling. . . . I have only written now lest you should have misunderstood my silence tonight, but I really felt I *could* not talk about it.

There are however few who will feel more anxiously than I shall for you or who will hope more earnestly that any step you take may tend not only to your happiness here but hereafter—in that future world which all these chances and changes seem to bring so very near—Ever yours affly M. T.

Her next letter to him must be later, when his plans were shaping. It too breaks a silence. Although they were both of them still at Battersea Rise it is addressed to him up at the Bank.

The children's incessant entreaties that I would speak to you my dear Henry have induced me to do so, though I know too sorrowfully that it will be of little use. But is it quite beyond hope that you should return here after your marriage, instead of remaining an exile in a foreign land? I cannot understand how to you, an Englishman and a Churchman, there can be any difference in the right or wrong of living on one side of the Channel or the other. And surely your inducements are great to remain here amongst your family your occupations and your friends. It is such a bad age to take the Children abroad—if they were younger it would not hurt them and if they were older their characters would be more formed. So much depends upon the society that surrounds them. English *residents* abroad are mostly people of broken fortunes or broken characters, and travellers do not stay long enough for friendships. To one of your kind disposition too, I am sure it will be a great drawback even in your happiest moments to remember how many people you make miserable by your stay on the continent, who have never injured you and would gladly forward your wishes if they could. I am not pleading my cause this time, for I have resolved under any circumstances to have a small habitation of my own at Clapham, but if I could only think of you and the Children as still dwelling under the shadow of the old home, so full of solemn and holy recollection, I should feel grateful to you and Emily every day I lived. I can hardly help fancying that I see the forms of our own father and mother amidst the scenes of our infancy and imagine what they would have felt at their child and their Grand Children becoming exiles in France.

[*194*]

Henry Sykes Thornton
(about 1860)

Another lovely letter, and its reference to Miss Dealtry most courteous. Yet it irritated him—he found it too skilful perhaps—and he answers sharply:

My dear Marianne,

You cannot understand the marriage question or you would not write as you do. I will give you the substance of what the Archbishop told me was his advice to a friend of his—It is allowed by scripture and the prayer book is silent, but it is made void by the act of 1835. If however you like to go abroad to obtain a bonâ fide residence there, it is without doubt a legal marriage.

If I were to go merely to be married and return its legality would be doubtful, and I am quite determined to have no doubt.

Your plan would be a very pleasant one if it were right.

I have quite made up my mind that I shall be much blamed for breaking up my establishment and going abroad. The person who has housed his sisters till he is 50 and has never crossed the channel is the very person who must expect to be blamed on these heads.—As to meeting people with broken fortunes, I have no pleasure in large establishments or the society of the rich, and I much wish that I could have my fathers opinion on these matters, not for my own satisfaction for I have no doubt on the matter, but for that of my friends.—He would not have avoided Z. Macaulay's society when he became poor.

I very much wish you would talk to me instead of to the children. Moreover the Lords may pass the Bill this session so that all this excitement may be quite uncalled for.—at all events it is clearly a question of time.—Ever yours affectionately

H. S. THORNTON.

The rest of the family now became active and combined against Henry and tried to weaken the bonds of affection that connected him with Marianne. Letters flew, and on May 12th the Rev. Charles Forster addressed a truly deplorable

one to his wife. He was returning by train to his Essex rectory, and had purchased his second-class ticket at Liverpool
Street Station when he was "touched," and " 'twas my Lord
of Rochester":

'Are you going down?'—'Yes'—'Shall we travel in the same
carriage?'—So I had to change my ticket for a 1st. The Bishop
went, meanwhile, and secured places vis-a-vis, and there came
for me, a full and most satisfactory talk about the Bill. The
Bishop began himself about the affair in Archdeacon Burney's
parish—whose courage you know a little surprised us. But
you'll not wonder when I add: 'twas all the Bishop's doing. 'I
directed the Archdeacon to treat the man as *excommunicate*
and to reject him from the Communion; to refuse to church the
woman; and to register the children as illegitimate.' This *is*
discipline: and we owe it to the Marriage Bill. I was so glad.
He says he don't think they can get the Bill through the Commons, 'twill be so badly received. It's greatly damaged beyond
a doubt and will be more so (D.V.) next week.

While in London my grandfather had seen Sir Robert Inglis
and others, and they too were confident of victory. Parliament regarded the bill with "abhorrence": they all used the
word "abhorrence" and in Sir Robert's opinion it was the
only word that expressed the truth. The danger had been the
sluggishness of the "right side," who had slept and snored
whilst evil got to a head, but they were awake now and as
for Wortly the introducer, he was "a mere tool as much as
is a child" in the unscrupulous hands of Henry Thornton.

The letter then reverts to my Lord of Rochester, now in
saintly mood.

He spoke so kindly about poor Henry, saying Be kind to him
while you can, he's not gone yet. He said this with such feeling. I told him how I kept St Paul in mind: 'yet count him not

as an enemy but admonish him as a brother'. But though full
of kind feelings, he is firm as a rock about the path of duty.

My grandfather was notably courageous: thirty years
before, as a young clergyman in Ireland, he had thrown himself "like a levin-bolt into our churchyard" to prevent blood-
shed between two rival gangs. But he does not appear to
have admonished his formidable brother-in-law at Battersea
Rise. He did however appeal to the Archbishop of Canterbury.

Henry Thornton had already got into touch with the
Archbishop and this led to a good deal of confusion. For the
Archbishop replied to each of them in prudent terms and
each interpreted the reply in accordance with his own wishes.
The confusion is reflected in the following letter from Marianne to Laura; I print it with its abbreviations—they indi-
cate her agitation and haste. (The Mrs. Whitmore of the
opening sentence was a connection of the Dealtrys who was
also a friend of the Thorntons and in agreement with their
attitude, and consequently useful as a go-between.)

My dear Laura,
   Would you write Mrs. Whitmore a few lines, enclosing the
Archbps. letter to Mr. Forster, merely saying that you know
how much she is interested in the question, & that as Henry
seems to have quite *misunderstood* the Archbishops opinion,
you enclose it to her. Mind you say *misunderstood*, however it
may go against your stomach. It must be a letter wh. may
be shewn to Mrs. D.ᵞ & if so it must go on to Emily & finally
to Henry. The Dealtrys are all persuaded—at least they pretend they are—that all our objections arise only from my being turned out by what is happening, & that if *I* were not dis-
composed no one wᵈ interfere. *So* I mustn't be the person to
have shewn Mrs. W. the Arch's letter.
   H. Venn has been here today, he spent 2 hours with Henry

yest.ʸ & says that if he had only *him* to deal with he thinks
he should succeed, but that he is the veriest slave of Emily that
ever lived—& *yet*—he says he isn't in love with her—not one
bit. He says he feels he has damaged her & owes it to her to
make her retribution, & having been baffled in altering the law
in a sort of mad passion he listens to her wishes of going
abroad—for H. V. is convinced that the foreign scheme is hers.
He says he thinks it possible he may make her & her mother
ashamed of the part they are acting, wh. will make them willing to delay a little. He says the only ground on wh. he could
move Henry at all, was his conscience. He kept asking him how
he could answer to God when he was on a dying bed, having
done such a thing. He says H. is very unhappy wh. you might
not have thought, but he says his Child.ⁿˢ feelings are one great
blow to him & the other was the Archbps letter to Mr. Forster
wh. he shewed him contradicting every word of it, & asking
H. Venn to go with him to the Archbp to talk to him, but he
never let out one word of his own letter from the Arch—wh. I
shewed H. Venn, & wh, H. Venn won't believe he has ever received, but I feel sure he has. He says Henrys excitement is
dreadful, & that he must be *gently* dealt by, or he will be worse
—if he means mad, he is that already I'm very very sure. H. V.
gave me what I've no doubt is very good advice, absolutely to
prohibit the subject to the Child.ⁿ however much their father
sets them talking about it, always to stop it in my presence.
He says no good can be done by setting them against going
abroad, or against the marriage, its better to let their own
natural feelings come out to their father undisturbed by word
or look of ours and that besides . . .

The rest of the letter is lost. With its flurried style and
its spinsterish anxiety for something to be shown to someone
so that it may be shown on to someone else, it is not typical
of Marianne. As a rule she is detached and even amusing. As
in the following letter to Sophia:

Other people will be at Roehampton when I come to see you tomorrow evening, and as I suppose no discussion can go on before them on the Danish question I will write a few lines now so far to relieve your mind as to tell you I will do nothing except by Sir Robert and My Lady's advice; and with much love, and reverence too, for Mr Forster I must think them much safer guides than he is. Indeed to own the truth he is one of the very last people whose opinion I should take on any question in which his feelings are much interested, for he works himself up into a degree of excitement that is hardly sane, and a reaction so often follows the other way that I was saying not long ago I should next expect if Laura died that he would ask me to go to Denmark to marry him! He has changed as much on other subjects. Once he rode like a maniac out of Dover because he found Mrs John Jebb was in it, and he declared he could not speak to her, she was 'a dishonest daughter and a wicked wife' because she had persuaded her husband to refuse Ash. This year he has been staying with her. He used to say that a man was guilty of a sin who sent his son to such a wicked place as school and now he has four at school. But I need not go on on this subject, for I am sure you are as much aware of it as I am.

However, though hot he may also be right you may say, and I will go on to tell you why I think he is not.

And she expounds her position to Sophia in long leisurely sentences, and explains why she has decided not to break off relations with their brother, whatever happens.

I believe that Henry has done very wrong, so do not fancy that I am defending either his conduct or his principles, but he has done fifty worse things before and yet I did not leave him—you would have wondered if I had. I really think his behaviour at the time of your marriage was more wicked than anything he has done now, and it was without the temptation he now has, but we all 'pieced together' again.

The above agitations and alarums are nearly all of the
year 1850. The next year, that of the Great Exhibition, involved her in pleasanter matters and her letters contain no
reference to the impending disaster. She could put her troubles aside to enjoy herself because she shared her enjoyment
with others.

The crisis came in 1852: the Ides of March, it could be
called.

The first letter to be quoted is an unexpected one: from
Tom Macaulay to his sister. Tom, already a statesman and
soon to be a Peer, bounces back into Clapham circles with
vehemence, and concerns himself for a moment with the
problems of his old friend.

March 1st

I was at the Bank today about business. The moment that
I came, Labouchere and Melville began to talk of this miserable
affair. They seem to be most uneasy about it. I plainly told
them that I thought it a serious matter as respected the Bank.
They said that they wished me to speak to Henry and talked
about my influence. I told them that he knew my opinion and
that he carefully avoided the subject in my company. I could
not with propriety introduce it, nor should I do any good by
such officiousness.

They then asked whether I knew Wm. Dealtry enough to
speak on the subject. I told them that I hardly knew him at
all. . . .

We all agreed that he never will be able to bear a prolonged
exile to the Continent. I told them that if they could get him
to go abroad alone for the purpose of taking a house and
making preparations, he would come back so thoroughly sick
of Bonn or whatever other place he might try, that he would
give up the whole scheme.

While we were talking, he came. He looked unlike himself,
gloomy anxious and irritable. He tried to talk on ordinary

subjects, but seemed constrained, and so I have no doubt did I. I went away in two or three minutes after his arrival.

Marianne to Laura:

It is such a strange sensation to me to conceive of an existence outside Battersea Rise that sometimes I scarcely feel awake, but have a giddy misty sensation that I am hallucinating, but 'alas recollection at hand' drives me—no, not to despair, I am sure no one has less need to do that—but to feel that I must prepare for a great change in everything 'a rehearsal of Death' as Reginald Heber said when he was going to India.

On March 4th she writes to Mrs. Wedgwood from Henrietta Synnot's house at Clapham: she has taken refuge there from the turmoil of Battersea Rise:

Its strange how familiar I seem already to have become with what appeared so impossible to bear—but there are many extenuating points now, chiefly and mainly in Miss Franks' going with them, and in the blessed obstinacy of Henry's partners refusing to let him go out of the country for more than 6 months at a time—I am trying to stun myself with the din of my new establishment, which feels such a mixture of going to be married and going to die; generally it seems so little worth while to care where one lives if it isn't at that dear old home, the only *home* I can ever know, tho' enough has passed there of late to make me well content to quit it—This is a sort of half weaning living at Ettas with her Girl; a Child that *won't* be spirited away from me feels so stable, after those poor dear things whom I am so soon to see vanish, and who are now so unconscious of their fate—I quite hope however that Miss Franks going with them,—and their certain return will make it a very different thing from what it was before—But all I meant to write was about maids—I think that a Cook has turned up—I suppose your married lady would hardly like to find herself ladies maid, footman and housemaid all in one for thats what I want—When will you come—It shall be to Etta's where we shall be free from callers, and I'll take you to see my rambling old gloomy new house—It looks like a half way house between ones cradle and ones grave, as it is—but yet I expect to be very happy in it. How would Monday do—You know we are nice and near the Omnibuses which I soon mean to frequent so constantly you'll see me whenever you pass the Plough—

About the same date she asks Miss Louisa Inglis's advice over "taking things away as Isabella proposes": there is at least a week's work before she can clear out. She feels that she can legitimately remove the contents of her own room, Lucy's bed, Mr. Bowdler's marble-topped table, and the little library stools, which she and the elder Miss Inglis once worked, but she is anxious to avoid any appearance of pillaging in Henry's absence.

From Sibylla Grant to Marianne:

March 10

I received your melancholy little note yesterday, and hasten to answer it. It is very very sad, that abode to be deserted, and for such a cause. You may be sure of the utmost sympathy from us who knew your house in the older time and its inhabitants in those days. 'Twas then of just and good he reasoned strong' &ct. How you will miss the lawns and groves where you have lived so long. I can hardly yet believe the event will really happen. . . . I really believe he himself is not conscious of doing wrong, but is probably making great sacrifices for what he thinks right. . . .

I can only sincerely trust that the lessons learnt in your early home may accompany and cheer you in every future abode. And I hope B. Rise will not be dismantled or rendered unfit for habitation. You will want it again, I think.

From Marianne, back at Battersea Rise, to Henry, the day before his departure.

[*202*]

March 11

My dear Henry—Though I did not feel equal to speaking to you on the subject, I cannot refrain from writing you a line to tell you how very much I am obliged to you for the offer you sent me through Miss Franks of taking any furniture plate or linen that I liked from hence, towards setting up my new house. I will gladly accept the contents of my own room, and three or four other articles that are particularly associated with those that are gone.—and the sight of them will often remind me too of your kindness which during far the greater part of the seventeen years that I have been your inmate, made mine such a very happy home.

I will also gladly accept a little plate and linen but everything else that I remove will be what I have either bought myself or what has been given me by friends, and you would be quite surprised, as am I, to see how much has accumulated during the half century that I have spent under this roof—Ever your affec^{nt} M. T.

The following day Henry Sykes Thornton and Emily Dealtry left their native land. One would have expected to have no details of their departure, but by a fortunate chance a couple of first-class gossips were stationed at Dover. They were Mrs. Georgiana Raikes, who had married into another branch of the family, and Georgiana's mother. They got wind of the event and Georgiana actually witnessed it. With her father at her heels, she hurried down to the harbour and was just in time. The following letter of hers (to a cousin) has an earthiness—or should one say a saltiness?—about it which is a welcome relief after so much high-mindedness, fair-mindedness, discrimination and recrimination. Here is exactly what we want, namely an ordinary woman on the gape.

March 12

You will be interested to hear I am just come from the Pier, after having seen all the Dealtrys and H.S.T. embark for Calais. The train came in at 2.0 p.m. and the steamer left as soon as the mail bags and Passengers were on board. I saw Mr Way the station-master coming and then a Porter carrying some *new* Carpet bags, and a card on them directed H. S. Thornton, Calais, so I told Papa, and in a few minutes Henry came up with a strange lady on his arm. Papa went forward and shook hands with him and then he came and spoke to me. He seemed in excellent spirits. Then followed Mrs Dealtry, Emily, the girls and Miss Franks. Emily looking better than I ever saw her in her life, splendidly dressed in black velvet Polka coat trimmed with sable and Cuffs and Boa to match, a violet velvet bonnet with black lace trimming. She told me it was 11 years since she had seen Dover, admired the Castle and said how beautiful it looked, then asked after Mama. She said 'Good Bye' in such a cheerful way I was *quite surprised*. I don't think she knows we are aware of what she is going abroad to do. . . .

The girls looked out of spirits, poor children and underdrest I dare say it had cost them many tears leaving their old haunts at B. Rise. Mrs D. came forward to shake hands. She had a nosegay in her hand—some relics of B. Rise I suppose. They had a foreign servant with them. The sea is not very rough but the wind against them so they will not have a smooth passage but it is such a short one there is not much time to be ill. Henry had bespoke a cabin to themselves, but *that* they could not have as there is only a Ladies and Gentlemen's Do. in those vessels. . . .

I hope you will not be very angry with me talking to E. D. but I could hardly avoid doing it.

On the same date, Georgiana's mother wrote off to Isabella Harrison, repeating her daughter's account of the departure, and adding "E. D. thinks Dover such a pretty place. I only hope they will not come and live here—we shall leave if they do. I shall be so glad if they fix upon Hamburg as a Residence instead of Boulogne—I think there are so many undesirable Families resident at Boulogne whom they may get acquainted with."

The Ides of March are now past. It is surprising that so many letters should have survived from them. And there will be more letters to come: the whole of 1852 pullulates with correspondence. The biographer feels inclined to pause at this moment, as the Channel packet carries away Emily in her Polka towards the uncertainties of the continent, and to survey, one hundred years later, the general scene.

Battersea Rise had been abandoned. That is the point that most horrified the family. Servants had been left in charge, and though no one would be more loyal than Mr. Harrison, the butler, or more shocked by the course of events, he was no substitute for the Master, the Inheritor, who had betrayed his trust. It was the loss of Battersea Rise that distressed them most and exacerbated their genuine moral distress. They had been accustomed to return to it and to show it to their children, or at any rate to think of it as functioning. Now they were excluded for ever—unless they bent the knee to immorality, which was unthinkable. Their outlook wavered; they did not know whether they wished Henry to return at once or after an interval or never. They did not know whether they wished the house to be sold and to vanish off the spiritual face of the earth, or to stand as it was, an empty and dishonoured shell. I understand many of their feelings: it has so happened that I have been deprived of a house myself. They will not be understood by the present generation.

Round the deserted shrine were grouped the dispossessed.

Marianne, the worst sufferer, prepared to make herself a new home at the other end of the Common. Henrietta already had a small house at Clapham and Sophia a huge one a few miles away at Roehampton. Further still, in The Precincts, Canterbury, dwelt Isabella. Laura in her congested rectory felt anything her husband felt, and Watson in his Hereford rectory was presumably indignant too. In Bedfordshire brooded the Inglises. Sir Robert Inglis, in the House of Commons, had already expressed his mature disapproval of such unions, and no doubt he resented the loss of an establishment where he and his womenfolk had once reigned with benignity.

In cataloguing those families most affected I must not omit the Dealtrys. Since Dr. Dealtry's death they had continued to live at Clapham, and according to the Thorntons had gradually insinuated themselves into Battersea Rise with the intention of possessing it. Whether this is so I have no idea, I have no evidence. They certainly welcomed the alliance—the genial departure from Dover proves that—and may have taken, as many decent people did, a more critical view of the law. But they too must have been puzzled when they looked into the future. What ever was going to happen?

And what was going to happen to Henry's children, particularly to Harti and Emmy? Marianne was just shifting from the position of sister to that of aunt, and she regarded her little nieces with passionate concern, she longed to protect them and she overestimated their troubles, and sometimes turned "Di" into a heartless stepmother. She could bear the loss of Battersea Rise, she could tolerate the distasteful marriage, but the children, oh the poor exiled children! Oh their pet guinea pigs and rabbits! Henry had actually ordered them to be killed! "Does it not shew that there is not a vestige left of the kind and over-indulgent father of other days?" She rescued Emmy's favourite doe together with three babies which had been born to it since the child's departure to France, and she discovered that ten guinea pigs had not been killed but had been sold by the gardeners for 1/6 to a man from whom she managed to retrieve them at 8*d*. each. "It was too bad to part with them for they belonged to poor Edmund Stainforth who was blown up in the Amazon."

Behind all these emotional problems lay a practical one: the Bank. Henry was not prepared to renounce his beloved profession, and his partners' refusal to allow him more than six months' absence from England impressed him greatly. He might wander over the European continent and even buy a house there, but he would have to come back now and then to the Bank, and his wife would want to come too.

The fugitives had escaped but the complications in England increased. Only four days later a Mr. Thomas Jackson took up his pen in Oxford and addressed the following ineptitudes to Marianne.

Is it can it be true? Has my friend and defender indeed left England? Harty governess, and Emily, Dealtries and their belongings all gone to swell the Hansa Town League, German Zollrevision and Altona marriage fees?

Do tell me what am I to do?

I am like the men in Greek tragedies around whom difficulties gradually thicken and who at last say nothing but interjections.

Give me just one line of information and tell the fugitives that I am always your and their obliged friend.

I think that I must get the good Bishop of Sodor and Man to look after me.

More serious than Mr. Jackson was the problem of the Infant School Treat. Henry insisted that it should take place at Battersea Rise in his absence, but Marianne declined to be present. What then should the Vicar of Battersea and his wife do? They wanted the children to have the usual fun, and they did not "take the same view some may of the marriage question," but they felt unable to attend themselves and they were anxious not to offend the powerful Miss Thornton. Mrs. Whitmore, that good friend to all parties, counselled them to go ahead. Their letters show how fluid public opinion was on the subject of the Deceased Wife's Sister, and how many people, perhaps most people, were trying to remain neutral and to behave as if nothing unusual had happened.

And now came an ignoble squabble over furniture, such as often happens when two people part keeping house. Marianne had to start her new establishment, and it may be that she exceeded the permission given her by Henry before his departure. Nothing however can excuse him for writing to her as follows:

Paris, May 15, 1852

My dear Marianne—I did not know till the other day that, with the exception of the pictures of Emily and of her father and mother, Harriet's dressing room was dismantled.

It is one of the many advantages of marriage with a sister in law, that all things connected with one's former life, instead of raising feelings of jealousy, acquire an increased interest and form a new bond of union. I certainly feel a much greater feeling of affection than I did for all the articles of furniture in that room where Harriet's state of health compelled her to spend so large a part of her waking hours, and I would gladly pay you the value of them if you would have them replaced.

Emily readily complied with your request to have the childrens' likenesses taken—Ever your affectionate H. S. THORNTON.

[*208*]

In consequence of this insulting letter she took further counsel with Mrs. Whitmore, who managed to convey to the Dealtry faction that she "did not think Henry could have married into any other family where a little bed furniture would be grudged to a sister who had lived so many years with him." She advised Marianne to take whatever she thought herself entitled to, but to make a complete list, down to the smallest item, and to send it to Henry and Emily without a single word. No doubt the exiled pair were in a state of suspicion and irritability, and had worked themselves into a panic lest Battersea Rise was being rifled in their absence. Mrs. Whitmore also suspected them of cupidity, and had been confirmed in her suspicions by her Bible which she opened by chance on the Sunday after their departure, and lit upon at Ecclesiastes v: 13.

Behind the contest over furniture lay the graver problem of the investments. Marianne's sisters held that she had been shabbily treated in the share-out and had been compelled to sell out securities disadvantageously. She was certainly less well off; she had lost the amenities and facilities of Battersea Rise and was obliged to run her own establishment and engage servants for it. An air of cheerful poverty pervades her letters for the next twenty years. But she was an excellent woman of business, she had the gift of attracting money as well as the habit of generosity, and she had plenty of money to spend on herself and to give away, right up to the end of her life.

Did her brother treat her badly? Yes. She was his favourite sister, and the only one of his family who stuck to him. He ought to have been gentler with her and more tolerant—he who was in such need of tolerance himself. All that can be said in his favour is that he was irritable and anxious:

irritable with his relatives because they disapproved of the
marriage and disliked the new wife, and anxious about the
future. He had spent large sums in trying to get the bill
through Parliament, he had weakened his position in his
Bank, and displeased his partners, he had left his paternal
home to wander over the unknown continent, and in the
midst of all this strangeness and newness he was proposing
to found a second family. How could such a family be
financed? Every penny must be diverted to the purpose. No
doubt he would have worried less if his only son had shown
signs of shaping satisfactorily. But the boy (then aged 12)
was already aggressive and unstable and had been arrested
for fishing by the French police, and in later years he caused
graver anxiety. Henry could look for no help from his son
nor from his poor little daughters, snivelling their hearts out
for the paddocks and ponies of Battersea Rise. To the mor-
alist, so much discomfort will seem appropriate. To the
amoralist it will offer yet another example of the cruelty and
stupidity of the English law in matters of sex.

I do not know where the continental marriage of Henry
Sykes Thornton and Emily Dealtry was solemnised: possibly
in Denmark. The Thorntons continued to deny her the style
of wife and insolently referred to her as E. D. She returned
in the summer to England on what they called an "experi-
mental trip," in order to see how many people could call on
her, and "had the face to come on Clapham Common last
Friday," writes Henrietta, "and to call at Battersea Rise:
but Harrison won't receive her and made Mr Abbott open
the door." With her were the two little girls. She soon
whisked them back to Boulogne—Harti carrying a cage full
of birds to comfort her, and Emmy a cage full of guinea
pigs, who had survived in sufficient quantity. All rejoiced at

the shortness of Emily's stay: it looked as if she had been sufficiently snubbed by decent people, and would never return.

In one's indignation at the way in which she was treated, one is inclined to elevate her to a heroine. She will scarcely fill that role. She was a diffident pleasure-loving woman of the clinging type, shrewd where her own interests were concerned, but devoid of conversation and wit and indifferent to public affairs. The charge that she alienated Henry's money as well as his affections is probably true; she had to look after herself, no one else would. She appears to have been nice to his children. Presently she had children of her own, and her duty of feathering her nest increased. She may be summed up as an ordinary woman who married into an unusual family in an unusual way. Further to sum her up: she made her husband happy. I never met her, though dates would have allowed it; and my great-uncle died when I was a baby.

During that odious year Marianne underwent further trial. She had been promised that her nieces should come and stay with her in the autumn, and in July Emmy had written her a charming sprawling letter about it, beginning "My dearest Mony"; Mony or Monie was the name by which her nieces and nephews began to call her. "There was a circus at Strasbourg but it was too low for us and so we didn't go. I shall be so glad when I get on Puss dear Puss back again. I quite long for a ride. I am getting on with my stool for you so very fast. Scarcely 2 months now and you'll see my sweet face at Clapham again."

The promised day arrived.

From her new home on Clapham Common she thus describes it to Mrs. Wedgwood:

Your enquiries about my affairs, I have hardly the heart to answer—The very day and hour were fixed, and I spent the whole of it you will believe at the window, expecting in vain that every moment would shew me their dear old faces once more—but in vain—and the next day I heard that owing to a most 'artful dodge' they had been prevented coming at the last moment. They were suddenly told they were not coming to me at all—but were to live in an Hotel in the City! with their Governess for 6 months—but if they would give up coming *now*, they should visit me for six weeks at Christmas. The poor children fell into the trap, and offered to give up England on those terms—and she writes to every body 'how much she has been gratified to find they prefer remaining with her! to going to their Aunts'! I only know the truth thro' private letters from them, and were they detected they would be prevented from writing, so I hear her version of the story circulate in silence, and tho' Henry has twice been to see me, I have never alluded to the subject—I should not so much blame him, if differing as we do about such marriages, he chose to put a stop to all communication—but he does not dare to do that, and this thimble rigging scheme is too bad—but happily so utterly unlike him that one is at no loss to whom to attribute it—Don't talk of it please for the above mentioned reason. I was very bad at first about it all—but have happily had a flight of Forsters here, filling up every nook and cranny of my house and my thoughts, or at least my time—

Anyone who has waited in vain for a beloved person will understand what she felt. A wound has been inflicted which no subsequent reunion quite heals. The insecurity against which we all struggle has taken charge of us for a moment— for the moment that is eternity. The moment passes, and perhaps the beloved face is seen after all and the form embraced, but the watcher has become aware of the grave.

One of the most remarkable of the letters of censure is from Isabella. Writing from The Precincts, Canterbury, on April 20th, she states her attitude to Hannah Macaulay "in a few words" and succeeds in doing so in eight pages:

I do not see that sisterly affection has anything to do with the matter. Mine towards Henry is unabated. From the time he announced his intention I have avoided all intercourse with her but shown him what kindness I could. He has been very angry with me for *ignoring* her (I have done nothing more) but I could see that in all his letters to me his affection continued, and nothing could be kinder than his manner when last I saw him above a year ago. . . . I had far rather he should remain abroad than that he should live at B.R. with the sort of rabble who would collect about him there and I believe it would be far better for the children. . . . I had far rather respectable strangers lived there than such as E. D. I should feel less excluded. Why do you not take it or your Brother Tom if it is let. . . .

What a strange fatality has attended the eldest sons of the Clapham Sect! Henry and Tom Babington expatriated and W. W. excluded from respectable society. I am sure in this world some such stunning events are needed to remind us that this is not our true home. My lot has fallen to me in such pleasant places that I specially require some warning voice.

The danger of the house being sold now became acute. Why should Henry and Emily settle in a country where Isabella, Sophia, Henrietta, the Forsters, and the Inglises were organising hostilities against them? Rumours of a sale presently reached Herefordshire, and yet another relative, Mrs. Watson Thornton, wife to the Prebendary, gives tongue.

My flesh curdles and my blood boils [she informed Marianne] at the bare idea of B.R. being sold, and worst of all, out of the family. To think of that place hallowed by so many associations being knocked down to the highest bidder! Where can H's feelings be gone? They don't seem merged in E. D. or he would never be so much away from her. I don't wonder at *her* having no affection for so sacred a place (for really B.R. has religious associations which Abbotsford and Strathfieldsaye are exempt from) and what possible advantage can accrue from such a step? I think you *could* not have acted otherwise than you have about calling. No doubt it has been an experiment to see who would call, and no one of consideration has called, but who would be likely to, at the Adelaide? . . . I never wished for money before, but I wish now that amongst us we had sufficient to redeem that dear old place. Couldn't we each invest something and so buy it as you would a railroad, by each having a share, or couldn't Melville buy it as an investment, do talk it over and contrive something so that the place may remain in the family.

And the family continued to dance on hot bricks, letting the old home, selling it, forbidding it to be let or sold, and only uniting in the advice they offered to Marianne. She was the weak link, and the fact that she had been the greatest sufferer only made her the greatest danger. Through her affection for her brother and her nieces she might recognise E. D. and all would be lost. My grandfather prescribed her duty for her as follows:

As for M. T. visiting B.R. for the children's sake, it would be wrong in principle and could not therefore be right in practice. We are not to do evil that good may come. If we do, the evil is done but the good is sure *not* to follow.

Then look at the weight of responsibility incurred. The weak and the worldly, in such cases, only wait for a pretext; this pretext may be supplied then by *a single visit*. That visit will be magnified into *countenance* and approval by a leading mem-

ber of the family: and every artifice be employed to draw others in. In short there is no end to this beginning. In the mind
of society the family may become mixed with the offenders: and
real injury be done without any resultant benefit. 'Be ye separate' is the only safeguard for one and all.

Looking back at her conduct during that crucial period,
I am overwhelmed with admiration. She behaved like a
statesman—a woman statesman. She temporised. She would
push nothing to a conclusion even in her mind. She was affectionate without weakness and moral without asperity. In
the end, the good fortune of Elizabeth I rather than the ill
fortune of Catherine de' Medici awaited her, and she saved
something from the wreck. Much was lost. But her sisters
lost everything. When the storm cleared, and Henry and
Emily settled back into Battersea Rise, as of course they
did, he often called on her in her new abode and occasionally
she went to see him. Seven years later she could write: "I am
sure he fancies he is not only doing right himself but that
he is trying to help others to do so. To pass that Bill has
become with him a 'furore'—it is almost what the abolition
was to us, but unhappily he has a personal interest in the
matter." And seventeen years later she could sit peacefully
for an hour with him in their old beloved garden, while "Di"
chattered harmless nothings to Emmy in the distance.

A poem entitled "The Tulip Tree" shall close this sorry
chapter of our family chronicle. It was by Charley Forster,
the precocious schoolboy at the Charterhouse, where he contributed so frequently under the initials C. T. F. to the
Carthusian that he became known as Cackle Too Fast. The
Battersea Rise tulip tree, which Napoleon had coveted, had
lost some of its limbs after Henry's second marriage, and

Cackle Too Fast hastened to point the moral and widen the breach.

The Tulip Tree

Under a tree whose ample shade
    Harboured the violets fair,
And golden daisies, fringed with white,
    Which children love to wear,

Walked erst upon the grassy lawn
    The wisest and the best
Of Britain's sons, whose happy soul
    Is gathered to its rest.

But no one, now, upon the lawn,
    Beneath that old tree's shade,
Doth ever walk, for its sere leaves
    Fall off, and drooping fade.

While stood the honour of that house,
    The glory of that name,
While still unstained remained its worth,
    Untarnished its fame,

That old tree stood upon the lawn,
    And cast its shade around;
And sweetly bloomed the violets
    Upon that hallowed ground.

It seemed the Genius of the line,
    The Guardian of the race,
Had made that ancient tulip-tree
    His sacred dwelling-place.

When fell the honour of that house,
    The glory of that name;
When stained its spotless purity,
    And tarnished was its fame:

[*216*]

Then died the spright, and drooped the tree,
  The withering branches fell;
The barren stump alone remains
  Its story sad to tell.

                                C. T. F. October, 1852.

Henry was right in thinking that it was only a question of time before his Marriage Bill became law. But the time was not in his lifetime. Not until 1907, long after he and Emily were dead, was their position regularised. The 1907 act made such marriages as theirs valid, and valid retrospectively. I can remember the indignation of Orthodoxy when it was passed. A man is permitted to marry his deceased wife's sister today, and the particular situation which brought so much unhappiness to my family cannot recur. A woman is still impeded in marrying her deceased husband's brother.

AUNT

1852-1879

When Marianne left Battersea Rise the ages of the Thorntons were:

Marianne	55
Henry	52
Watson	49
Isabella (Mrs. Harrison)	48
Sophia (Mrs. Melville, afterwards Lady Leven)	46
Henrietta (Mrs. Synnot)	44
Laura (Mrs. Forster)	43

Some of their children:

Henry's: Harti, Emmy
Watson's: Marion
Henrietta's: Inglis, Henrietta
Laura's: John Jebb, Charley, Doanie, Laura, Eddie (my father)

ONE

East Side

AFTER THE CRASH, after Marianne left Battersea Rise, her address became Number One, The Sweep, The Pavement, Clapham Common. It was a graceless address and "East Side" was generally substituted. The Pavement was a convex curve of houses into which was nicked the concave of the Sweep. Both of them survive, but all the houses are new.

No one managed to love The Sweep. The three houses in it formed a single block; Miss Thornton on the left, Dr. Spitta in the middle, the Williamses on the right. The Williamses attracted no attention except when their drains smelt, but with Dr. Spitta there flickered faint suburban warfare. He wanted a better semicircle of grass in front, and suggested that the trees should be lopped; Miss Thornton would not have the trees lopped, she liked trees. He wanted the three houses painted alike, which would have conveyed the impression of a single residence with his surgery door in the centre; Miss Thornton did not mind how shabby anything looked, and her nephew drew a line of paint in the night from top to bottom to remind Dr. Spitta of his limitations. It was not much of a place to live in for thirty-five years, or to die in; still it served; it had a sideway squint of the Common and the Cock Pond and the church, and she liked to fancy it was "within sound of the Battersea Rise Dinner

Bell," half a mile away. The original Thornton estate was close, with cousins still living on it, and behind her was the amusing growth of Clapham. Modernity never frightened her. When she was asked to sign a protest against the introduction of horse-drawn trams, her comment was, "Not if I know'd it," and she wished she was well enough to use the things herself.

To Patty Smith, soon after moving in:

There had been much during the last four years at Battersea Rise to lessen its charm to me, & the comforts of a house of my own, once more surrounded by my Sisters & by my old friends tell upon me more every day. Indeed my living alone so far has ended in my never being a minute alone day or night, for I have had Henrietta's Girl to keep away from her brother's scarlet fever, & she has prevented my feeling so Rachel-like when I have lost my own poor Girls. I had all sorts of kind offers of homes in every direction, but I know you will think I was right in chusing one of my very own, & going to it at once. It is more homes, not more inmates that we want in our spreading family particularly now that Battersea Rise has evaporated. I wonder whether I shall ever see you here, I fancy my rambling ragged old house would just suit you—four rooms on a floor, opening into each other, & looking East & West, almost next door to Battens, & close to the Church, a fragment of what was once a Clapham Palazzo in the olden time, with a large vacant room down stairs, in which I hope there will be many festivities amongst high & low.

I will postpone further details of this house until I come to my own recollections of it. From the first it was an asylum for nephews and nieces. Chief in importance were the two Synnots, who demand immediate notice.

She had only been settled in a few months when her sister Henrietta fell ill ("I electric-telegraphed all my sisters who were around me in a few hours with their husbands"), died (May 1853), and there she was saddled with two orphans. Inglis was "a spirited boy of sixteen, and I feel like a fly on the back of an Arab Courser when I look at him—However like an Arabian he is gentle and affectionate, and I trust I may get on well." Henrietta was thirteen.

Anyone who could describe Inglis Synnot in such words was likely to get on with him. He had a fire and a strangeness unusual in Thorntons, he was a rare creature who has already appeared to us at Amiens, haranguing the French in his French, and it was he who drew the line of paint down The Sweep. Besides loving adventure, he was interested in science. He wanted to know how the world was made and why it worked. The Thorntons had never cared to know that; they had confined themselves to being good and doing good, and to being generally intelligent. With the arrival of the Synnot boy a window bangs open. He did not live to be an old man or to make a success of his profession as a marine engineer. But once seen he was never forgotten. His aunt Monie adored him. He was the proto-nephew, his successors were substitutes.

The health of the two children—particularly little Henrietta's—was her first care, and three months after their mother's death she took them off to the Isle of Wight bathing, boating, riding, and as a crowning excitement there was the Spithead Review. This, according to contemporary newspapers, "presented a spectacle of oceanic grandeur. The power of steam renders these fearful batteries moveable at pleasure" and much is said about the wonders of machinery and the presence of the Queen. Marianne describes it from her own point of view and with more poetry than usual; with a touch indeed of the magic of Thomas Hardy. Her large party decided on the expedition at the last minute—no

conveyance except butcher's cart, donkey cart, one donkey.
Mr. Harrison, the butler from dear Battersea Rise, had been
lent to them or had lent himself (it is not clear how he was
available) ; but Mr. Harrison proved more hindrance than
help, for he wanted to pack fourteen knives, forks, plates,
glasses, wanted to know where the knives were to be cleaned
on the top of the Downs and "looked as if we proposed to
dine on cold missionary" when the utensils were drastically
reduced.

A merrier breakfast there never was than at 10. o'clock on
the top of Bembridge Point, we almost seemed suspended in the
air with the sea and sky all around, the sea covered with little
white sails like shells, and the enormous ships all dressed for the
Queen. We saw them all steam off, and only send us a deafening
noise and a volley of smoke that turned all the green and gold
around us into a November fog. But to those who were upon
the water and not sick it was most beautiful they say. What I
did see and thought the finest sight possible was 'the enemy'
chased into Portsmouth as we were going home. They had every
sail set, and the sun shining on them made them look as white
as marble, while the deep blue of the sea was all around them.
'They walked the waters like a thing of life.' We got home at
7.0 in the evening in time to see Portsmouth bombarded, which
was a very pretty sight too, and altogether tho' tired and burnt
the day was well worth the fatigue.

Poor dear Henrietta was so like her mother about it. Liked
the drive to Bembridge (6 miles) because she could walk wherever she pleased, and would have enjoyed the being there very
much if 'there hadn't been such a squash of people and such a
noise'. (there were 9000 they say) made me sit on the grass
where they managed to plant two umberellas over us, and she
laid her head on my feet and went nearly to sleep.

The party went on to The Precincts, Canterbury, to stay
with Isabella and her Ben. A different atmosphere succeeds.

Popery is suddenly the trouble. Miss Stanley, sister to the Dean, is around all the time, and has got hold of the children, and "if she isn't an R.C. she certainly ought to be one." The Forster children—"*they* are safe enough but in Henrietta's sensitive morbid state I think there is much that w^d be very attractive to her in Romanism. I told her that she should go to the Cathedral as often as she wished but I should always go with her." The child confessed that she had been there twice with Miss Stanley, but hadn't prayed, had only listened to the music. "I quite hope no harm will come of it." Isabella and the Archdeacon adored pottering in and out of the Cathedral; it stood at the other side of their lawn, a huge booming toy with which they could not play too much. "Love me, Love my Cathedral." Marianne, whose deepest religious experience was family prayers, felt no sympathy. Even while she was writing her letter the bells started and caused her to exclaim, "And now here comes the Cathedral again, certainly I wonder how anybody gets anything done when their day is cut up so."

The Isle of Wight visit had lasting consequences for young Synnot, for he found the girl of his heart there. He stayed on with a tutor at Brighstone, a romantic and secluded village at the south of the island: "nothing can equal the loveliness of the place, the bluest of seas seen through such festoons of roses and thickets of myrtles as one only believed lived in Italy." There he became acquainted with two ladies who took care of children from India, and with their charges, particularly with a Miss Mary Preston. He went on to Oxford (Christchurch) and then to Canada. Whence at the age of 22 he despatched a gay and gallant letter to his favourite aunt.

Lewistown.
Aug. 30. 1859

Dearest Mone

Niagara falls are just the finest sight I've ever seen, & I've seen a good deal for my tender years. I saw 'em all how & all over, morning, noon & night, & they're great—and improve on acquaintance; its not merely the enormous size but the extreme beauty, they'd be beautiful if they were a 20th part as big, & they'd be big at that. I went right under the falls on the Canada side & thats a sight worth seeing. As soon as I had said I meant it, I ceased to be a free agent for I was delivered over unto a nigger who bound me hand & foot with waterproof clothes & then took me down an evil-looking 'precipidge' & we went down & down & down, & the water roared bigger & bigger & then we passed along a ledge of rock where great rocks as big as mountains fell on our heads, & cataracts fell over all us, at least this is what my terrified imagination fancied, for I ought to have said that I had by this time lost my senses, & followed my nigger in blind faith: then we got to a corner which seemed the end of the world, only the nigger said I must go on & my faith became absolute infidelity, when I saw him walk round, but I had to do it, & then I saw the fall falling its wickedest close ahead, & the main body of the water falling about 6 feet clear of the rock. I went right in, only saw nothing, at first, as the spray was so strong I had to turn my back to it. By this time I was in such a state of fooldom (between the noise & darkness & water dashing in my face) I'd have jumped down, if my nigger had commanded it, but he didn't & I went on till he said I might stop wh. I gladly did. By degrees my senses were restored to me, & I assure you they were worth having, for the world can't have got such another sight. You seem quite under the sea, only thats a small way of describing it, as the water goes roaring down, & the sun just shines thro' making a queer green light, very evil, & making yr. nigger look awful, & then theres a break in one part where you see a rain-bow in a complete circle. Then

[*226*]

I went back & wrote down my name somewhere, & somebody gave me a certificate, that I had gone under.

N.B. There's not a ha'porth of danger or difficulty in it, only one feels such a fool.

Montreal. Sept* 2. My paper runs short so I'll only give a resumé of the rest. Saw Blondin walk over the falls on a rope, saw Steven's big balloon, stayed at Lewistown for a 'raising-bee' at a farm-house, great fun. I'm going to buy some land if I can, I think near Lake Michigan but I shall see. The climate is wonderful, I've never been so well since I was born. There you see its all couleur-de-rose! so goodbye.

Ever yrs. affect*

R. H. I. Synnot.

How tame were the Niagara Falls when I saw them, and how tamed in comparison myself! I saw them from the Canada side, as my cousin did, but it is now all mussed up with a rose garden, and walks under the cataract are impossible or discouraged. The orderly waters of the river curve like a glass roller and turn into fluff. One watches them do it without wanting to know how it is done. Further down, where the river bends and makes a grim pool under precipices, the scene gets more exciting and nearer to the past.

He did not buy his land near Lake Michigan, but returned to England and married his Mary Preston: as Maimie she was to be my own beloved, and she was also to become the centre of a small Thornton storm. The quaint couple never had a home; she trailed about after him to Dover or Plymouth or Holland or wherever his work called him.

Here are some extracts from his aunt's letters to him. The first two mingle gossip with the American Civil War.

April 17 [1863]

Good boy to write me that pretty letter. Yes, I'll boil up the papers for you, but they will make but very shaking jelly, I fear. Why don't you take in Public Opinion. Mary and Maggie ought to be kept up to things. I could shew you quite an edifying paper written 60 years ago by your Grandfather and my father 'On the duty of young people being interested in public affairs' as tending to stop 'gossip' . . . the reason of *that* is I suppose that people get spiteful and uncharitable towards individuals, but it isn't personal abuse if you run down the American armies or the French Chamber or even the obstinate old Pope—*as* he's infallible he counts as an army.

Well the Southerners I guess are done for, Richmond being evacuated, but I expect they will give the Yankees a good deal of trouble. . . .

May 1st, [1865]

Dearest Inglis,

I should think theres news enough for you this week, but it must have penetrated even to you. We've a fresh horror daily, the last is the suicide of Fitzroy, the weather prophet. Tayloe has just declared that it's because he'd said the Thames would be frozen over in April, and lo it was fiercely hot, and so he shot himself. I think any mans head is wrong, who professes to know anything about the weather. The wind bloweth where *it* listeth, and thats all. What a donkey the Revd Archer Gurney must be in Paris, to ask the Confederates there, Slidell and his set, to come and sing a funeral dirge and the penitential psalms over Lincoln, in order to shew the North that *they* hadn't murdered him! I thought Slidell's answer very good.

Yes we shall be delighted to see you for as long as you can stay. I don't know when I have been so long without a sight of you, and I rather 'weary' for you as the Scotch say. . . .

About the Budget? Cheap T and a lenient income tax will please you, its pleasant to see all one's dividends come in a little bit higher, and one's insurance a little bit lower. But I'm afraid you would have been for malt being relieved. Y^r Uncle Henry was here on Sunday and asked me what 'those fellows' were paying you. I said I didn't know, he says Telleard told him they liked you very much, which sounds favourable.

Y: Uncle H.s carriage being full of children in London driving in the streets, the horses took fright and ran away. He tried to help Joseph to stop them and couldn't and they got on the pavement and were just turning over when an immensely strong navvy dashed at their heads and stopped them. Such was y: Uncles gratitude he asked the man to B. Rise and he brought a friend with him who had assisted in getting the child: out of the carriage and then they had a jolly supper and 2 Sovereigns—30s. to the Navvy—10s. to the friend. Well Henry went the next day to call on them and found the wretched Navvy had got so drunk with the 30s. that he then and there died! Theres a story for you to recount to your Navvys. Its horrid to think of, they say he was apparently such a very respectable man. The new President of the U.States has been made to take the teatotal pledge. He'd been drunk for 6 weeks when Lincoln was killed and he became president.

Ever yours aff.

M. T.

Only got yours to-night.

Later in the same year:

Yes to be sure—Dine here on Christmas day, who ever could expect you to dine anywhere else—and this year as far as I know there are no stray Governesses to harbour, but will get the Southeys and be jolly.—Henrietta has been asking whether there's any chance of Christmas day being good to us as it was last year and coming on a Sunday again. So many odd things happen, perhaps it may. Well we shall see. What storms & tempests do blow. The Bp. of B. & W. was at Folkestone & he says the wind *has* blown him into next week, really and metaphorically, for though he had his house for another week he wouldn't stand the wind and came up to town. . . .

Mrs Dealtry seems to have found out *her* true level, she sent to beg 'for a few toys to amuse herself with' which of course the Battersea Rise nursery afforded her.

[*229*]

I'm emigrating a boy to Queensland chiefly because he is such a plague to his mother and grandmother. The former however hopes I'll allow her to go to him when he's ill, which I assured her she should, for thank goodness she's not been taught geography. His grandmother, less tender-hearted, besought me to send him to the farthest off place that ever was made, 'but please Miss Thornton let him have a Pilot Coat—you talked of a Cord jacket but he swears if he has he'll not go—no nor unless you'll let him have some ties and braces'. So I've kept his outfit here and packed it, and if the sight of it makes him throw himself over board well let him.

N.B. Henrietta says her monetary system is in the greatest confusion till you'll tell her what she owes you for Guardian shares. Do.

I say—persuade Mary to do her Christmas here—I'll not have roast beef or mince pie or anything nasty if she will.

Ever yrs affectly M. T.

The subject matter is unimportant, but isn't her style improving? Isn't there from the 60's onwards, a terseness and brightness which were lacking in the long leisurely epistles from Battersea Rise? The loss of a home may mean a gain. She certainly gained much from the friendliness of a lively young man.

But he was ready enough to laugh at her behind her back. He writes to one of the Forster girls:

Money and Aunt Isabella have been writing nasty letters to each other on things in general. Money sent an extra nasty one shutting up Bella all over; and B. writes back to say she has accidentally burned M's letter so can't say what there was in it. I do think my dear we have 2 very superior aunts.

You have rather a superior cousin too I think; for finding my lavender water and hair-wash disappearing rapidly I am going tomorrow to put nitrate of silver into the first and depilatory 'for the removal of superfluous hairs' into the second, which I should say w.^{d} mark the thief: (nit. of silver turns folk black you know) so the first bald headed negress I find about the house, she'll go to quad.

And the letter becomes progressively untypical with "It's a nice book the Boys Own Book. It tells one how to put a mouse under an air-pump when it will expire in great agonies." Later on he describes how he has made a snob feel uncomfortable at Lord Leven's. There was an element of the brash joker in this charmer.

When he died his little widow gravitated to lodgings in Clapham. It was believed that she was too feckless to look after herself, and that she should remain for the rest of her life under the supervision of her sister-in-law and of Miss Thornton.

And now I ought to describe the sister-in-law. I shrink from the task. Henrietta Synnot the younger is much the hardest pebble on the family beach. How was it that someone so gifted, so warmhearted and unselfish and intelligent and witty could go through life causing little but discomfort to herself and to others? There must have been some early frustration, which a trained psychologist would analyse. She had a hateful temper: that is my inexpert conclusion. She could sulk, she could flare and thunder, she could be icily dignified, and then she could display goodness and imaginative kindness of the highest order. To those who did not know her changeableness the benignity in her was adorable: to those who knew it only inspired anxiety, for it might leave the adorer with a dart through the back. She was always taking people up and dropping them. There was a time when she would see no one but Caroline Stephen, Leslie Stephen's sister, and would do nothing but play chess with her. There was another time when she would see no one but Hesba Stretton, authoress of *Jessica's First Prayer*. She was devoted to animals. In this, as in other things, she differed from her aunt, who took dogs, cats, horses in their stride and reserved her emotions for her own species.

Henrietta was so young when her mother died that it was natural she should go to stay with her aunt; to both it seemed the perfect arrangement, and she ended by becoming resident niece at The Sweep. Miss Thornton and Miss Synnot. The phrase acquired the prestige of a combine. In some ways she was an appropriate companion, for she flung herself into her aunt's benevolent and educational schemes, and when Milton Bryan became Thornton property she enjoyed staying there and supervising the village. Life in the house at East Side suited her less. So much went on there that she could not control. Cousins came or wouldn't come, stayed too long, left too soon, tired Monie when she should not have been tired, her sister-in-law might do something foolish, and Battersea Rise was always close, a permanent irritant. Nor did my own tiny form, when it came upon the scene, bring appeasement. My brief encounters with her shall be described in due course. I saw her last during the present century, at Milton Bryan, where as Lady of the Manor she ended her unquiet life. "Requiescat in pace" comes to one's lips, but she may not have wanted peace.

It is a change from these two enigmatic Synnots to the ten Forsters, who were as good as bread and gave no trouble except when they were ill. I have already mentioned Monie's visits to Stisted and theirs to Battersea Rise; now that she had a house of her own they came endlessly; the 'fifties, 'sixties, 'seventies, even the 'eighties, are aflitter with the friendly swarm; the boys with their angelic rather weak faces, the girls with their genuine loveliness. She was a tower

Inglis and Henrietta Synnot
by George Richmond (about 1848)

of strength for them all. Her conduct over Doanie Forster's illness is characteristic. The lad was at the Charterhouse. In 1855 he collapsed, and his condition was only revealed by the good sense and loquacity of his brother Charley. Charley sneaked to their aunt, she descended, had the invalid removed to Clapham, and entered into a correspondence with the master responsible which left him little quarter.

Miss Thornton presents her compliments to Mr Miles, and in reply to his letter begs to state that she cannot alter the opinion which she expressed to Mr Forster, and which she supposes he may have communicated to Dr Elder—that on Sunday the 1st when she brought away her nephew from the Charter House, he was so very ill that he ought to have been in bed, instead of having been ordered that morning to go into School and Chapel. The bleeding was not a slight but a very severe one, and most certainly came from the lungs. It continued accompanied with high fever for many days, and is of so very serious a character that he will never be able to return to the Charter House, and will require the greatest care and attention for some years to come.

Miss Thornton is sorry to have said anything which annoys Mr Miles, especially under the circumstances to which he adverts, but his note only confirms her impression that he was not aware of the dangerous nature of the illness with which Mr Forster's son was attacked.

Doanie never recovered. His death two years later was the occasion for dramatic grief. Long accounts of his symptoms and of his dying homilies were compiled and circulated. One notebook runs into forty pages: its pietism makes painful reading, for one cannot catch in it the remotest glimpse of a real boy. Painful too, though aesthetically successful, is a George Richmond drawing: "The Forsters mourning for Doanie." My grandparents are shown grouped at the foot of a cross, he looking upward in prayer, she with a child sleeping exhausted in her arms, and another kneeling beside her. Doanie also has a death-mask medallion in Stisted church. He was the first of his generation to die and the last of any generation to receive protracted obsequies. The threnody which began over the elder Henry Thornton in 1815 ends at last.

Eddie Forster, my father, became Marianne's favourite nephew after Inglis Synnot's death. Youngest but two of his family, he shared their happy insanitary life at Stisted Rectory, followed his brothers to the Charterhouse, and followed some of them to Cambridge (Trinity). He did fairly well there, read classics, and won a Greek Testament prize: Macaulay's Works in eight volumes, full calf. When he came down, he took up architecture. He encountered opposition here from his father, who required him to become either a clergyman or a lawyer; these were the only tolerable professions—the army was brutal, the civil service ungentlemanly, India unthinkable. Architecture was finally conceded, and he became a pupil at Mr. Blomfield's office (afterwards Sir Arthur Blomfield). There had previously been another pupil there: by name Thomas Hardy.

It is one of Life's Little Ironies that I should have got to know Mr. Hardy and stayed with him at Max Gate, and should have never known my father, seven years his junior. My father then went abroad, and my treasured relics of him are the architectural sketches he made of churches in France and Italy. He developed a charming, niggling pencil; the further up a spire a detail is, the more clearly it shows, and he was also clever at putting in birds to give height. Objects on the ground, particularly human ones, are failures. Whatever the merit of the sketches, they certainly stimulate one to visit the church portrayed, and I have never paid such a visit without disappointment—the church has been neither as gigantic nor as delicate as I hoped.

As an architect he was promising, despite his retarded start and his rather unpractical character, and the only house by him I know has great distinction externally. He was beginning to get work through the family connections—a restoration here, a row of cottages there. Aunt Sophy gave him a little job at Roehampton, which caused Henrietta Synnot typically to remark to my mother: "What a thing it is to have a fool for an aunt!" My mother rushed trembling with rage to my father; he said, "Why didn't you reply 'And a knave for a husband'?" He was quick at the uptake, amusing, sarcastic, could always make old Monie laugh, and he had integrity and unselfishness. How these qualities combined to make him a real person I do not know. He has always remained remote to me. I have never seen myself in him, and the letters from him and the photographs of him have not helped.

It is the Synnots and Forsters who meant most to their aunt—they, and of course her beloved Emmy, who had married a Sykes cousin at Weymouth. Watson's children and Sophia's children do not come into the picture so much. Watson lived away in Hereford, and it was not until he and his wife died that their daughter, the well-liked Marion, frequented Clapham. Sophia lived close by but in aristocratic amplitude: it was more natural that Monie should visit Roehampton House than Sophia The Sweep. Sophia, now Countess of Leven and Melville, entertained, she even handled royalty, and Marianne gives us a glimpse of the Victorian court:

Roehampton House 1865

One day here we had an influx of visitors from Windsor Castle. Lady Augusta Bruce asked leave to bring two of the

Princess Alice's maids of honour and their Equerries *because* they were so dreadfully dull. They were merry rosy German girls and played the whole day at croquet and Aunt Sally. The latter they had never seen before and were so delighted with it that Ronald has made them a present of it to take to Osborne if the Queen permits. I wonder whether she will—one of the Equerries said 'It is very expensive, it breaks so many pipes.'

The entertainments at Roehampton were not always a success, and in one of the gayest letters she ever wrote a semi-disaster is recorded.

They had asked Ruthven to get Christies Minstrels but he couldn't, but said he knew of a *most* respectable woman, a Miss Young, only she was called Madame Violante, who could dance on the tight rope and do the ascension business 150 feet high. Aunt Sophy objected to female rope dancing, but Ronald and Norman replied the rope was to be only just above the ground, so it would do no harm. Well they didn't put it very high, and they first sent a little child to paddle backwards and forwards, but then her mother (let's hope she *is* Madame Violante) went off on it, petticoats above her knees, flesh-coloured silk-stockings, decidedly dirty drawers, and there she strode kicking her legs up sky high—on which Aunt Sophy said she couldn't stand it, and told Ronald to tell her to get down. Ronald said she was furious and wouldn't get down, Aunt Sophy said she'd have the rope cut, and after many high words she was made to give up her antics, and then good Miss Duckworth, who thinks it right to do good, proposed to Aunt S. to go and speak *seriously* to her.

So they did. She said we were all much too 'near' that at the theatre she was thought so very proper. Miss D. asked whether she had a Bible and prayer book, yes, ever went to church, yes constantly, then they sermonised her a little, and she promised next time she performed to make her petticoats two inches longer at least, and so far recovered her good-humour as to give us another performance *and* a decent one too. She and her 2 daughters danced on stilts all about the lawn. Henrietta thought it the pleasantest party that she had ever been at. I could hardly get her away though I could hardly get her there either.

Sophia had always been a stickler for propriety; she was an innate conservative, seldom read a book, and could make such remarks as "It's very presumptuous not to believe what you are told," which earned her the ridicule of the rising generation. The temper of her mind was simple and serious; when she became friendly with a Sikh Maharajah she enquired from my grandfather whether the Sikhs were Nazarites. He replied that the Afghans certainly were—he had proved it—and the Sikhs lived so close that they might well be too. At the same time she was intelligent, forceful, witty, and could write most entertaining letters. There is one to Marianne which begins with the wedding of Princess Alice as seen through the eyes of the Sikh Maharajah (Duleep Singh), and ends with the misfortunes of a Lady Ruth at a cattle show. Lady Ruth had sat in too hot sun but would not move because she was surrounded by French royalty and English dukes, then she cried, "I'm going to be ill, take me home," met more dukes on the way which revived her, and was deposited in the corner of a cowshed with the Duke of Athol on a milking stool and Jenny the dairy maid. Aunt Sophy's gown was completely spoiled ("dirty straw and wet grass close between 2 cows"), and Jenny had nothing but milk to wash it with. "From the remarks of the crowd close behind us I am sure they thought us all mad." A letter like this makes us realise the consistency of the Thornton outlook, and by a happy chance Roehampton allowed the outlook to be directed upon high society. Nowhere else shall we meet a Lady Ruth.

Although so generous to her family, Aunt Monie could be firm on occasion, and a nephew-in-law who tried to touch her for £500 gets a very dusty answer. He had asked for the loan of the money to help him over one of his many temporary difficulties—this time over a farm, and she replied that she would lend it him "if it could be proved to her that he was living within his income." If he was not living within his income he would start living on her £500, she would never see it again, and this—with ten Forsters to provide for—she could not tolerate. A further turn of the screw follows. He would have to prove that he was living within his income "to some better judge than you or I of such matters," *i.e.*, to some partner in Williams Deacon's Bank, whom she nominated. She then reminds him that he was in debt when he married, that all his debts were paid, that he instantly got into debt again, and she rallies him mercilessly over his optimism in connection with his farm.

I know that you are perfectly convinced that all your plans will turn out well, that your cows and horses will never die, that rain will never spoil your hay, that your pigs will always be eatable, and that your potatoes will never fail whatever other people's may do. On a large farm one thing balances another, but even then a man who has not a capital to stand losses gets thrown over, and what is to become of *you?* You will say it is not your fault if the creatures died and the seasons were unfavourable, but it will be your fault if you are not prepared for it.

She fears that her letter will make him and his wife angry, and she apologises for not sparing him as his wife does. She signs herself "Ever yours affectionately." The nephew-in-law in question was of unusual size. "He would make two ordinary men," someone said, to which she replied, "But what very ordinary men they would be." She had no patience with persistent insolvency, and very little with amateur farming.

Her family and its connections were so numerous by the latter half of the century, and on the whole so satisfactory, that she had little room for outside friends. The most notable addition was the Wedgwood-Darwin one. Her old friend Fanny Mackintosh married Hensleigh Wedgwood, and had thus become sister-in-law to the great Charles Darwin himself. There had been and were to be other alliances between Wedgwoods and Darwins, and the two families combined into a clan as distinctive as the Thornton clan and publicly much more distinguished. Like the Thorntons, they were provincial and nonaristocratic. The Wedgwoods came from the Potteries, the Darwins from Lichfield. Like the Thorntons, they were high-minded, generous, reliable, and prone to self-complacency and to valetudinarianism, and they formulated their clannishness rather more aggressively: after all they had more to talk about, especially after the publications of the *Origin of Species*. Marianne's affection for Mrs. Hensleigh Wedgwood was extended to her three cultivated daughters, Snow, Hope, and Effie. As for Darwinism, she usually made fun of it, becoming hostile when compelled to be serious. I do not think that Charles Darwin ever came to see her, or that she made the pilgrimage to Down.

Another addition to her circle—a bizarre one—was James Knowles. This remarkable man had started as a Clapham architect and builder. He had little education, but possessed a restless and many-sided mind, a natural flair for anything and anyone who was interesting, and a passion for organised controversy.

At the age of nineteen he founded *The Clapham Magazine*. It expired after three issues. Then the Great Exhibition of 1851 startled him into sociology and science and philosophy, and while on holiday in the Isle of Wight he managed to secure Tennyson. From that moment his pace quickened. He built the bard a house, persuaded him to change his publishers, helped him to found the Metaphysical Society, and became its secretary. "When we first planned it Knowles did not know a concept from a hippopotamus," writes Tennyson. "Before we had talked of it for a month he could chatter metaphysics with the best of us." He became editor of the *Contemporary*, quarrelled with it and founded in 1877 the famous *Nineteenth Century*. This is his great, his deserved, claim to fame. Before he died, he was the friend of royalty and the recipient of a Knighthood, and the Queen of Holland had called him "Le quatrième pouvoir de L'État Britannique." *

It is natural that Knowles's roving eye should have fallen on Miss Marianne Thornton. She was interesting in herself, and she was the representative of an important local tradition. He sought her acquaintance in the early 'seventies, much as he had sought Tennyson's, and called on her, and talked to her eagerly about modern movements and anxieties: it was the age of serious worries and deep thoughts. She listened with appreciation and a little amusement. She was much wiser than her pleasant pushful visitor, and this no doubt he knew and it was partly why he called. When he tried to make her flesh creep over the state of the world, he failed: she who had thought Napoleon would cut down the tulip tree at Battersea Rise—she was not going to be worried by trifles. Rather later (1882) she writes:

Here Mr Knowles has come in, in a perfect storm of terror about the tunnel under the channel tell Laura, he is persuaded that 20,000 soldiers will be able to force their way through,

* This account is adapted from Mr. Michael Goodwin's essay on James Knowles in *Nineteenth-Century Opinion*, a Penguin volume. His magazine, now *The Twentieth Century*, is edited by his granddaughter, Miss Skilbeck.

all ours are in Ireland, England is no longer an island, and tho'
as Britannia able to rule the waves she could not manage the
tunnels. Mr Chamberlain has some dreamy notions of universal
brotherhood, we are to form one of the United States of Europe
and the Board of Trade will be the great power amongst them.

Tell Laura to ascertain whether we had all better invest in
South Easterns [i.e., in the railway from London to the Channel ports]. I will send her the 'Nineteenth' when it comes in,
tell her.

There is a glimpse of one of her intellectual dinner parties
with Knowles in the middle of it—it occurs in a letter of
1875 written by (Miss) Laura Forster to Miss Darwin:

Knowles so absorbed me I did not see so much of the Pauls' as
I meant. He is wonderfully good natured. He is a snob, but I am
more and more struck with what good talk he draws out; he
doesn't shine himself but there is sure to be light in his neighbourhood. . . .

Mone drew him out finely at dinner for Mr Wedgwood's benefit, and excused herself afterwards by saying it was the only
way of making all her guests happy since Knowles liked talking nonsense about great people every bit as we did hearing
him. So he went on assuring us that Manning was a really good
fellow to whom he, Knowles could speak his mind, and that he
should insist on Gladstone doing this that and the other. . . .

He also advised the company how to stop the architect
Waterhouse from pulling down the old Hall and court of
Pembroke College, Cambridge. Here he failed, and the hor-
rors Waterhouse perpetrated remain unto today.

Marianne's real link with him was one which with all his
flair he could not have anticipated: she and Miss Synnot
became attached to his little daughters. Beattie and Milly
Knowles figure affectionately in her latter days. She felt that
they were lonely in their smart journalistic home at Queen

Anne's Lodge, she interested herself in their education, she sent them presents when they were ill.

Another acquaintance—a slight one—was Florence Nightingale, who, she declared, went to the Crimea because she was tired of picking up her mother's spectacles. In 1873, still worried about her mother, Miss Nightingale writes about servants: "We have found a maid for my mother, but have you such a thing as an *upper housemaid* perhaps from dear Lady Inglis' household?" She goes on to describe her own household, smaller than her mother's and, she thinks, *very* easy: no housekeeper and no manservant to be sure, but "a man comes in to do the work. Forgive my worrying you and believe me yours very sincerely." I have another letter from her somewhere, and a more characteristic one: about nursing.

Samuel Wilberforce, Bishop of Oxford and finally of Winchester, must also be listed. He was the only son of her old friend with whom she kept in touch, and though her allusions to him are irreverent she was fond of him and she did not forget how his piety had soothed the last hours of Nurse Hunter. They shared a common dislike of Disraeli ("Yes, Lothair is all you say," the Bishop writes), and she would have been on his side in his controversy with Huxley. He died—thrown from his horse—on a visit to the Farrers at Abinger.

Finally there are the lame dogs—indoor and outdoor—ex-governesses, indigent gentlewomen, etc. Suzanne Gobert serves as an example. She appears from France in the late 'fifties and is petted and trained with indifferent results. She grows up sulky, unhelpful, does not keep up her French, her one pedagogic asset. Wrestling with a chest of drawers, Suzanne is heard to say, "Ce n'est pas locké, c'est seulement stuck." Beyond her are the more definite objects of charity —Miss Synnot's errand boys, for instance.

Throughout these decades Marianne kept tolerable health, gradually becoming less mobile. In the 'fifties and 'sixties she was still rushing everywhere, then her activities declined until her longest expedition was from Clapham to Milton, then even that became tiring, even Sophy at Roehampton, even Henry across the Common were an effort, and by the time my recollections of her start she was wheeled about the room in a chair. When old people become immobile criticism of them is stimulated, and we are reaching a period when she will be widely discussed behind her back.

The intelligent young women of the new generation—and it is they who did most of the discussing—do not compare gracefully with their predecessors. They are captious, unsure of themselves, interminable on the subject of their ailments, and such Darwinism as they imbibed is of the nature of secret drinking. Early in the 'seventies a group of these semispinsters formed and cohered for about twenty years— Laura Forster, Henrietta Synnot, Marion Southey, and athwart them some Wedgwoods and Darwins. Many letters have been preserved from Laura Forster to Charles Darwin's eldest daughter, her lifelong friend; Miss Darwin became Mrs. Litchfield and she is the immortal "Aunt Etta" of Gwen Raverat's *Period Piece*. Miss Forster never married. Released from Stisted by her parents' death, she followed the Thornton pattern of intellectual and philanthropic activity, but she could be censorious of her elders, and is constantly taking them up and dusting them before she replaces them, with a word of commendation, on their shelf. In her later life she changed—became gentler, wiser, greater.

Darwinism was of course anathema at the rectory, but my grandfather had become so remote from events that he had not realised its full enormity. It was otherwise at Clapham, where Marianne, as sharp as a needle, read what she wanted in the way she wanted to read it.

Miss Forster to Miss Darwin (April 8, 1871):

It rather consoles me to hear that my writing has the single merit of being easy to read, its so ugly to look at, and what Mony minds more is 'so unimportant'—the defect she finds hardest to bear in men or women.

Did I tell you that my character for orthodoxy got a most welcome rise before I left Clapham? Mony began recommending F. Galton's Hereditary Genius to me, to my astonishment, for it is not the least in her line. I said I had read and admired it, 'but do you agree with it?' said she. I said I was not a good judge, but he seemed to me to have proved his point thoroughly, and asked if she had read the book, she said no, but she was glad I had, as it must quite confute the Darwin theory that we inherited things from animals if F. Galton proved we got them from our fathers and mothers! Isn't that a nice bit of logic! Just that rather pleased me, but it is provoking to hear judgments dogmatically pronounced by people who won't take the trouble to go skin deep.

Another letter begins in gay conspiratorial tone; Miss Darwin, safe in scientific Down, has proposed a showdown in Evangelical Clapham.

I cannot picture to myself anything more appalling, my dear Harriot, than your proposal for a Clapham explosion. My life wouldn't be worth a minutes purchase. Inglis Synnot is always declaring it is not here, and that he expects every time he comes down to see me hung up on one of the large oaks opposite our house but I must say I should prefer that alternative to being drowned in the Cock Pond. . . .

What a very odd turn of mind it is in Thorntons to object to the only thing that in my mind annihilates impropriety, i.e. the details that build up a theory. I am so impressed by the whole that I can only see the details thro' it. **Mony** is so impressed with the details that she thinks a whole made up of such must be a climax of horror which only the depraved can understand. She thinks me very perverse and cannot conceive why I should have gone bad upon one point, when in the ordinary relations of life I am what she thinks too particular to make either a good nurse or invalid.

She has here indicated a weak point in the family outfit: its indifference to experiment—exemplified at the philosophic fête at Battersea Rise in 1808—and its refusal to accept the results of experiments if they are unpleasing. She herself agrees it is "against one's taste to come from furry animals, tidal or otherwise," but she could bear it for the sake of the general grandeur of the scheme. While remaining a devout Christian she believes "it is of practical use to get a just estimate of one's place in creation," and she has been helped to do this by Mr. Darwin's books, particularly by the *Descent of Man;* "I suppose your Father is not likely to moderate his demand for time by allowing sudden changes or jumps of any kind?"

It is a thoughtful letter, and shows a profound difference of outlook between the generations. There were also differences of temperament, and these receive copious and petulant expression. Miss Forster, like her Synnot cousins before her, had been offered a home at East Side. She wisely refused; a short visit was more than enough, in fact it was too much:

This is such a restless house with all its charms. Mony is so over anxious about me and I cannot express how it worries me to know beforehand whenever she enters the room that whatever I am doing will be criticised. I have a great deal of rather tiresome business and I like to give 2 hours every morning to clearing it off. Mony knows that it is inevitable, yet she will come in every ¼ of an hour and try to interrupt me with anecdotes, a bit of newspaper, or insignificant notes 'for fear I should overtire my head'! The whole thread of my reasoning is broken, and I have hardly recovered it before she is at me again.

Two years later, when she had a cottage of her own, and her aunt had inherited Milton, she writes in the same strain, and indicates further cracks in the family fabric:

Milton I believe was not unsuccessful, except that I was rather overdone there and went in for bad nights and Dr Southey made me realise more keenly than usual the hopeless crookedness of Mone and Henrietta as a couple. He says he never saw 2 people wearing each other out so much—certainly Mone's ceaseless going over of her accounts and arrangements to no very great purpose, made me feel she was older than I thought. She has still great power and judgment I think, but seems less able to give the final screw which would settle every-thing in its place firmly. I felt that we were going up steadily till just the last, and then the final touch not being given, the whole was begun from the beginning the next day.

The rest of the correspondence between the two young women deals with other family matters. Laura criticises her Aunt Sophy's children for their appalling lack of intellectual in-terests, but has to admit that they are good-tempered, well-mannered, and kind, and that this is something. She criticises and excuses her cousin Emmy Sykes on the same grounds. She criticises the three Wedgwood sisters for being too in-trospective. She criticises her youngest brother for his inter-est in sport, and particularly in racing, a vice which she presently defines as "rowing in an 8." Miss Darwin agrees: one of her own brothers once rowed in an 8, and has regretted it ever since. Miss Forster sends on Miss Darwin's warning against 8's to Master Forster. Master Forster takes no no-tice of the warning, does what he likes all his life, is athletic, amusing, vindictive, selfish, idle; models himself, he alleged, on Inglis Synnot; makes a breakaway from the family pattern.

Since the younger generation have started sniffing at old Monie, let us hear what she says about them. Not that she ever criticises her nieces—it had become a sacred duty to keep the family peace, even to the extent of ignoring quarrels. But she does let herself go on the subject of their erudite friend Snow Wedgwood.

> Great Cumberland Place
> February, 1867

I do find myself so wicked for finding Snow such a dreadful bore. She will sit next me at every meal, puts her trumpet over my plate till I can't get a mouthful into my mouth, and then begins to discuss fate and free will, the plurality of worlds, objective and subjective influences, till she drives me wild—all clever and eloquent, but so tactless a woman I never came near, and gets worse I think, its odd in a family that is all tact except herself. Then she bears footstools, screens and little politenesses all about the room after me, till she infuriated me just now into telling her I'll try to get her a place about court.

Stylistically there's no doubt as to which generation wins.

Snow (Julia) was an intellectual heavyweight who became a contributor on ethical topics to the *Spectator*, where her writings were said to be indistinguishable from those of Hutton, its editor. She also wrote *The Message of Israel* and *The Moral Ideal*. Here we touch my own literary career, for I assisted her in the revised edition of the last-named work (1907). She was an old lady then, and most pleasant to devil for. Indeed most of that group matured when they had passed middle age.

TWO

Educational

THE FAMILY CHATTER with which the previous chapter has abounded gives but an imperfect picture of Marianne's daily life. For now comes the main period of her educational activity. The facts relating to it are not easy to come by. I do not know what schools she started and financed, or partially financed, or how often she taught in them or what she taught. Her business correspondence, unlike her private correspondence, is exiguous. A school for Tradesmen's Daughters, in Acre Square—"my Middlings," she called them—is the most definite of her institutions; the girls attending it paid. And there is also mention of a school for Raggeds and of another for 2/8s—which may mean for infants between the ages of two and eight. After the passing of the Elementary Education Act of 1870 the scene so far clears as to reveal her coping with a new type of human being, namely the School Inspector. But the schools remain obscure.

Her educational tradition derived from Hannah More and from her parents. As soon as she had learnt anything, indeed almost as soon as she could talk and walk, she was taken to any handy school and encouraged to impart her knowledge to the less fortunate. The early nineteenth-century scene was of an educational simplicity that we cannot imagine. The carriage stops, the pious occupants get out and teach, and drive on. We have come across her "baby settlements" (p. 142), and Anna her schoolmistress (p. 85). To the end of her life she felt herself entitled to make informal inspection of elementary schools, and some of her relatives retained the feeling into the present century.

There were two motives for her zeal over education. First and foremost was her dislike of ignorance and her eighteenth-century faith in reason. If children knew more, they would grow up happier, healthier, and more helpful. And by "knowing more" she meant fuller knowledge of the way in which to get the best out of their lives. They must therefore—and now we approach her second motive—be educated according to their station. Like Hannah More, she assumed that the existing structure of society was satisfactory and would continue, and since the section of it to which she belonged required servants and governesses, she was anxious that education should produce servants and governesses of good quality. If this second motive is accented, she can be shown as craftily defending her own class, and as breeding up servitors for it. The accent (I believe) should be on the first motive.

To begin with the governesses—where we shall not find her at her most charitable. She knew a great deal about the unfortunate creatures, for there had been a long series of them at Battersea Rise, and a shorter, cheaper series at Stisted. Anxious to transmit her experiences, she now composes a jobation of over 4,000 words in which she addresses an imaginary specimen of the tribe and advises it how to behave. It is an amusing, clever, and discreditable piece of writing. The employer has too much the whip hand in it, and flicks too knowingly at the sore places. When she was advising an actual living governess (my own mother will be a case in point) she could be charming, sympathetic, and subtly on an equality. When she generalises she becomes hard and superior.

The jobation is undated. 'Fifties or 'sixties? Some of the MS. must have been lost, for it starts in midstream:

But you will ask whether I mean a poor Governess should have no rest or respite from the worry of the children throughout the day: and you will be surprised if I tell you that I believe many of the sufferings of Governesses arise from vacuity of mind, and having too much time to dwell upon the little troubles and indignities incident to their position—in a way which would never occur to persons whose whole thoughts were devoted to their occupation. When school hours are over and the Children dismissed to play—the very time when *real* education goes on— the Governess feels tired with teaching and indisposed for much mental exertion, new and amusing books are not often placed within her reach, so she takes to fancy needle-work or letter writing, and either employment leaves her thoughts at liberty to ponder over every little incident that has lately hurt her feelings—'Certainly Mrs —— is offended about something— she helped three of the children before me today at breakfast. The very pudding I disliked is the one we constantly have now —and boiled mutton which always makes me rather sick is ordered oftener than ever. The children were all taken out this afternoon and I was never invited or even told they were going.—Old nurse gets more impertinent every day, she called out the two little ones without even asking my leave to have their frocks ironed, and Mr —— who was so very kind and cordial when I first came, used to light my candle in the evening and ask me how I did, now goes on reading as if he did not know I was in the room. . . .'

And so on. Marianne's remedy being that the governess, when her teaching is over, should follow her little charges into the garden or playroom, and take an intelligent interest in their affairs, instead of an unintelligent interest in her own. A severe remedy: and throughout the jobation it is always assumed that it is the employee who is to blame, whereas the impertinent servants, unreasonable mamas, and naughty children could not be any better than they are. She is further charged with not taking care of her health—to the grave detriment of her utility.

It is very rare to find a strong Governess, partly I believe from depression arising from their triste position and partly from the absurd manner in which many manage themselves. Removed from a mother's affectionate care—or a sister's watchful expostulation—in the matters of eating and drinking, of going to bed and going out, they will often do just what is sure to make them ill, tho' they will not allow it, assuring everyone that to act in these respects like the rest of the world would kill them. It is part of that morbid strangeness which often belongs to the profession.

And the attempt of a governess to make herself interesting by "being different" from the rest of the household, and by manufacturing peculiarities, is shrewdly analysed, and severely reprimanded.

When she stops nagging the governess about the conduct of her private life and considers her as a disciplinarian, she has some valuable things to say.

Do not tempt children to say what is false by questions and cross-questions upon all that has happened, when timid and nervous children will always appear guilty, and bold and hardened ones seem innocent. Tell them that you leave them to their own consciences. . . . It is better that twenty guilty children should not be punished than that one innocent one should be unjustly suspected. Above all—on this and on other occasions, beware of giving a child what is called 'a good talking to'. I do not believe that any child ever yet was the better for 'a good talking to'. A volley of words rouses their little angry hearts and confuses their little weary heads. And the scripture rule of telling our brother of his fault 'he and ye alone' is above all true with children—it is often needful for others that an offence should be noticed publicly, but I do not believe that the culprit herself is ever mended by anything that does not pass with her alone.

One wonders for whom this pessimistic and acute treatise was intended. Was it to be printed? Was it to be circulated amongst prospective applicants? It must have filled middle-class girls with despair, and inclined them towards any profession except teaching. But for most of them no other profession existed.

Turning from governesses to schoolmistresses and pupil teachers, we find the same anxiety that they shall be sensibly trained, and the anxiety finds more agreeable expression. Back in the 'fifties she writes to Miss Louisa Inglis about an institution called Whitelands which might provide a suitable under-mistress for the little village school at Milton. As a rule she is suspicious of institutions, but Whitelands is an exception:

The system of training there seems to me perfect and they make a very great point of needlework, particularly cutting out, and shirt-making and gown-making as well as fine work. There seems such a desire to make them really humble unpretending Village Teachers, making them clean and cook and iron (not wash) that they mayn't fancy themselves fine ladies *because* they teach them Geography & History and so on. The only things they don't set them to are scouring and washing, and they say 'The nature of these employments (scouring and washing) is such as to unfit the hands for fine needlework in which it is absolutely essential the mistresses should excel. But every effort is made to give them just views of the worth of humble domestic duties on the performance of wh. so much of the comfort of both rich and poor depend—a happy change may be hoped for in the race of young servants who issue from our schools if we obtain mistresses able and willing to instruct them in the proper method of performing the simpler offices of their station. . . .' I have copied this bit out, I think it sounds so sensible.

It does; but it must be observed that the two motives above mentioned are again at work: the desire to educate the poor combines, in varying degrees, with the desire for a good supply of servants. Significantly it is the education of girls that most concerned her. Boys, though she liked them—well, they could emigrate, they could plough, they could rise in life, they were less requisite domestically. She conceived of society as an agglomeration of homes and of helpers in the home. She had little perception of the industrialism that was rapidly engulfing both girls and boys, and it was only at Hereford during the visit to John and Emilia Venn, that the existence of a shop-assistant class became vivid to her.

As for the schoolchildren, they figure most when there is a school treat; we seldom meet them at their lessons. When the Synnot boy and girl were young themselves (1855) a rollicking Christmas party took place, described by their aunt with gusto. Henrietta had returned from her Aunt Isabella's a little bilious as usual, but was well enough to go to the school, where the festivities were held.

Inglis was the life of the party, he did his conjuring tricks for them, made a smoking pudding in Suzanne Gobert's bonnet, hid the Missie's gold ring in the centre of an orange, burnt Miss Combe's pocket handf. and then made it right again, handed round a glass full of ink and turned it into water before their eyes, and a number such performances which made them scream till I was all but deafened, then we fed them, then we toyed them, then we drest them, the two latter were at Henrietta's sole expence and wonderfully she managed it.

The tea and cakes she and Sarah managed for £1.5.—holly was 2^s (how I grudged it), and the 3^s over of £1.10 she persuaded me to give Sarah for her trouble, for she had sat up so late doing the cakes. Dough and baking were 8/2, currants 5^s, butter 4/8, eggs 2^s, sugar 1/6, tea 1/10, milk 1/6. There was a great plenty. The Bowyers helped us to feed but weren't able to get to the conjuring wh. was the best of the 2. Inglis took his dog and set it up on the chimney piece with a cap and a pipe in its mouth to their infinite delight. Inglis isn't well to-day. . . .

Fifteen years later there was another school festivity which deserves special mention:

Last Tuesday Knowles brought TENNYSON to call on me, and not finding me at home led the unfortunate man on to the school where I was, and where he really was very pleasant, investigating all that was going on, especially the Infants, for whom he left 2/6 for sugar plumbs. As soon as he left the room I told my Misses and Teachers who he was. I kept my senses thro' the visit, but they lost theirs entirely. Annie flew down to 'Tell mother to look out and see his back' and Mary Lee exclaimed 'It's he that did that piece about the six 'undred. Oh if I'd known I'd have shown off our Tommy who isn't 2 and yet can fight and march and do all like a soldier.'

They ruled that sugar plumbs were too evanescent a memorial of the Laureate's visit—one proposed gingerbread nuts as more consequential, another a picture and I expected some one would propose a brass to be inserted in the chair where he sat, as some one did for Gladstone. However it ended in 2 lbs of ginger nuts and a dreadful little Toy man who squeaks and beats cymbals, and is to be shown to the babies once a week.

On one occasion the schoolchildren do come to the front and take political action. It is during a No Popery scare in the 'fifties. There had been a Catholic settlement in Clapham, described by Cardinal Wiseman as a "Little Paradise of cheerfulness, comfort and respectability," but otherwise described by Miss Thornton. I do not share her rabid anti-Catholicism any more than her mild anti-Semitism, but I am writing her biography not my own, and what she says is: "On opening a cottage door I can instantly tell whether the inhabitants are Cats or Protestants, and very odd it is that this should be. I never could discover the connection between dirt and popery. And I cannot take Catholic children into the Schools for their thieving propensities." She does not however take the Papist threat seriously when she thinks "to what shifts Pio Nono has been reduced of late"; a reaction is probable "and the fear will soon be that we will recede into Puritanism."

She then turns to her schoolgirls:

You will think my head very full of those people but I have just been writing 'my Pastoral' to my 'Middlings', my tradespeoples' Girls School, who I hear from their Governess are in a state of fever heat on the subject and I am afraid call the little papists names, and incite their brothers to chalk the walls, and certainly assisted in dressing some Cardinals and Archbishops for burning.—Now I have no objection to seeing Guy Fawkes flame as in olden times, he was a sort of hobgoblin, and whatever reality there was in him deserved it, but I cant approve of Bishops being so used, or indeed anybody, for the thirst for flames is one that grows with what it looks upon. So I have begged they will confine their protestant spirit to avoiding the Cat. Chapel which they like very much to look into as a spectacle, and to avoiding all the faults of popery, idleness, deceit &ct. in their own conduct. They are a set of nice girls, but no doubt are led away by the popular clamour that is so strong in that class of life.

This leads her to discuss the conversion to Catholicism of Henry Wilberforce, a son of her old friend, who had previously been a clergyman in the Church of England; nothing could have surprised her more:

He was a sharp clever well read rather sceptical man, a match for any priestly humbug one would think. I said this to T. Macaulay adding it would have surprised me far less if *Sam* had been induced to believe in the winking Madonna and such nonsense. 'Oh' says Tom M. 'if Bishop Sam had given up his Bishopric there would have been no miracle in the matter, the Madonna would *really* have winked I am sure'. Oh dear! to you and me it is more a matter of crying than laughing that their fathers' sons should have run such a race. . . .

It is curious to compare her reaction with a similar reaction today, when we may observe one able person after another embracing dogmatism and sneering at reason. She felt (as some of us do) the ground slipping beneath her, and it is to her credit that she could still say "the thirst for flames is one that grows with what it looks upon" and could still keep her feet upon the uneasy path of religious tolerance. Would that her Pastorals to her Middlings had been preserved! They would have been amusing and shrewd and something more.

Henrietta Synnot took a prominent part in all these educational activities. It was a strong link between the two women. The difficult creature never showed her difficult side to her social inferiors, she was charming to mistresses and pupils, she ran a "Popular Book Club" at Acre Square which included a personal delivery service at cottages. She could comfort the superannuated. When Marianne was not well enough to entertain old Annie Chambers, Henrietta "promised to do her thoroughly and so she did, for A. C.

did nothing but praise her when she came in to me, but the old are easily flattered by the attentions of the young." Her energy was endless. Once she tried to own a school of her own and would have put down £500. Moreover she had a rollicking sense of the ridiculous and could bring back ludicrous tales of what was going on in the world of education.

>Horry Zontal
>Perpen Dickler
>Here's a Mangle
>Here's my Mother

sang the children making angles with their fingers. Or:

>See the maid a milking going
>   How she wags about her tail
>Now she's kicking now she's lowing
>   Now she's overset the pail

Or Henrietta herself sang:

>Whene'er I take my walks abroad
>   How many poor I see.
>I scarcely ever think of them
>   And they never think of me.

In later years, as her ascendancy increased, she involved her aunt in some unwise schemes. Sensible Laura Forster came across one when she was staying at Clapham in 1875, and unburdened herself on the subject to her Darwinian confidante:

Dearest Harriot, it would be uncommonly nice if we could have a week together at Down. . . . Here I am shivering at the idea of 6 workhouse girls coming to be trained here under all sorts of impulsive methods, yet even Mone doesn't see the elements of defeat. Ten days ago H^{tte} was full of tempting a capital woman away from a very satisfactory employ, separating

her from an ill daughter and establishing her at the Home with
a high salary. . . . I was obliged to advise her to say nothing
till at least the present matron had her warning to leave. H.
scouted the idea of uncertainty but now comes a letter to say
the girls can't be legally sent except to an *industrial school.*
So now H. writes off to say it will be that, and she'll have a
certificated mistress, and her plan is to transfer the Infant
school-mistress, a girl of 5 or 6 and 20, unrivalled in her present position, to the Home. She may be and is a very nice girl
but I can't see that the power of keeping 60 babies good and
happy proves her competent to manage such difficult creatures
as Mrs Senior's report shews these 6 girls to be.

Mone doesn't like my hinting this, but says the only reason
the Home did not do was because there were too clever women
on the Committee. . . . This scattering about of brilliant
ideas and ingenious contrivances, without any consideration being given to the working of them out, frightens me to death.
It will give the impression that women of necessity work hap-
hazard and dont care what they go at so long as they go.

Whether the six workhouse girls arrived, who controlled
them, and where the Home was I do not know, but the letter
shows that aunt and niece had something new to face, namely
Officialdom with its rules, regulations, prohibitions, and dis-
tinctions, and—it must be added—with its superior expert
knowledge. The aspect of Officialdom that most concerned
them was School Inspection. It gradually developed and
became more intense after the passing of the 1870 Education
Act and they were constantly involved in it for the next
fifteen years.

Marianne behaved very well, considering that she was an
independent lady who had become accustomed to getting her
own way. She managed to consider each Inspector on his
merits, and to give praise wherever it was due.

I dont think I caught cold the examination day, for anxiety about our 2/8s kept me warm enough, they did very well on the whole, but as each child was trotted out, imagine our feelings. H. says next time we'll give a breakfast to the Inspector and his Assistant. They enjoyed their luncheon, but what was the use, the children were all marked by that time. Tinting is a first rate man, but it was not his civility to us or his cleverness that I valued so much as his seeming such a really good man, so anxious to improve the school as he has done I'm sure for the rest of its life.——He suggested some very good alterations in the religious instructions which I *will* have carried out, tho' he says its difficult to make pupil teachers believe that knowing the genealogy of the Kings of Judah and Israel will not take the child^n to Heaven.

Two letters to my mother (March 1878) describe a grimmer visitation: "We had our first inspection, that in the 3 r's yesterday, and atrociously the child^n seemed to me to do—— but I gave our Spectre pigeon pie for lunch, and hope for a good report. Hernaman comes tomorrow to see about our ——" The next word is illegible, unfortunately: for it might have thrown light on the organisation of the school. On the following day Hernaman arrived.

We've been examined all the morning by that horrid Hernaman. H^{tta} was there first and when I came she whispered to me 'I have wrung that man's neck twice over already' and so she had, convicted him of mistakes about the New Code wh. she'd studied more than he had, but it was a pity for it put him into such a cantankerous state he didn't know how to scold hard enough, said the child^n knew nothing, nor the teachers either, and were so fidgitty—why he kept the wretches 3 hours and $\frac{1}{2}$ doing nothing whatever, who wouldn't be fidgitty. But matters changed when we got to luncheon. The Rector, Erskine Clarke and Mr Sharp and I propounded the fact that most of what was taught was nonsense, specially grammar——because Herna-

man had rated the child[n] for not knowing a predicate noun
from an absolute or some such rot, and all joined in chorus
except Hernaman, and now they are all gone.

It was in connection with the New Code that she went into
authorship, and appeared for the only time of her life in
print. To her biographer the event is an important one and
must be described carefully.

She contributed to a series of reading booklets for children, the precise title of the series being *The School Man-
ager's Series of Reading Books Adapted to the Require-
ments of the New Code.* Before I discuss the extent and the
character of her contribution, there is a letter of hers to
be quoted (May 1869) which refers to the origin of the
project.

We've had Allister here for three days, as inoffensive a visitor as one can possibly have, I think, for at the expense of 2^d
for a Pall Mall he will read steadily the whole evening. Yesterday tho' we'd a sort of miniature dinner party in the interests
of the School Managers' Reading Book which Strahan has un-
dertaken, and Knowles declared he would take twice as much
interest in it if we had him to dine, which Enty, who had met
him at Knowles declared he was too dirty a little bookseller to
sit by a clean table cloth.

"Allister" is Canon Alexander Grant, recently Inspector of
Schools, and editor designate of the proposed series: he was
connected with the Grants she had known and loved at Bat-
tersea Rise. Strahan the bookseller was the publisher of the
Contemporary, with which Knowles was still connected.
"Enty," so snooty about Strahan, is Henrietta Synnot.

The *Reading Books* consist of an Introductory Primer
and six "Standards," designed to cover the corresponding
classes of an elementary school. All seven booklets were pub-

lished separately in 1874 by Messrs. Lockwood & Co., 7 Stationers' Hall Court. There is a short preface by Canon Grant, whose share was limited to revision and suggestion; the items for reading are chosen or written by various authors "who have had opportunities possessed by very few people of gaining an intimate knowledge of the character and capacities of those for whom they write." In the loose atmosphere of the nursery I used to be told that "Aunt Monie wrote the Reading Books." She did not. The series is a hotchpotch. It opens with the words "ba be bi bo bu by." I do not believe that she wrote these, or the poems by Coleridge and Campbell, or the sections on geology and astronomy, or the historical and geographical sections, or the heavy mawkish stories. It is only in the dramatic pieces that I detect her. I could swear they are hers. Even in the Introductory Primer her voice is recognisable, though it is speaking to tiny tots:

Master What is the rea-son Jim is not at school today?
Frank Please, sir, he is gone to pri-son or at least to the lock-up house be-cause he threw a stone at a train.
M. And he is right-ly serv-ed too. I think I saw you, Frank, throw-ing stones as I came to-day by the Long Pond.
F. Please, sir, I was only do-ing it to make the ducks and geese swim quick.
M. How should you like to have stones thrown at you to make you run quick? The poor ducks and geese mind it as much as you do.
F. I did not think of that.
M. That is just it, you do not think. I know a la-dy who was in a train in France, and some boy that did not think threw a stone at her, which cut her eye—.

The lady is Lady Inglis, hit by a stone at Boulogne in 1851, the Long Pond is on Clapham Common, and the hu-

manist attitude, the appeal to thought, the quiet repartee,
are Marianne's own.

Mother   Tom, come here, I want you. What made you be-have
so to my Will and throw him down?

Tom   Be-cause he call-ed me names: he said I was a guy, and
I said if he call-ed me names any more, I would pay him
for it; and he did, and so I gave him a push, but I did
not mean to hurt him.

Mother   What tire-some boys you are, that you can-not go
to school and back with-out fighting. Why did you call
Tom a guy, Will? What did you mean by it?

Will   He has such an old coat, and then he rub-bed out my
sum at school, and I had to do it a-gain.

She found boys like Will and Tom irresistible. "Silence
in the pig market, let the old sow speak first!" shouted a
nephew as he rushed into her crowded drawing room. When
she rebuked him, "What did I tell you. I knew the old sow'd
speak first," said he, and she collapsed.

By the time the Fourth Standard is reached, tiresomeness
has taken an intellectual turn. Shades of the prison house
begin to close around the growing scholar, and we have two
tense dialogues between Mary Saunders, a pupil teacher,
and the rebellious Sophy Williams, aged twelve.

The Inspector

Mary   You must look sharp, Sophy, or you will not have
made up your attendances before the Inspector comes.
What has kept you away so much from school?

Sophy   I don't know—one thing and another—sometimes
mother wanted me, sometimes my shoes were bad, and
my sister has been at home from service, and I wanted
to be along of her . . . Never you be afraid. It's only
the three r's that the Spectre comes to see about isn't it?

M. I do wish you would learn to pronounce your words properly. 'In-spect-or' means one who looks *into* a thing. 'Spectre' means a ghost.

S. And the best name of the two, for the thoughts of his coming seem to frighten everybody like a ghost—but I am not a bit afraid. I can read and write and sum and that's all that's expected.

M. But if you read so that nobody understands you, if you write such a bad hand that nobody can read it, and if your sums are always wrong; what's the use?

S. Well and what's the use of this Inspector as you call him coming here? Haven't we teachers enough already? What right has he here?

M. Well you know what taxes are, I hope. They are the money paid by the people to the Queen which she spends for their good; some of it on prisons in which to punish offenders, some in police to detect them, and some in schools, hoping that when the poor are better educated there will be less need of police and prisons. Now of course it is right the Queen should see that the money is properly spent.

S. That's it is it? This horrid spectre comes from the Queen. Well I expect I shall pull through, and anyhow you know you say I have a very good memory.

The Day after the Examination

Sophy Was there ever such a shame, teacher, not to pass me in anything? I am sure that the Inspector took a spite against me.

Mary Well you made three mistakes in reading, four in spelling, and every sum but one was done wrongly: not always worked wrongly but you did not seem to understand the question.

S. Its such a horrid shame not to set us regular sums, but to give us questions in words, enough to puzzle anybody.

[*263*]

Its so hard when I know the multiplication table so
well; and then my geography was the shamefulest thing
of all. I had learnt the names of all the countries of
England, and——

M. Not countries but counties.

S. What a fuss about one little letter! What's the odds?
Well when he asked me what I knew about the geography of England, I rattled out the names of Northumberland, Cumberland, Westmoreland all as perfect as perfect, and would have done the rest, but he stopped me
by asking me to tell him what there was in the room that
came from Northumberland, as if it mattered: and
then he wanted to know if I had a friend in Durham
which way I should go, and what counties I should pass
through. I have no friends in Durham and mistook it
for Devon. And then he wanted to know where knives
and scissors are made, and tea-trays and things, and
I was to find them all on the map.

M. What! the knives and tea-trays?

S. No, I tell you, but the places. Who cares what comes from
those bits of painted paper they call a map? Its all
such rubbish. Bible lessons and all, too, it was all alike.
I had learnt up all the kings of Judah, and a heap of
dates, and knew the names of the parables and miracles;
but because I couldn't tell him anything to be learnt
from the story of Joseph, he said I might as well never
have read it . . . Well I do think school is dreadfully
dull work, and to tell the truth that is mostly the reason
I don't come oftener.

M. I thought so; dull it must be, when you don't care a
farthing about anything I am teaching you . . . It *is*
stupid work to learn strings of names like a parrot,
without ever caring to enquire what they mean.

S. Well, teacher, you always have been very good to me
when I did come, never knocked me about as some do,

       and I will try now to come constant, and perhaps I
       shall pass the examination.

M.   I have no doubt you will if you take to liking your lessons
       from a wish to get on, and to improve yourself; but if
       you only care to pass in the three r's I am afraid you
       won't.

Poor Sophy's problem afflicts others in our educational
system including university dons: it is the old problem of
the letter that kills but seduces, because being a letter it can
be easily memorised. Marianne believed in the spirit, the
pursuit of which must be continuous and may be tiring.
Another dialogue, "The Candidate for a Pupil Teacher-
ship," inculcates the same lesson. In form, and sometimes
in sentiments, she was indebted to Hannah More, but she
had a lighter touch, and sketched rather than underlined
her religious and moral conclusions.

The longest and liveliest of the dialogues is "On Emigration." It handles a subject that had always interested her.
Its tone is mischievous and indeed irresponsible: we assist
at the baiting of a simple countrywoman, a Mrs. Jones, by
her son, her husband, her daughter, and her doctor, who
want her to take part in a family migration to Australia.
Gallantly does she resist, alleging snakes and savages, and
even making capital out of a kangaroo. "Ah those machines
I suppose they have got out there too," she cries, when her
son has compared a kangaroo's pouch to a perambulator,
"I never saw but one, and hate the lazy servants that won't
be at the trouble of carrying the precious children, but shove
them around like bad fish." (One hears in passing the voice
of Nurse Hunter.) Mrs. Jones abuses scholarship, which
puts such ideas into her son's head, and machinery, which
those who invented it will be punished for—also how's she

to get the cows drove that distance—think of the keep—and
all the shell fish and rubbish to eat.—And anyhow she will
not leave Mrs. Smith—they have hung their clothes on week
days on the same lines—not that she ever sees Mrs. Smith
now, who has been taken away to a place hard to get at
seemingly, and called Yorkshire.

This last remark was unsound, for Mrs. Smith and her
husband are also known to be discontented with agricultural
conditions in England and might be persuaded to join the
emigration to Australia. Mrs. Jones then yields, but with
conditions:

It would make all the difference certainly—Mrs Smith, and
the cows. Well I never did stand out against father yet in the
long run; he's been a good husband to me, and I am no scholar,
and so, I suppose, can't be a judge—only of what I do like.
But I seem to begin to feel that if matters went worse next
winter I should reflect on myself for speaking my mind so out
and out about not going. After all, if I have you all about
me, and little Tottie does grow stout, besides the cows and
Mrs Smith coming, I shall be able to make myself comfortable.
So father, dear, I'll go. Only one thing more; let me go as far
as I can in Willings' cart; I know he will lend it: but don't
ask me to get into a train. It may be quicker and I never saw
one near; but as it roars and skurries along by Hayes Hill it
frightens me to death. I am sure all the people that get into
it must be killed, for how should that senseless engine know
how to go or where to go? I am pretty stout on my legs, and
can walk a good bit, and Willings' cart will do the rest.

This is pleasant comedy, but does not the writer of it reveal a divided purpose? She wants at the same time to poke
fun at the working classes, and to encourage them to read.
Perhaps they were more easily gulled eighty years ago than
they would be today.

I do not think that the series was much used, though the press was favourable. "Simple without being at all Silly," said the *Athenaeum*. "Impossible to speak too highly"—*John Bull*. The *Spectator* found (which I do not) "a skilful gradation of lessons and a judicious choice of extracts," and the *Literary World* exclaimed, "If books like these do not make the young folk eager to read we know not what will." Today, neither the Library of the Ministry of Education nor the original publishers * can find any trace of the little venture and the only copies I have seen are my own. Aunt Monie has had the seven booklets bound into two volumes and has inscribed both volumes to my mother for my use, and dated them 1883. I also have an MS. dialogue in her handwriting; not a remarkable one—Mama starts to explain the facts of life to Mary and Charlie and naturally does not get far—but it provides stylistic evidence for her authorship in the series.

* I should like to take this opportunity of thanking them for the trouble they took.

Milton Bryan

MILTON BRYAN or Bryant in Bedfordshire has flickered on the edge of Marianne's life ever since 1815. In 1873 it moves to the centre and faintly illumines her declining years.

Let me recapitulate Milton's mild story. Sir Hugh Inglis had inherited it through his first wife, Sir Robert had inherited it from Sir Hugh, had failed to found a dynasty there, had left it to Milady for her lifetime, and, after her, to Marianne. His interests lying in London and in foreign travel, he had used the house as a dumping ground for his womenfolk. His sister, the tenuous and timid Miss Loo, spent much time there, so did his wife, and they were constantly visited by various Thornton sisters. Thus the house acquired a character it never lost—that of a resort for aging ladies, who pottered about the garden and the little village, and drove through the quiet lanes. As time went on, Sir Robert made additions to his will, and arranged that after Marianne's death the property should go to his godson Inglis Synnot, and, when he died, to Henrietta Synnot. Sir Robert died in 1855, Milady in 1873, and Marianne plus Henrietta now entered into possession. They knew the house inside out already, so it was possession without thrills. Marianne's age was now seventy-six, her niece's thirty-three. "It is possible," said the lawyer at one stage, "er—is it possible that Miss

Synnot may some day—er—contract some more intimate relationship?" It was thought unlikely, and consequently Inglis Synnot's little widow got inserted into the sequence of inheritance. She was appalled: "If I ever own Milton, whatever shall I do?" she gasped. "Oh how I do hope Henrietta will live for ever!" The lawyer finally extricated her, and what happened to the estate after Henrietta's death I do not know. I think it now belongs to the Duke of Bedford.

The Manor House of Milton is a pleasant countrified gabled building, looking south over a garden and sloping fields. Much timber. It backs on to the churchyard and the village. The site is huddled and unimpressive. The great park of Woburn Abbey is close and Milton is ducally dominated. Sir Robert did however become Sheriff of Bedfordshire, and was benevolent locally, and he did his duty by education. He supported two schools: an elementary one and another for boys. He inspected them when he was in residence, and in the elementary one he allowed no corporal punishment. Mrs. Brittan, the mistress, might at the most impose a fool's cap for inattention or a red-cloth tongue for talking, and even then Sir Robert would say, "I feel sure, Mrs Brittan, this little girl is very sorry for having been naughty, so I hope you will ob*leege* me by forgiving her." Joseph Paxton, first the gardener and then the friend of the Duke of Devonshire and the creator of the Crystal Palace, had been at the school and Sir Robert had given him a prize, which he is said to have cherished. Jane Burrows, the Forsters' nurse, had also been at the school. Jane Burrows' mother kept the village shop, Mother had once kept the Red Lion, now Mother keeps the village shop, there is a dell in the garden, there is a Temple of Vesta in the garden, Leighton Buzzard Station is almost eight miles off. . . . The slow rustic stream trickles, sometimes thickening into commitments. Little snags abounded. Concerned at what her aunt might be letting herself in for, Miss Laura Forster wrote Miss Darwin another of her competent letters:

I go to Milton tomorrow to meet Mony as she fancies I can help her to arrange matters there. I am so thankful she is likely to make a good arrangement about the place, without my having to go there—she offered to pay me handsomely to live there but I am one of those wonderfully well to do women who want neither a larger house nor a bigger income, so I begged off. So she is going to lend it to a Mrs Havart an old friend of the Inglises and a very practical sensible woman who is fond of the people and likes the place and her son was the only popular clergyman there of late years, and he died after he had been there a year.

She is to keep a bedroom always at Mony's disposal and to vacate the house for 3 months every summer. She takes in Indian children [*i.e.*, Indian-born English children] she is most grateful for the large house rent free, and will be sure to see that Mony is not cheated by her workmen. So that is a great weight off my mind.

The introduction of an extra old lady into Milton did not solve its problems or abate its heritage of "paupers and pensioners." Mrs. Havart's Indian children damaged the furniture and before long she departed for Bournemouth "with her cow and her horse and her ass and all that is hers, and that's nearly everything." An attempt at a seasonal let to a hunting man fell through because Henrietta's invalid horses occupied too much of the stables. An attempt to make a change in estate management nearly led to a lawsuit with a neighbour. There was a flare-up with the rector because Aunt Mony's groom left before the Church Militant prayer in order to fetch her pony: "he is in an irritable state, the church is so thin and the chapel so full, but I can't help that." There was extravagance inside the house, there was theft, there was scandal when an upper housemaid was seduced by a churl of low degree. But if the function of Milton was to provide an old lady with a summer resort for a few years, it certainly succeeded. She got more pleasure than worry, and she could afford the wastage, for Milady had left her a substantial legacy. The following letter, headed "Sunday, Milton, pouring!!!," defiantly states her case.

We've settled to call this 'the Cripples home'. It's absurd to see the dinner table set with a low chair for Mrs Wedgwood, a soft cushioned one for me, a high-backed prie-Dieu for Aunt Sophy and a soft backed for Emmy. And there's such a clatter of sticks and crutches when we move. Allen and Gibson, the gardener and coachman, carry Mrs W. and also me up and down stairs. I go up good when they arrive, but Aunt S. told them to go away altogether—she and Emmy could quite well carry up Mrs W.

We *are* full but I think it does a house good sometimes to stretch it like an Indian rubber band. Besides our staff of 6 maids, we have Ing's daughter, Mrs Wedgwood's cook, Mrs Wedgwood's cook's husband, the Farrells, Emmy's maid, Mrs W's maid, and my sick nurse!! Staines is in a state of intense hilarity because I told her to feed them on what she thought they liked, so there's pork, goose, beef, steak puddings and pies without limit. And I dont know why a house with 17 bedrooms should have been left me but to give pleasure to somebody, and I prefer large parties in the kitchen to having them in the first class waiting rooms.

Two other letters of the time, though not written at Milton, strike the same lively note. In the first she is visited by the Director of a Hospital:

He told us that they had 30 cases of typhoid in the Middlesex owing to bad water for the cows in Devonshire, and said they are invisible insects in the water, but when milked into the pails in Devonshire they are great grandmothers by the time they get to town. Oh, says Mr C, *I'm* told they don't take three minutes for their accouchements. Nurse was bringing in the tea and I thought all my best china would have been smashed, she laughed so.—And now perhaps I'll tell you that Trollope is the *real* cause of my neither attending to my duties or pleasures. Why I stick to the book [the Autobiography] like glue I can't imagine—a series of the most horrible cruelties perpetrated on him by every body who came in his way.

Thanking a sporting nephew for fish:

There arrived today at 3 oclock a fine bag of trout as many as the sands by the seashore reminding me of the miraculous draught of fishes. I ordained first that my maids should have a feast and sup on them at which there was a great hallelugh (badly spelt but you know what it means), then I sent a dishful to poor old deaf Tayloe and was going to send a basketfull to Aunt Sophy and then I've kept a lot for self and niece for dinner today and breakfast to tomorrow and I've sent cook for a book called 'fish cookery' which will enable us to pot them or pickle them.

Consequent on this summer arrangement, Milton generally appears in the documents through a haze of hot weather, flies, squashy fruit, wasps. My mother, who could also wield a lively pen, has described a sultry workhouse treat in the garden:

We were all dreadfully tired and wanted tea and sandwiches, and horror of horrors I ate a large spider which was on my sandwich, being dark I did not notice it. Henrietta marched about like a dragoon all the afternoon with her hat well over her nose, parasol under her arm, and dress hitched up on one side.

This dominating figure, always changing her plans, moves through Milton like a lost spirit. She ordered one of the invalid horses to be killed, went to Clapham to escape the execution, had a reaction, telegraphed countermanding, and became hysterical in case she was too late. The telegram arrived in time, the invalid's life was saved and its troubles intensified. Aunt Monie bore her restlessness with patience and dignity, she was never a grumbler or a regretter, and she was further helped by one of her defects: her refusal to allow that she ever made a mistake. To most onlookers the joint life with Henrietta represented a bad blunder. To her it was something upon which she had decided and in consequence nobody's business. Her niece's bad temper certainly was a serious problem. Every now and then that clever tongue said something wounding and gave offence to relatives or friends. Here the best the old lady could do was to prevaricate and confuse the evidence; it was called "Monie's deceitfulness" at the time, but deserves a more charitable title.

With this brief reference to Milton I close the period assigned to her aunthood. It may have been noticed that as her life proceeds it is becoming less distinguished socially. She had been born amongst public figures of eminence, and after her father's death there was anyhow Sir Robert Inglis, a reputable second-rater, and there was the prestige of an established household. With the withdrawal of Sir Robert and with the loss of Battersea Rise, she tended to consort with people who were from the worldly point of view less important. She was intimate with the Levens but only as a sister: she would never have dreamt of climbing into the aristocracy with their help. And she resisted the kindly efforts of Mr. James Knowles to push her up his own flight of stairs. All this (I'd say) is part of her fineness: she kept to people she liked and to work she could do. But it makes her biography decreasingly imposing, and I must warn the reader that in its final section she will consort with still smaller fry—including myself, who was almost too small to be fried.

GREAT AUNT

1879-1887

At the date of my birth the ages of the
surviving Thorntons were:

Marianne	82
Henry	79
Isabella (Mrs. Harrison)	76
Sophia (Lady Leven)	74

My Arrival

I WAS BORN at my parents' house, 6 Melcombe Place, Dorset Square, London, on January 1, 1879. Two months later I was taken down to Clapham to be christened, Miss Henrietta Synnot standing as my godmother. I had already been registered as Henry Morgan Forster, and that was to be my name. The party walked over from Aunt Monie's to the church on the Common. On the way the old verger asked my father what the baby was to be called, and he, distrait, gave his own name, Edward Morgan. This the verger wrote down upon a piece of paper. My maternal grandmother held me at the font. When the clergyman asked her what I was to be called she became afraid of the sound of her voice in a sacred edifice, and indicated the piece of paper. My mother, in a distant pew, heard the announcement with horror. I had been registered one way and christened another. What on earth was to happen! It turned out after agitated research that the christening had it, so Edward I am. Aunt Monie's reaction was characteristic. She had never liked the name Morgan, it was not a Thornton name, it was a Forster import, and to the end of her life she declared that I had been given it by mistake.

My mother, Alice Clara Whichelo ("Lily"), was the third child and the eldest daughter of Henry Mayle Whichelo and

Louisa Graham. She did not belong to Thornton circles, and
the story of her entrance into them is interesting. My grandfather was a drawing master. He had the delicacy and the
inclinations of a creative artist, and his brother, born to
easier circumstances, painted pleasing pictures of the Claude-
Turner type. He himself had to teach in Stockwell Grammar
School and other institutions of the Clapham neighbourhood.
By all accounts he was a delightful character—unselfish,
considerate, sensitive, handsome, cheerful, and alive to scenic
and architectural beauty—and the pretty verses he addressed
to his children recall those which Henry Thornton had once
addressed to little Marianne. I never had the luck to know
him. In 1866 he suddenly died (one now surmises appendi-
citis), leaving my grandmother with no money and with ten
children.

My grandmother was a lovely, lively woman, most amusing and witty, fond of pleasure, generous and improvident,
and by no means inclined to regard trials as blessings; it
may have been possible to do this at Battersea Rise, but she
had too many trials and too little room. She was always
popular and her friends helped through the disasters as well
as they could, but they were not influential or wealthy. She
had to take lodgers, Germans, whom she undercharged, and
to employ a sorry series of maids-of-all-work, whom she
scolded and spoiled. The children had to earn their living
almost in their childhood, the boys as clerks, the girls as
governesses. It seems terrible as one writes it down, cushioned
by the Welfare State, and Dickensian catastrophes did occur.
But there were good looks about and good taste and good
spirits, and it may be that these qualities form as sound a
defence against Fate as a solid education and a considered
morality. Anyhow the Whichelos muddled through. They
had no enthusiasm for work, they were devoid of public

spirit, and they were averse to piety and quick to detect the falsity sometimes accompanying it. "I told her I hadn't much religion but what I had belonged to my own religion" was the typical remark of an aunt. Typical too was an uncle who filled up his census form with a mapping pen, in the hope that he would be unreadable; typical another who grumbled, "I can't be in two places at once bar I were a bird." How I adored my grandmother!—we played for hours together. In later life I became high-minded and critical, but we remained friends, and it is with her—with them—that my heart lies.

Amongst those who tried to help her in her trouble was her doctor, Mr. Tayloe. He was also Miss Thornton's doctor. He was furthermore Henry Thornton's doctor at Battersea Rise and Marianne was able through him to send messages to that lost paradise and to get news in return; absolutely trustworthy, Mr. Tayloe did much to soften the alienation between her brother and herself, and his death after thirty years' attendance on her was deeply mourned. In 1867 this good man took my mother to call at East Side. Perhaps he wanted to give the child an outing, perhaps he hoped to get her a job, and he certainly knew how fond Miss Thornton and Miss Synnot were of young people. The visit was a success. Both ladies were delighted with her and she for her part was fascinated by them, thought them so kind, so amusing; indeed she talked so much at home about Miss Synnot that my grandmother prophetically cried, "I'm sick of Miss Synnot already."

"Lily" was then twelve years old—small, lovely to look at, with a delicate complexion, and full of gaiety and charm. In this she resembled the rest of her family, but she had one quality which some of them lacked: a sense of responsibility.

[*279*]

As the eldest daughter she had had to mind the little ones, and there is a pathetic photograph of her with six of them around her at Margate, on a long day's outing for which she had been insufficiently financed. Perhaps this had matured her; certainly her integrity and independence persisted and prevented her now from being carried off her feet by her wonderful new friends.

As early as 1869 Marianne took this new protégée to Weymouth to stay in the leisured society of Emmy and Major Sykes. She writes to Miss Laura Forster:

Lilly is a great success here—its useless to say beauty isn't a great advantage tho' I think her pretty manners tend as much to her popularity—and I reckon I have added to it by insisting on shabby dress against Mr Tayloe's offers of help to any amount to make her 'to appear respectable', but strays and waifs are never liked unless they show their lowly estate. Nor will I let her dine late or accept croquet parties by herself, for Emmy says on the Esplanade the young artillery officers were enquiring who she was and whether she was staying on here.

My mother was delighted with Weymouth, though bewildered to find that her elegant hostess had never heard of an apple pudding, here was indeed a new world! Marianne's letter sounds patronising, still it is a responsible letter: she never took up people to please herself, spoiled them and dropped them. She took them up to please herself to be sure, but also to help them. As soon as she was assured of my mother's deserts, she began to consider how they could be utilised. The child would have to be a governess—nothing else lay open for her—so let her be an efficient one, and the first step towards that was extra tuition. The school chosen was one kept by a Mademoiselle Collinet at Brighton and was not altogether successful, but my mother enjoyed herself, picked up some French, acquired social assurance, and made friends, and in the holidays there was the expanding circle of the Thorntons. Everyone liked her, she was helpful and happy, and when the time came to start her off as a governess there was no difficulty in finding her a place. Her first pupil was a daughter of James Knowles; then she was with Marion Southey, and became lasting friends with her: she was then with Mrs. Farrer (Effie Wedgwood) at Abinger Hall near Dorking: here again friendship survived. This engagement was more ambitious than its predecessors. She was to be in charge of the little stepsons for two years, but before she had been there long, she and my father fell in love, became engaged, and married.

My grandmother's delight may be imagined. More surprising and very charming is the delight of Marianne. Eddie was her favourite nephew, Lily her trusted protégée, so what could be better? She cared not for a "good" marriage but for a marriage of true minds. The rest of the Thornton circle followed her powerful lead, and their conduct was decent and cordial, though there must have been reservations. In a letter which has escaped the family censorship some of these got expressed. It is from Mrs. Farrer to Miss Laura Forster, and is dated November 7, 1876, from the Farrers' town house:

Fancy our surprise just after our arrival as we were sitting in the drawing room having just said 'we *neednt* say not at home, no one will come', to see the door open and Lily and Eddy appear. I was as innocent as usual and thought no evil, and Eddy had to tell me plainly 'Lily and I are engaged' before I took in the situation. She was half wild with excitement —fell upon Ida's neck kissing and ejaculating and looking quite lovely. The two girls soon fled and left me and Eddy by the fire and we had *such* a nice talk together. He was not wild

[*281*]

like L. but as befitted his seven more years all aglow with
happiness, and having looked 'things' steadily in the face I
should say. One of the first things he told me was that he
thought you were come round to like it. Dearest Laura, this
was my one shadow in seeing so much charming happiness—
the disappointment for you. How I hope and trust it may turn
out better than you think it. He seems thoroughly to have
faced the want on the intellectual side, and I do think there
is stuff and character in her—witness her dealings with her
own people. I feel sure they'll be very happy, but your question
is couldn't he have kept up at higher level. But oh the chances
of marriage. . . .

Aunt Monie extended her graciousness to all my mother's
family. She liked them, as did most people. She was charming to my grandmother, who adored her, invited up the
various brothers and sisters, and tried to help them, and
they often required help. Through her connections she sometimes got them more satisfactory jobs, and in some cases
they kept them. In all this she comes out as a great lady who
has a good heart.

Unfortunately another side of her began to develop—the
tendency to interfere—and from it proceeds what is tiresome and unacceptable in her old age. Thorntons always had
known best—it was part of their moral integrity—and as the
circle of her activities narrowed Aunt Monie knew best better than ever. Once an idea was lodged in her head, she would
support it with ability and duplicity. The desire to be right
can become a poison which corrupts the integrity out of
which it sprang. Melancholy to relate, in a few years my
mother was saying, "Monie is a very wicked woman," and
"Well well—I hope in the next world there will be a com-
partment labelled 'Thornton' and that it won't be anywhere
near me."

Typical of her interference is the enlightened but nagging letter which she wrote my mother when she was expecting her first child (December 1877). My mother was not enlightened. She had never had a child before, and she did not want to talk about it, and if she did want to talk about it she had her own mother and her sisters. On to her the following avalanche descended:

My dear 'Ostrich'—I didn't try to lift your head out of the sand when you were here on Friday, because I want you to like coming here, and if you were always in fear of an allusion to that improper topic you might stay away. Still, I must answer your note, and my dear 'it beats me all to shivers' (as the Americans say) to know how to order your bassinette (it shall be such a beauty) when you won't tell me when you will want it—Also its beyond my power to imagine what *added* impropriety there is in mentioning when you expect to want it. I was obliged to answer an enquiry from a friend of yours last week by saying you would not tell anybody!

My dear child, do shake the sand off your head and start off and run with the rest of the flock of birds on the beaten high road, where nobody will notice you or talk about you. As long as they see two feet and a feathered tail sticking up out of the sand by the roadside, they must and will wonder what it means.

I have known you a goodish bit of time dear Lily, and one of your attractions to me was your never setting yourself up, as if you thought you were wiser or better or prettier than the rest of the world. Governesses are generally supposed to carry a flag and to strike out some new and superior path, but during your brief taste of the profession you never did. Why should you unfurl one now—that of being more 'proper and particular' than all the rest of the creation—of the female part of it at least. It's never wise to be in a majority of one.

"Majority" is a slip of the pen. Aunt Monie corrects it to "minority" and proceeds. She prefaces her new subject with "Mind you needn't take any notice of all I have said so far. I shall think you very nice and good tempered if you are not affronted with me, but yet I couldn't help saying it":

As to the £50, leave it if you like till your Xmas bills come in when you may be glad to square them—except that I shall spend a little of it in your bedroom sofa and arm chair. No bedroom—not even a maiden lady's—is furnished comfortably unless it has both, so don't turn them out with ignominy if they come in, *they* won't betray your prospects. You tell me not to be afraid of your doing anything foolish. Its the last thing I should have been afraid of, but for this hiding in the sand.

Then she changes the subject again, tells of a wedding where there are to be eighteen bridesmaids and an extra-long train to keep them at a distance, tells of the misery of Mr. Knowles who has just discovered that his children know nothing, absolutely nothing, signs herself "ever yours affectionately," and concludes, "I shall look in The Times for the announcement of the Bassinette being wanted."

The bassinet never was wanted: the child died at birth. But this was the sort of letter that exasperated the unfortunate women who had married into the Thornton clan, and made them feel hunted and cornered. It was not exactly a patronising letter, it was not snobbish, it was openhanded and warmhearted and amusing, but it left the victim no outlet and it was written without the slightest consciousness that it was appalling. No wonder Lily grumbled to Maimie and Maimie to Lily, and Lucy, a third immigrant, referred to herself as "and me a poor young bride." My mother's insubordination did not go down ill with Aunt Monie, who never minded being opposed as long as she got her own way.

She liked spirit, while counselling moderation: "Long before you are half as old as I am, my dear child, you will see that nobody hardly is as black or as white as they seem. There are more greys and browns than you imagine, and the more people will see that, the more influence they will have on everybody about them—the more hotly they take things up the less people care what they think."

To turn to a more harmonious topic, next year my father and mother went to Paris—I don't know where they had been for their honeymoon. Streatfeild [*sic*], a friend of my father's, went too. Paris always inspired and softened Aunt Monie and the thought of a new generation going there and particularly of my mother going there for the first time filled her with sweetness and light. Of course she subsidised them. She writes to "My dear Eddie" informing him that she has placed £30 to his account—£25 should be enough for their proposed week, and the extra £5 is "on condition of its being spent on Lily being drawn about in any conveyance she chuses, but by Jengo I won't have her walk. It would be a bad investment having her laid up in a Paris hotel and no Lady companion except Streatfeild who is very nearly one I own, but not quite." If the £30 isn't enough, Eddie is to let her know: "its only discounting your own money and at very short interest."

To my mother she writes soon after their departure, and reports a further donation of £10 from Aunt Sophy for shopping purposes, "but if it takes the form of staying a few days longer Aunt Sophy wont mind." Continuing:

You good child to write me that nice long letter from Amiens. I enjoyed your account of your dinner, but if as you say you eat it all 'I doubt love you'll be very sick' as Percy's grandmother said to him.—However everybody can and does eat enormously more of the light French cookery than they can of our domestic dinners at home, and I know Eddie holds that he never met with a bad dinner in the merry land of France. I am so rejoicing in this lovely day for you on your entry into Paris. That Gare du Nord is not a picturesque first view, but I hope you will have mild moonlight nights, and that Eddie wont be too old-maidish to walk you down the Boulevard Italienne at night when Paris is en fête, and then if the Café de Mille Colonnes is alive still you must go in for an ice.

Then her mind switches back to 1816 when she first felt Paris's healing, civilising power.

I seem to be very frivolous in my recommendations, but one's earliest impressions are always the most vivid. We (my Uncle and Aunt Dan and 2 jeunes hommes were our party) got late into Paris and my aunt ordered me to bed, and I obediently got in, but my uncle, a steady Yorkshire country gentleman, came in just as I got to sleep and told me to get up and dress and he would take me out. That was sixty three years ago my dear and I hope you may have as much pleasure 63 years hence in thinking of your first sight of the Boulevards. I have been there many many times since, but nothing effaces that first view.

Ever yrs affly M. T.

Old French novels I believe are generally good, such as Cottin,* de Staël, or Genlis. It's the modern that are many of them at least so dirty and wicked.

My mother lived for those required sixty-three years more, but I doubt whether in 1941 she looked back to her first visit to Paris with vividness or love. Remembrance of the "Happy Memories" type is an art which the Thorntons had cultivated. She never acquired it, moreover Paris was then under the heel of Hitler, and neither she nor I expected to see it again.

* Authoress of *Elisabeth ou les Exiles de Sibérie,* etc.

Milton. August 1878

Your Paris letter of yesterday, dear Lily, did me as much good as a drive round the Boulevards. There's some old song about 'you go courting with your boys and I make conquests with my girls'. I think I go travelling with you, and even fancy myself once more at a Café chantant in Les Champs, or wandering about the Palais Royal. You seem to be enjoying it so much I cannot bear to think of your coming home yet. I wonder how your money holds out and whether your Hotelier keeps to the charges he promised. Is St Cloud quite burnt to death? It used to be so pretty. I'm glad you were going to Versailles. Did you see le petit Trianon—perhaps not for it isn't much worth looking at except to people who had gone mad about poor Marie Antoinette, which I had in my schoolroom days. She was so tired of the state and size of Versailles that she persuaded the King to let her have this cottage built where she used to dress en paysanne and milk the cows and make the butter, and by so doing poor child brought her reputation under a cloud that never cleared up. How does your French talking wear by the way—are you not glad you kept it up, but I believe Ed. is very glib at it.

There is a big packet of letters from Aunt Monie to my mother in 1878. At the turn of the year I was born, to be christened as related. The family seem to have been pleased, though ominous rumbling began to be audible inside my godmother. My father was getting on in his profession, he had acquired a beautiful and acceptable wife, a son and heir, a pleasant town house. Then he developed the disease which had carried off so many of his brothers and sisters, and within four years of his marriage he was dead.

Aunt Monie recognised the ominous symptoms all too well. My mother did not. She was accustomed to young people remaining alive, and although she dutifully carried out instructions, she could not take her husband's illness seriously.

This laid her open to criticism, and also made the end harder
for her, when it came. He died at Bournemouth (October
1880). The shock was terrible. Apart from her grief, she
felt that her life had ended before it had begun. At twenty-
five she was left with a small baby, and without any support
except what was extended to her by her husband's relatives.

It was at this time that she made the great friendship of
her life, and how she would have survived without it I do
not know. It was with Inglis Synnot's widow. They had of
course met when my mother entered the Thornton circle, but
Maimie was then still vague and immature, and a hanger-on
of her husband's relatives, to be loved, but to be laughed at,
and ordered about. My mother's disaster drew them together,
and she developed the spiritual delicacy and strength that
distinguished her later years. She had always been devoted
to my father, and had come down to Bournemouth to stand
by in his final illness. She stayed on to help my mother ex-
tricate herself from the great furnished house she had taken,
and went into lodgings with her for a time. She wrote to her:
"We don't like to think that time can ever soften our grief—
but mercifully it does or we couldn't live. By my own past
agony I can feel for you, who are now going through the
same, but I am thankful to say my life is not empty as I
feared it might be. I have so many to love." The only reason
that the women did not set up house together permanently
was that Maimie (they agreed) was too devoted to the baby
and would spoil it.

Aunt Monie's sympathy was more philosophically expressed, and I doubt whether it brought much comfort. She
had had too many losses to be startled by death, and, generally speaking, old people are disinclined to lavish emotion
for fear of upsetting themselves. She thanks my mother for
all the happiness she brought my father, and especially for

her cheerfulness through his months of "languor and sickness," and she rejoices that my birthday had been happy, and that I should never know of the additional happiness I had missed. All is graciously and affectionately put. But it makes one realise how little mourners can enter into each other's minds. To the older woman Eddie Forster's death was an extra step in a long descent, to the young one it was an abyss. They had no common ground in their grief, and whereas my mother was dazed and wanted to slink away, Aunt Monie was already fertile with plans.

They centred round me. I succeeded my father as the favourite nephew, just as he had succeeded Inglis Synnot. I received the deplorable nickname of The Important One, and when my mother showed signs of despondency she was reminded that she had me to live for. My comfort, my talents, my toys, and my health fill innumerable letters. As soon as we got back from Bournemouth, she was importuned to bring me to stay at Clapham or Milton, and this went on for the remaining six years. Too much affection in a world that contains too little is ironical: *"ordina questo amor . . ."* comes to my mind as I read the plan-crowded correspondence. Sometimes my mother behaved like a saint, sometimes not— that is to say she behaved as any other decent person would. On one occasion she became so exasperated that she burst out to Maimie in dramatic form. She was trying to clear out of Melcombe Place and find a house in the country. She was desperately busy, still she brought the baby to Aunt Monie's for a few days, only to find that she could not remove it.

Pharoah has again triumphed and we don't go until Saturday. The horrible torturing I have endured passes all comprehension. I will give you the Daily Dialogue:

Mone   Oh I do hope you are not going to take that dear child away from me not only on my account but his.

Lily   —obstinately—I must go on Tuesday.

M.   Why must? London is very bad for that child.

L.   —aside—Dr Southey thinks it better than Clapham.— aloud—I don't think a fortnight can do him any harm.

M.   Yes it can. I thought you *promised* you would not *go* near London.

L.   No. If I thought it bad for baby, there would have been no object in my leaving Bournemouth at all.

M.   The North East winds are so bad.

L.   No worse than Clapham.

M.   Yes they are. People go abroad to avoid them.

L.   If the North East winds are confined to London then they could avoid them by going to some other part of England. They go abroad because they can't avoid them.— But it does not much matter as Baby does not go out in North East winds, and he may just as well be in the house at Melcombe Place as anywhere else.

M.   By no means. Your rooms are so small.

L.   I am afraid I shall never have such large ones again.

M.   I am sure I hope you will.

L.   —mildly—The sitting rooms are 12 ft. high and 20 ft. square.

M.   Well that is something.

L relapses into moody silence and knows nothing is any good but just sitting and enduring. Mone said she would like the baby for her birthday so again I have feebly given in, and let us hope it will be the death of me for flesh and blood certainly ought not to be able to hold out against such worry.

The real problem at Clapham, as I have already hinted, was the growing hostility of Henrietta Synnot. My mother never discovered what caused it—they had started such friends. It was perceptible before my father's death. It got worse yearly, and by 1887 the situation was so tense that the two women were not on speaking terms. Messages would arrive through the maids: "Miss Synnot's coming down to the drawing-room, mum," which meant that we had to clear out of it, and once my lesson books were thrown like infected objects into the passage. She incited Aunt Monie to sell all the family silver, and when my mother looked disconsolate said, "Let's hope Morgan won't inherit *that* vulgar craze." The explosion came when she complained of my mother to Aunt Monie: hitherto the poor old lady had managed to pretend that her nieces still loved one another. "Oh then Dick's anger boiled and I was Dick," writes my mother to Laura Forster, "and I fired such a letter as will I hope make her hair stand on end." A draft of this letter has been preserved: "Now that you have thought well to enlighten Monie as to the true state of affairs between us, and have by so doing worried her very much there is no longer any reason why I should remain silent . . ." etc. Dick's anger had certainly boiled, and Henrietta ceased to talk in what was called "her fat military voice" for quite a little time.

To end on a gentler and more appropriate note, I will quote two letters that passed between Lily and her benefactress. I don't know their dates.

Dearest Monie: It was a very great pleasure to get your letter saying you had been glad to see me. I thought you would be but still I feel very happy that you should tell me so, and that I was glad to see you you know without my saying, for nearly if not quite all the happiness I have had since I was 12 has come through you and Henrietta. I have indeed reason to thank Mr Tayloe for taking me to see you and H. when I was a little shy girl, and such happy times I had in your house. I am afraid my mother was quite jealous in those days.

[*291*]

Aunt Monie replies:

Dearest Lily—Your letter was almost as dear and nice as your visit—not quite as no letter can quite come up to the living presence. I am so glad that while I live we have got to understand each other better. Soon I shall be only a memory but I should like M. to know how much of the happiness of my later years came from him and his mother. I believe I misunderstood you—you have sometimes seemed so anxious to get away that I had got to fancy you really didn't like being here and preferred your home & I had no blame for you if you did only I felt very sorry and wondered what I could do different to make you like being here better. But the sight of you on your little visit on Monday as well as a dozen lines like your letter has made that mistake at an end for ever.

As to your mother I think she behaved without knowing it like an angel from heaven—not because she did not feel having her child kidnapped for she did but in bravely making us quite welcome to you. If I consulted her in any way about you she always answered me by saying 'Lily is your child Miss Thornton now—never ask me about her. I only feel so thankful it is so.'

The Death of Henry Sykes Thornton

THE ABOVE SQUABBLES and softenings become ephemeral when they are set against the immense length of Marianne Thornton's life. Born in 1797!—it is incredible, it begins to assume the proportions of infinity, and Henry Sykes Thornton had been born in 1800. Their companionship had endured; thanks to her wisdom he had continued to come and see her and she had sometimes gone to see him. The visits on both sides must have been brief and are seldom mentioned, but she happens to describe, to my mother, the last time she saw him at East Side.

Fancy—no you can't fancy—how I felt yesterday when Aunt Sophy being here at 5 oclock T in walked her brother and mine! unannounced, and when he saw who was there he said he couldn't stay or keep the carriage out, and she did the same and said the same. I said I was going away so soon, they must sit down, and they did, and conversation flowed on very tolerably for half an hour. I believe it's the first time they've been in a room together for 20 years or more—but I think life is too short for quarrels, and if brothers and sisters don't stand by each other do what they may—who will? Henry outstaid her, thought her 'terribly altered,' much older apparently than I am which certainly isn't true.

There was a subsequent meeting in Battersea Rise when she was carried upstairs to the room where he was confined. He died in 1881, worth £330,085. Battersea Rise was left to his daughters by his first wife, Emmy and Harti. They could not afford to live in it, and would have found it inconvenient to live in, so they proposed to let it to his widow at a rent of £800 a year. Marianne was unreasonably upset. She cherished the illusion that at the death of her brother the sacred house would be released from its bondage and return to the true succession. She writes about it (to Emmy Sykes) with unusual bitterness:

Harty has seen Di who apologised for not wearing a cap but said she had one upstairs—she is putting her curls back by degrees, she says. Ba called Harty's attention to the fact that she has no crape or other sign of mourning on—for says she 'Henry was always saying sisters-in-law are no relations so I don't see why I am to mourn for him'.

It breaks my heart (what there is of it to break) to hear you say you can't keep B. Rise—but if you can't keep it don't let that Di have it to make merry and hold high festival over her triumph over the first family—Why it would have killed old Abbott and I'd set my mind on once more being drawn round the garden before I died, while it was yours and Harty's. If it is to be hers I'm sure I've done with it and never wish to see even the outside any more. The latest person on the subject is Aunt Sophy, who ended her visit yesterday by saying 'Well I shall go home and look over my accounts and I am sure I can prove to Cam and Emmy how very cheaply we live at Roehampton and B. Rise isn't so large. We've only 2 housemaids and 2 footmen, and economise in so many ways you can't think compared to what we did.' Much she knows about it, but I know our mother was going to live there on £1500 a year, only she died before it was fairly tried.

I think Di has lost honour and peace both. She'll always have a train of harpies after her like sharks that follow a ship, and the peace will be greatly troubled that depends on people not begging of her.

She was ill at the time with the malady of her declining years and the doctor had been dosing her heavily. This may explain her lack of restraint. She was indignant that Emily had inherited a large fortune, and even more indignant that by the terms of the will the heavy succession duty on it was to be paid out of the estate. Since the Marriage Bill of 1850 had never become law Emily's legacy would be chargeable at 10 per cent instead of the usual 1 per cent, and this would mulct the estate to the amount of £17,000: "all thrown down the drain." She talked and wrote unwisely and wildly, and her supporters did the same. Suddenly she became scared by the possibility of a libel action, counselled caution, and calmed down. What her brother's death meant to her, how much passed out of her with him, we cannot know. It must have recalled her further and further into the past, and made recent events dim.

Soon after his death she wrote as follows to one of the partners of the Bank: the letter is still preserved there together with its accompanying photograph:

East Side
Clapham Common
7th Feb. 1882

Dear Mr Williams,

I wonder whether you and your partners see likeness enough in this photograph to wish to keep it in Birchin Lane. If you do, I shall be so glad to give it to you. It is all we have of him for he never would sit for his picture to any one but some years ago Cam Sykes managed to take him without his knowing it, when waiting in his gig for somebody on his way to town. Cam gave it to me, and I have had a few copies made, and I thought you might like to have this slight as it is, if it reminds you of the old friend to whose comfort and enjoyment you all so largely contributed during his declining years.

Ever yours most truly,
MARIANNE THORNTON.

Only one letter of sympathy to her has been preserved: from quaint little Archdeacon Harrison:

I miss him much at Festival times and Quarter days when we exchanged greetings, and also condolences on the alterations which time does and must bring in Church Services & ornamentation so called. But I have lived to see many improvements here in the warmth of the Cathedral & its beautiful illumination by countless lines of gas jets.

The same disastrous winter she suffered another loss. It was not an intimate loss, but it meant the disappearance of another figure from the friendly past: Mrs. George Richmond, whose elaborate funeral caused her to reflect on her own end, and to express her revised views on the subject of mourning.

A very interesting sight it must have been [she remarks to my mother]. There was quite a pyramid of flowers crosses and wreaths on the coffin, a canopy was held over it black embroidered with gold. Mr Richmond as chief mourner walked next to it, looking so white and bent, Sophy said he seemed to have become 20 years older. Then followed all the married girls and their husbands, Willie and his wife, then all the grandchildren, such a long string as took up all the length of All Saints. There were crowds of people.

married a gay life Guardsmen at
Quebec Chapel they retired to Hampton
Court where a house had been lent
them for honeymooning. They had
had their dinner & were wondering
which of the two ought to propose tea
when a Carriage drove up in double
quick time & out stepped the awful
old Governor Genl of India, announcing
that they were not married, & he had
come to bring her home again, they
had been married at a wrong Church
The Portman estates had been divided
into three parishes & Quebec Chapel was
not theirs. on which ensued a scene.
The Groom insisting on keeping her there.
He would bring her back the
next day at any hour for a 2d
ceremony. but the Gov. Gen. of

Marianne Thornton's handwriting
(May 1885)

I hope nobody will ever think it necessary to imperil their lives at my funeral or to bury lovely flowers in the earth.

Throughout all these sorrows and partings her handwriting—so often an index of decay—remained firm. The letter reproduced facing page 296 illustrates this.

My Recollections

THE TIME has come for me to put down a few recollections
of the house on East Side. Family life was led on the first
floor. Aunt Monie had a bedroom at the back, and she would
sit on the edge of her low bed of a morning and entertain
me to breakfast. Her deshabille was dainty—("My dear, an
old woman's bad enough, but a dirty old woman——!");
clean dressing gown, pretty cape, cap with a pale blue ribbon—and in the kindest way she would invite me to share
her egg, dipping a bread-and-butter finger into its yolk and
popping it into my expectant mouth. I enjoyed this for a
time but alas for too short a time. I was growing at the rate
of a month a day, she was static in her 'eighties, and she
could not realise that eggy-peggy-leggy-jeggy would soon
stale and might even nauseate. I behaved fairly well, thanks
to my mother's admonitions. She would urge me to be nice
before I went in, and she has recorded my attempts to get
into intellectual touch with Aunt Monie, and my dejected
expression when I realised I had failed. Anyhow I minded
eggy-peggy less than my corkscrew curls. I had to wear
these for the old lady's pleasure, and must have been almost
the last of the moppets thus to be tormented. A pupil of
Mr. Richmond's made a repellent drawing of the curls and
of me in their midst.

Henry Sykes Thornton in his gig
(about 1860, from a photograph)

The bedroom communicated with the big front drawing room which looked over a corner of Clapham Common. There were two wheeled chairs: one of them had great wheels on each side, and when she was strong enough she propelled herself in it, and she had "lazy-tongs" which darted out and nibbled ineffectively at objects she had dropped on the floor. Once I came on her all alone in her chair shouting "Nurse, nurse," and I slunk away frightened. I often wondered what was wrong with her. The room was covered with a Brussels carpet, in whose corner a cat made messes, and it had a fire-place in front of which an enigmatic figure occasionally stood: "Enty" (Henrietta Synnot) robed in a gown of plum-coloured silk with buttons all down it from the throat to the floor. I did not realise that Enty hated us, and was only there because she had had publicly proclaimed she should not be. I merely found her unresponsive. Once she gave me a Bible, whereupon my mother sobbed with rage. I learnt afterwards that when Enty disliked people she gave them a Hymn Book, and when she detested them a Prayer Book. So a Bible was the limit of limits. She also had a habit of sweeping out of the room uttering barbed words which were too incomprehensible to wound, "A tortuous path is always futile. Good baa" was a classic farewell.

Upstairs was the Important One's peculiar realm—a darkling region, often overshadowed by Christmas. I would lie awake in excitement and be unable to enjoy the stocking when dawn broke. And I remember a healthier excitement—discovering up there at the age of four that I was able to read to myself. From that moment I never looked back. Printed words spread around me. No one taught me to read and no one managed to teach me to write. Pothooks and hangers remained unattainable. It was the nice picture books in the Clapham upstairs that started me off towards freedom. "Tiresome to be interrupted in my reading when the light is so good," I would priggishly say. "Can't you tell the people I am busy reading, Havell?" I soon got on to the *Swiss Family Robinson* and loved it because the boys in it were happy, whereas Robinson Crusoe was always worrying over savages.

On the ground floor were the servants—a friendly enough company, and a numerous one, for Lady Inglis's legacy was still operating. Sarah Cook, Sarah Housemaid, White-faced Emma, Mrs. Ing etc.—I had tea with them and was usually popular, but when I cried, "Mrs Ing's a cat," she laid down the saucer from which she had been lapping and Sarah Cook looked very grave indeed. The most important figure of all —Nurse Havell—did not consort with us. She ate alone and worked alone. She was the power behind the wheeled chair and for all I know a beneficent one, but the letters of the period are full of anxious references to her; Havell has said this, that . . . Havell has told Monie when she had no right to that . . . has been playing fast and loose. She was certainly hand in glove with Henrietta Synnot, who has put up a tablet to her in the church at Milton.

Not much happened during these visits, which appear in retrospect as dun-coloured. I was not unhappy, I did not protest, but I caught the prevalent atmosphere, and realised without being told that I was in the power of a failing old woman, who wanted to be kind but she was old and each visit she was older. How old was she? Born in the reign of George the Fourth, my mother thought. "More likely Edward the Fourth," cried I. Occasionally cousins were encountered— Brian Southey my senior whom I admired, and nasty Blow-die Wags who blew a whistle in my ear. I screamed, I screamed. News of this outrage spread through the Thornton clan, and Blowdie was widely condemned. My mother was furious with him for upsetting her darling but also annoyed with me for being a crybaby. This horrid boy got me altogether on the hop, pointed his finger at me whenever we met, and was the first to demonstrate to me that I was a coward. Then there were some protective girl cousins, Ethel and Mabel Forster, whose pink dresses and kind offices won approval. But as I have already said once not much happened at Clapham, and I could say this again. I seemed never to see the sun there: "The room gets lighter or darker, but the sun never throws his rays in as he does at home." Thus I sighed to my mother.

The truth is that she and I had fallen in love with our Hertfordshire home and did not want to leave it. It certainly was a lovable little house, and still is, though it now stands just outside a twentieth-century hub and almost within sound of a twentieth-century hum. The garden, the overhanging wych elm, the sloping meadow, the great view to the west, the cliff of fir trees to the north, the adjacent farm through the high tangled hedge of wild roses were all utilised by me in *Howards End*, and the interior is in the novel too. The actual inmates were my mother, myself, two maids, two or more cats, an occasional dog; outside were a pony and trap with a garden boy to look after them. From the time I entered the house at the age of four and nearly fell from its top to its bottom through a hole ascribed to the mice, I took it to my heart and hoped, as Marianne had of Battersea Rise, that I should live and die there. We were out of it in ten years. The impressions received there remained and still glow—not always distinguishably, always inextinguishably—and have given me a slant upon society and history. It is a middle-class slant, atavistic, derived from the Thorntons, and it has been corrected by contact with friends who

[*301*]

have never had a home in the Thornton sense, and do not want one.

Aunt Monie had urged my mother to take the house (provided it was on gravel), so she had no grounds for complaint, and it had seemed to her quite proper that a beautiful young widow should bury herself in the wilds for the sake of a supposedly delicate son. All the same, there was this nagging desire to see us—me particularly. Her thirst for youth had become cannibalistic. My mother's letters fall into three classes—those in which she undertook to go to Clapham, those in which she excused herself from going, and those in which she fed the old lady with amusing bits of news about the Important One, in the hope of keeping her quiet. She was rather cynical—she held that it was as Morgan's mother that she mattered, and she could be proudly silent on the subject of Whichelo affairs. She was not very cynical—she was fond of naughty tiresome Monie, and grateful to her, and liked pleasing her.

Out of the endless trifles she now dished up I will select a few on the subject of Pink-Faced Emma. I might have chosen the Sailor-dollar sequence of letters, but it lacks variety. Pink-Faced Emma was our housemaid, and she was so called to distinguish her from Aunt Monie's White-Faced Emma.

Emma arrives:

Morgan got much excited on Thursday at the thought of the new maids, he would watch for Emma at 4, she not being expected till 5.30. When time drew near he picked a huge yellow pansy to make himself smart. He asked her her name the moment she arrived and took her up to her room. At tea he said 'She calls me *Sir*, mamma, it is really very awkward. She doesn't know my name and now will she ever. She might ask

My mother, pony and self in Hertfordshire
(about 1885)

me.' I think she must think he is mad, for he said to her 'Have you heard one of my long stories about things that have never happened except inside my head—I'll tell you one, it is called "Excited maids under the Clothes line".' I can't imagine how he thinks of such sensational titles, he will write for the Family Herald I should think.*

Emma's folly:

We do lessons after breakfast and after dinner and then M has his dancing lesson. I am teaching him the Polka and he is beginning to have quite a good idea of it. Unfortunately for me he instructs Emma in the afternoon and evidently she is but a sorry dancer—heavy footed for the drawing-room windows and doors rattle & the furniture screams. As the dancers grow wild they shout and play tambourines and musical boxes at the same time, so you may guess I pass a lively afternoon. Now they are very happy chatting, and he is determined the maids shall look for nineteen constellations this evening, poor things. He is quite annoyed with frivolous Emma for calling Jupiter a star.

Emma's further folly:

M. says to me several times today in a tone of mournful admiration 'how very sensible you are mamma, you can play games, Emma can't learn and does it wrong every time'. I can well believe it. I have always said (tho' not to M.) that she was deficient. The way she likes to amuse him is to make some foolish speech over and over again through the entire after-

* Titles of others stories were: Dancing Bell, Chattering Hassocks, Screams, Scuffles in the Wardrobe, The Earring in the Keyhole, and The Adventures of Pussy Senior. What relation would these bear to the pictures painted at Battersea Rise by my little great-aunts? A brief analysis of Chattering Hassocks has survived: fifty lions and as many unicorns sit upon hassocks, and the lions put forward a plea for tolerance and for variety of opinion which I still support. "Why didn't you finish baby's story about the talking hassocks?" Aunt Monie writes. "It's much better than Alice in Wonderland."

noon & then they both laugh as if they would have fits. The last speech is 'My name is Sir William Podgkins'. I ask what it means but they can't speak for laughter and then M. manages to say 'there is no meaning that is why we laugh'. Occasionally he wants variety, but E. could go on being amused by her own folly for ever.

Emma under instruction:

M. invited the maids to tea with him yesterday, and he said he must give them some amusement, so he armed himself with astronomical diagrams and said they had better do a little learning. He explained all and they giggled like a pair of noodles. He then proposed Hide & Seek. He then took them both into the hall and instructed them in moves at chess. He flew all over the hall carpet saying 'Now I go like a knight, now like a castle &ct. He is chalking a map of South America, and implored me to help him before I went out yesterday 'for I know Emma won't think it matters a bit whether I put Patagonia in the place of Ecuador'.

Emma under examination:

Did I tell you of the conversation I overheard (I was supposed to be asleep) between Emma & Morgan.

E. You know a good deal about stars, don't you Master Morgan?

M. (humbly) No not very much. Do you?

E. Oh no.

M. *What* do you know about? (What indeed!!! Long pause.)

E. Oh only what you have taught me.

M. Botany?

E. Yes, about the Great Bear & Little Bear.

M. —scornfully—That's not Botany, that's Astronomy. Botany is about flowers and *Cology* about shells. I don't know very much of both those.

E.   Oh I think you know a great deal, Master Morgan.
M.   —very self-satisfied tone—Oh, do you.

Emma leaves. My cleverness and rudeness were more than she could stand. The break came gathering primroses. I sneered at her for picking them with short stalks, she jeered at me for picking so few. I hit at her basket and upset it, she hit at mine. I hit her, she hit me and tore my little coat. "But I had to hit Master Morgan, ma'am, he hit me," she explained mildly. I was sorry when she left and rather ashamed, for I knew it was my fault. She was such a suitable companion, and our chant of

> Oh the corns and bunians how they do grow,
> They hurt me so oh oh oh oh oh oh

still sometimes rings in my ears.

Aunt Monie loved all this nonsense and the way my mother put it, and before long there was little in our simple life that she did not know and upon which she did not advise. Occasionally she discussed the defects of my character. I was not a bad child, but I had been noticed too much by grown-ups, and I could be hysterical, pretentious, and detestable. On this occasion I must have gone well over the edge:

I have not an idea what I should do if I had a child who in-dulged in that stile of talk, but I do think it ought to be stopped somehow, and I see no way of doing it except as Harti said 'Scold him when he's good and not when he's naughty', but when in one of his loving affectionate moods if you were to talk to him as if he were 20, and show him the evil consequences of saying what is not true for one thing and what will make mothers who have good children afraid of letting them play with a boy who says such shocking and such untrue things. You know I'm never for punishment which leads only to eye service as men-pleasers, but I do quite think that if you could

convince that precocious little head of his that it really grieved
you, he would reform—but if not with school looming in the
distance I suppose he must look forward to the time when you
will be his refuge from the torments his fellows will bestow
upon what they call 'cheek'.

Or she meditates on my financial future:

Oh dear how I wish we knew beforehand what children are
going to turn out, specially Mr Morgan Forster—as to getting
his money when 21 or 25. If he *takes* it as they call it at 21
no provision is made for his children. If he waits till 25 he is
to leave *his* money to you and his children, I'm afraid this will
put it into his head to marry—like Charley Sykes who is to
be executed on Tuesday next being just 21 & foolish enough to
reverse the figures and be 12. The Important One I feel will
have cleverness enough and to spare, & I could be almost as
certain of his goodness & his general promise of all that one
most wishes to see in a child.—His fits of crying for little
things I look upon as more weak nerves than anything else.

Part of the trouble was that there were too few children
in our lovely retreat. At the park gate dwelt Baby Plum
Bun or Sizzle, of inferior lineage and age, and through the
rose hedge was Frankie Franklin of the farm. I admired
Frankie when he attached himself to the wheel which turned
the hay-cutter, and whirled round upon it Ixion-like, but
did not get to know him well until later years: he only died
in 1949 and I have actually spoken to five generations of
that honoured family. Down in the rectory were nine daughters, to whom was presently added a future Lord Chancellor. And there were a few more children in the village, but
we did not visit widely, for the pony backed when he thought
we were going too far, and ran the trap into a hedge.

I depended a good deal for company upon the garden
boys. With one of them, William (Mr. Taylor), I am still

in touch and he remembers, as I do, how he led me on the pony into the wilds of Botany Bay. But it is Ansell whom I remember best. This was a snub-nosed, pallid, even-tempered youth who came to us shortly before Aunt Monie died. He was reliable but not too reliable; " 'e done it isself" was his explanation when the puppy arrived patterned in tar. My mother in her kindness let Ansell off every Wednesday afternoon so that he could play with me. We mostly played on a straw-rick which Mr. Franklin abandoned to our fury. More kindness. We slid and we shouted. Ansell hid and left his billycock as a decoy. Not finding him I jumped on it and stove it in, and this did ruffle him. Once we built a hut between the rick and the hedge: " 'ow 'ot it is in 'eer, I've got the 'eerdache already," said he. We stored apples there, and could not think what ate them.

Nor was his education neglected. I neglected no one's education. Each week, as we walked round the edges of the fields, I recounted to him what last I had read of the Swiss Family Robinson, and he retold it to me fairly well, except that he would call Fritz Frizz. Arithmetic defeated him. He never could state how many chickens his mother had, however much he waved his arms, and "Ansell and the Chickens" survived as a family saying long after we left Hertfordshire. For me he has survived in other ways. He was the good sweet side of the odious Blowdie Wags, and probably did more than anyone towards armouring me against life. That is why I bring him in. He faded when a professional armourer was introduced in the person of a snobbish Irish tutor who prepared me for a preparatory school which was to prepare me for a public school which was to prepare me for the world, and who supposed he had obliterated the world of Emma and Ansell for ever.

FOUR

The Aylward Incident

THIS IDYLLIC LIFE had not been such an idyll for the grown-ups, and I must now refer to a rattling row, which, all unbeknownst to the Important One, had been raging over his head. It is in its small way comparable to the row at the time of Henry Thornton's second marriage, though it did not involve important people or public issues, nor had it tragic consequences.

Since Inglis Synnot's death, Maimie had passed most of her time at Clapham and a little of it in the Isle of Wight, with her sisters. Her brother had entered the church and had become a curate at Salisbury. In 1883 she went to stay with him there, and—being passionately attached to music—she became acquainted with an elderly citizen, a Mr. Aylward, who shared her tastes. I think he gave her violin lessons. Mr. Aylward fell in love with her—though if I interpret him rightly "fell in adoration" would be the better phrase—and he made her an offer of marriage. I know too little of this early phase of the affair. Of its later phase I know too much and I must have torn up dozens, nay hundreds of letters from Aunt Monie, Aunt Laura, my mother, the Miss Wilsons, the Miss Prestons . . . up and down, round and round.

Maimie hesitated. Her love for Inglis never waned, and

to the end of her life she could not speak of him without a delighted laugh in her voice. Mr. Aylward was different, was noncomparable. He told her she could make him happy; he might be right, and she did not at once send him packing.

Then the panic began. And certainly her suitor was a tall order. Not only was he old, he was unwieldy and unappetising, he was a widower with a large grown-up family, he called his home 'Olmleigh, and worst of all worsts he was in trade. The Thorntons had been in trade too, but in the eighteenth century, and they had never stood behind a counter. No more, it turned out, had Mr. Aylward, but he was openly connected with Aylward and Spinney, the music shop on the Canal, in whose windows flutes and ocharoons and comic songs could be daily discerned. He was also a highly trained musician, who came of a family of organists distinguished since the early eighteenth century, and he was a close friend of Hubert Parry.* That was beyond their ken. They only saw the enormity of the *mésalliance*, and their panic increased when Maimie fell ill. She was upset by her own uncertainty and by the clamour of the Thorntons, with Aunt Monie at their head. She collapsed with neuralgia and neurosis, and had delusions; she was received for treatment in the house of a doctor at Bournemouth, and one of my early memories of her is in a darkened room. To Aunt Monie all was now clear; a wicked old man was forcing a wealthy invalid to marry him in order to get her money. She called in the family lawyer and put the case in his hands.

In a draft letter headed "To Mary but must be shortened" she addresses her nephew's widow with a mixture of personal affection and dynastic blackmail:

* Were the context relevant, I would quote a remarkable letter from Parry to Aylward, written from Bayreuth in 1876 after he had heard the *Ring* for the first time. It shows that both men possessed not only musical training but musical adventurousness.

It is my birthday and looking back at the way I have gone mostly in such green pastures and still waters, I cannot but reflect that there is only one heavy sorrow that seems to get heavier every day.

You will know that I mean you my dearest child, indeed I might call you the dearest, just as a mother always loves best the one that is in trouble. I do not know whether any one has ventured to remind you of dear Inglis, of all the love he felt for you or what he would have thought of your having an attachment to a person whom every friend and relation would give all they had almost if they could induce you to give up that which we all feel is a delusion owing to your health. . . . He had a great horror of women being talked about I remember thinking how safe he was in chusing you, the most sensitive retiring being that ever existed. You must be aware that not only marriage is out of the question, but *he* will hope to keep up intercourse with you as an avenue for pushing his claims further.

She wrote almost daily to my mother, as Maimie's closest friend, and poured out her hopes and fears and plans and second thoughts. Henrietta was laid up "partly with a cold partly with downright misery." Mr. Richmond had racked his mind for a parallel, and had found it in a lady of title who had married a gardener. "Enquiries and condolences" kept coming in. Laura had begged Mr. Aylward's name might never be mentioned to her. Too much music may have been to blame, and Aunt Monie is sorry to hear that a violin has been seen in the sickroom. And then she changed her tone and wrote charmingly and sincerely about the invalid's sweetness and goodness and of her willingness to consider whether her mind might not indeed be impaired.

My mother took up a line of her own, and it was an excellent one. Like everyone else, she deplored the attachment and hoped it would come to nothing. But she went to see Mr. Aylward, which no one else had deigned to do, and she found a bewildered and honourable old man, who had fallen in love with a woman much younger than himself and had received some encouragement and who—having been twice Mayor of Salisbury—found it difficult to regard himself as an adventurer. She came away convinced of his integrity and devotion. If Maimie really wanted to marry him, she must; it was a mistake, but her mistake; nothing to do with her in-laws. Her support won her Mr. Aylward's disproportionate gratitude. He wrote her a sweet letter of thanks. In after years he said to her, "My dear lady, they all thought I wanted to marry Mary because of her money, but my dear lady she has no money."

After this crucial interview she wrote in strong terms to Aunt Monie and urged her to call off the lawyers at once—they were making a sorry mess and were considering offering Mr. Aylward a bribe. She assured her that he would not worry any member of the family by calling—it was the last thing he was likely to do. She begged her to prevent Laura, who was ill, from going down to see Maimie in Bournemouth, and making the pair of them iller. Her general line was "do nothing and perhaps nothing will happen." Thereafter the situation eased. Maimie got better, thanks to the skill of her doctor, she became able to make decisions, and though her decision was marriage it was accepted with tolerable resignation by the Thorntons. They were too fond of her to organise a boycott. She and Mr. Aylward were married in London in the summer of 1884, my mother being almost the only person present. When my mother got back home that night she wrote to Maimie:

I am so glad to think that I was able to be with you up to the end. How very very good you were, you behaved as no one but yourself could have done—perfectly. You have suffered so much and so long—I trust and pray that you may be as happy as you always make all that you come near. Mr A. has found a pearl of great price, and I am so selfish I cant bear to lose you, for you and I have always been so much to each other, at least I know you have to me, you are my only friend. Keep well and *don't be unselfish* for your goodness is a snare to you.

I left 10 minutes after you. I took omnibus to Victoria & reached Clapham soon after 3. Monie was alone, Henrietta had been out all day to avoid us all. I only stayed ½ an hour. Monie was more than tiresome—said she hoped there would be another wedding soon as evidently that was the only way to bring me to London. I bore all patiently. I suppose when anyone gets to her age they lose all feeling for others. I came back by a quick train—5.15. Morgan and my mother did not expect to see me so soon, he was delighted to see me and immediately insisted upon my playing Lady's Toilet, a game which my mother has taught him.

I was then only five, and all I knew of the upheaval was that Maimie's name was not Mrs. Synnot as I thought, no it was Mrs. Aylward. Presently a Mr. Aylward stood in my presence. I disapproved, and told Maimie that he was a nasty, fat, waddling old thing. She took it well, indeed she was helpless with laughter. When they paid us a visit in Hertfordshire things went better. He and I had been schooled by our respective womenfolk and we met in a spirit of determined amity. Mr. Aylward invited me to stay at 'Olmleigh. I replied, "Fank you, I shall be pleased to come" and shook hands at arm's length in case he poked me facetiously in the stomach. Holmleigh proved to be a tall sun-drenched house balanced high above Salisbury. I loved it. I never loved Mr. Aylward, but he enters into happy memories. I can see my mother and Maimie rattling at the Erard—it is Spohr's String Quartet as a piano duet—and when they start the slow movement too fast, as they always did, I can hear the old man's sonorous magisterial voice saying: "Adagio, madam, Mary, adagio. . . ." It was a rumble in the grand manner. He has a further claim on my gratitude for becoming, by his first wife, the great-grandfather of my friend Joe Ackerly. There were no children to the second marriage. On its own lines it was a thorough success. He continued to worship the ground she trod on, she never called him anything but Mr. Aylward. Her brother had felt obliged to resign his Salisbury curacy when the scandal started, and neither the Close nor the county could call on her or go beyond bowing at bazaars, because she was Trade. So she was rather isolated. But she had plenty to do making her husband comfortable and helping people in Holmleigh and outside it, and enjoying the ravishing sounds and sights she found in the world—yes and the tastes, and the smell of flowers. Of the world to come, on which she set equal store, she would say, "Won't it be exciting, won't it be fascinating to *know*, and I have an idea that one or two who expect to be very highly placed may have some surprises." It is tempting to run on about Maimie. She was so rare and is now so lost. Let me anyhow quote: "It is a dreadful thing to say, but I do prefer people who are untruthful through sympathy to those who are truthful through hardness." And let me pop in: "Cultivate Snow Wedgwood, for you may be entertaining an angel in the dark."

Aunt Monie cannot be blamed for her foolish conduct over the Aylward incident. The facts as she heard them were disquieting, and she was confronted with a section of society of which Thorntons knew nothing. And her age was now eighty-seven. She had however come to enjoy interfering for inter-ference's sake, and I cannot help contrasting her conduct with what it might have been in earlier years, and with what it had been at the time of her brother's second marriage.

FIVE

The End

I WILL END her biography by transcribing all the letters—
nine in all—that she wrote to me. They show her at her best.
They are an extraordinary series to have been addressed by
a woman in her late eighties to a child under eight. I keep
on hoping more will turn up. I cannot remember receiving
them, and was probably crawling on the carpet or rushing
around while my elders read them aloud and implored me to
listen. The first was written when I was eighteen months old
and staying with my aunt. It is characteristically introduced
by a present.

May 6th 1880

My dear Morgan I send you a gardener's apron for working
in the garden, nothing will improve your appetite like being
a Gardener, so intelligent as you are you will soon be Aunt
Laura's head man. Tell her I went to my garden, that is my
school, and staid two hours there. I had my wheeled chair
taken there and was rolled about and the children laughed and
I don't wonder.—

Ever your affectionate MONIE.

The next is a post card of October 12, 1881. By that date
my father had died. It is addressed from the Cock Pond, and
the text is:

Dear Baby—If you will come to luncheon tomorrow you shall take away with you a cock-a-doodle-do called a pheasant. Do come. MONIE.

In the next we have moved to the country.

My dear Morgan,

I have got a new mechanical toy, it is a cat holding out a number of dead mice for sale. She is beautifully drest, a velvet gown and gold chains very pretty feet and she walks very fast. If I sent her to you, do you think you are old enough and care-full enough for me to give her to you, with the key to wind her up, and will you always put her to bed in the little box in which she will travel. There's two others you might have instead of the cat if you liked. There's a goat with a rake and a watering pot, a gardener. A rabbit, a green-grocer, offering fruit and vegetables for sale. I wonder which your own animals would like best for you to introduce to them.

I am sorry you hate your pothooks and hangers so badly but it is tiresome to keep on the same thing. Persuade your mother to give you ever such little words to copy, like your reading book. I am beginning to want to see you very badly.

MONIE.

The next letter has historical importance. Beginning with the usual gift, it modulates into reminiscences, and describes —I understand accurately—a scene which occurred at the opening of Parliament in the year 1804.

Dear Mr Morgan

I hope you will do me the favor of accepting a dozen of hyacinths that will all blow and grow in glasses in water— Lloyd of course is full of glasses, price half-nothing, but you could if you liked put them in earth in pots. What stupid names they give the poor things. I wish I could think of some better ones. I have just stuck the names on my glasses but I am sure you would find better.

I think its time now for you to write me another letter. Do you write every day. I can shew you a big thick copy book that when I was just your age I wrote for my father. He had not very good eyes and could not write much himself, and I was so proud of being able to help him. And what do you think he did to reward me. Why, poor old George the Third was coming to summon parliament. That means he ordered that all the members of parliament were to come to hear what he had got to say to them about making new laws and altering the old. He was a good man and wanted to do right, but he was very obstinate and used to get very angry and at last very ill, and he quite lost his senses and kept calling the people about him peacocks. When the day came for him to meet his faithful commons though very ill he insisted on having his own way so they gave it him, and he went, and I could see his carriage—all gold and glass, and I did so beg of my papa to let me go across Palace Yard and he carried me across and took me into the House of Commons, and they were ordered by the Lords to meet the King and hear what he had to say to us. And there he was sitting on his Throne with his King's Crown on, his robes scarlet velvet and ermine, held his speech written out for him just what he had to say. But Oh dear he stood up and made a bow and began 'My Lords and Peacocks'. The people who were not fond of him laughed, the people who did love him cried, and he went back to be no longer a King, and his eldest son reigned in his stead and Regent Street was named after him.

This is a very dull letter so I will finish.

> Your affectionate old
> AUNT MONIE.

Dull letter? I wish I could get many like it or write any like it! What a treasure to be thrown into the lap of an inattentive child! What a sequence—hyacinth bulbs, copy-book, mad King! How much has died with her which, properly evoked, might have lived!

My dear Morgan

Your letter was indeed a surprise and such a nice one. I had no idea that you could write real letters and I think I can see that you will write a very good hand, and if you do that you will like it. It is just like talking to people if you do it often and well it will come naturally to you but unless you write well enough to make it no trouble you will hate it—just as Enty does because she writes so badly nobody can read it.

Yesterday Aunt Emmy meeting Mr Richmond in town asked whether he was coming the next day to see me on my birthday. He said no, there would be so many callers, he meant to come here the day before and keep the Vigil—and so he did. Mother will tell you what a vigil—or as poor people call it a wigil—is. Tell mother that her shoes fit beautifully. They were exactly what I wanted. Ronald Southey has sent me such a pretty jug and basin, to hold flowers, with the Oxford Arms upon it. Aunt Emmy a new satin gown with lace to trim it. Aunt Laura a lace collar. Boxes of flowers keep tumbling in. I don't see why people should give so many presents for no better reason than my being so old.

> Ever dear Morgan Your loving AUNT MONIE

Now comes a comedy.

My dear Morgan

Two such nasty men came here last night and peeped in at the kitchen window and saw all the maids eating their suppers. Did you ever look at what is called a safe in which Sarah Cook keeps her meat? It is something like a very very big bird-cage only the sides are canvas, and it hangs in the passage that leads from the Common on to the garden. Mrs Reed my night nurse always comes to supper, but as she got to the door of the dark passage, she met two men coming out, but it was so dark she could not see them but one was bigger than the other.

This morning I was half asleep but was soon quite awake, Sarah Cook crying with all her heart and saying 'Oh mam I have something so dreadful to tell you'—'Oh do make haste' says I, for I began to be afraid that the maids had all gone and drowned themselves in the Long Pond.—Oh no says she, but it *is* dreadful—2 thieves have broken open the safe and taken off three chickens and a leg of mutton, and then she sobbed and cried as if she would never get over it. So I scolded her and said it wasn't dreadful, and then Aunt Emmy said she would send to Weymouth to get us some more mutton and some more chickens, and so we should not be worse off. I don't think anyone has such an Aunt Emmy as you and I have.

We had a man called a detective to help us to find out the thieves but he fears he cant though he thinks he knows who they are. When he came into the room he said 'Good day ladies I hear you had some unpleasant visitors last night—but tell your maids always to shut the shutters and not let the world see what they are about.' This is good advice I have no doubt. He went away saying 'You shall have my best attention ladies in any further alarm'.

From your AUNT MONIE.

The next three letters are dated.

Dec 18, 1885. My dear Morgan

I am glad you liked the book I sent you. I was not sure that you would like stories that are not true like Alice in Wonderland. But pretending stories are often very amusing. When you go to school you will have to learn Latin and Greek. Neither mama nor I know Latin or Greek. Do you think us stupid and silly for not knowing what we were never taught? * I wish I was quite well. I should so like to come to you for Christmas. Write again soon. When you can read writing I shall like to write to you very often. And so goodbye.

Yours affectionately MONIE

* But see p. 59 where her papa expects her to construe Ovid.

I am going to send you and your mama and Emma and Lydia and Wray each a present. What would you like me to send you all.

The following is directed to "Morgan Forster Esq. Upstairs", with an unused lilac penny stamp on the envelope. She was downstairs and had sent it aloft to greet me on my birthday.

Jan 1st, 1887.
Many happy returns of the day dearest Morgan—that is what everybody is wishing themselves and everybody they love, but we cannot make ourselves or other people happy by only wishing it—we must try to make them so and how is that to be done. You will be able to tell me because I see you already do a great deal because you think you can do or say something that some of us liked. Children do not know how much they can do for the sick or the sorrowful to help them to bear things or how bright and happy they can make us. I am giving you a magic lanthorne. Will you be able to light it up today. And now I must write to poor Millie Knowles who has been shut up for so many many weeks and is so good and patient. This is a dull note but the fog has got into everything I think. I am so very very old that I can hardly expect to be alive another year—to wish you a happy new year. *That* we cannot tell—but I do know what a joy and pleasure you are now to everybody about you and to none more than to his old old Aunt Monie.

She did not live to see the other year. But I had another letter from her in the summer, on the occasion of Queen Victoria's Jubilee. Following the lead of my mother and other respectable citizens I was violently anti-Jubilee. There was much more freedom of speech about royalty at the close of the nineteenth century than there is today. Many people—people who were not at all revolutionary—refused to contribute pennies towards a present for the Queen. When invited to do so my mother publicly protested; and my grandmother and I planned to spend the day together in strict seclusion. "Where will they find it?" Aunt Monie remarked. She rebuked my attitude and recommended deference, though I do not find her arguments for monarchy very sound.

My dear Morgan—I thought you would like this little geography book by which it seems you can always find your way about. The sun they say always is shining on some bit of the globe that belongs to *us* meaning by us all English people—and that reminds me that I heard you did not like the Queen—but I think that must be because you do not know her, neither do I as an acquaintance, but I do know she is the best Queen or King we have ever had. She has kept her crown on her head while everyone in Europe has had theirs shaken. Then she is the only King or Queen who has been saving—always paying everybody all she owes them—and she is so kind and full of pity for those who are ill and in trouble.—Absolute governors who do not care for the law, but help themselves to their neighbours goods—if she took to those sort of ways—why we should soon learn to be thankful for her, but I must end now for Dr Spitta has made me buy some little pots of tallow to be lighted up tomorrow—from

Your dear old AUNT MONIE.

My republicanism was but feebly rooted, and I can still remember my cowardly behaviour at Hatfield House. Queen Victoria was driving to visit Lord Salisbury on that year of her Jubilee, and together with other children I sat on a wall to see her pass. Our legs hung outside. The policeman made us hang them inside, for reasons of propriety. I boiled with rage and I determined that I would not take off my sailor hat and wave it, nor would I cheer. At the critical moment, though, I thought the policeman was looking at me, and before I knew what I was doing my hat was off, and my lungs were squeaking. I remember, too, consenting to witness the great Jubilee procession in London, and no doubt after it my mother took me on to Clapham. But no details of that survive, nor of our last visit, which was in September—only three weeks before the "dear old Aunt Monie" who had chosen so to love me died.

I can remember the arrival of the news. I knew that she was ill, and one gloomy afternoon I was walking with my mother towards our home across a corner of the park. Tall woodland (it still stands) was to the left, to the right was rough grassland. I asked her how Aunt Monie was, and she replied, in the strained tones then thought appropriate to the subject of death, "She is better."—"Is she well?" I asked. "She *is*" came the solemn answer, and I burst into tears. They were composite tears. I had not really loved Aunt Monie—she was too old, and the masses of presents she had given me had not found their way to my tiny heart. I cried because crying was easy and because my mother might like it, and because the subject was death. Of later years I have loved Aunt Monie better—best of all now when I have been trying to trace the unfoldings of her good life.

A week before she died she wrote an extraordinary letter to Emily Thornton. She asked for some milk. No biographer could have foretold such a request, no novelist before Proust could have invented it. After thirty-five years' alienation she asks for some milk. Her letter has not been preserved nor has Emily's reply. Both must have been courteous, for on October the 31st Marianne writes a second letter:

My dear Emily

I cannot let another day pass without thanking you for the very kind manner in which you have taken my rather free and easy request for milk &ct. I hoped you would take it as I did as a proof of my gladness that anything should occasion my hope that the long state of estrangement between our two houses should have passed away at last and believe me that no one can be more happy than I am that we are now to be on better terms. Believe me to be yours truly and cordially MARIANNE THORNTON.

The letter is confused but has a strangeness about it which cannot be explained by confusion. Emily replied:

My dear Mony

Thank you so much for your kind letter. It would have pleased Henry so much. I cannot tell you what a pleasure to me it is to send you anything you like from Battersea Rise. I am so glad to hear a good account of you today. With love, I am Ever your affectionate EMILY THORNTON.

These two letters survive in copies. The copyist (Marion Southey perhaps) remarks: "Don't you think there is something regal in the way Mony holds out the olive branch to Di? the wording too is not like hers generally. Or do you take it as an admission that the estrangement was *her* doing?"

The latter explanation is the likelier of the two. But it is more probable still that Marianne was writing not to a person but to a place. The milk was a sacrament. She knew she was dying and before it happened she wished to be in physical touch with Battersea Rise.

After some comfortable days and nights her end came— November 5, 1887. She left a paper of wishes behind her in which she said:

I should like to be buried at Milton, under the large spreading tree at which I used to look on Sundays when waiting for the

First Service to end that I might go in for the Holy Communion afterwards.

I do not wish for anyone to be asked to be present. I humbly hope I shall be in my better home above. I think too much attention is paid to the body, therefore I should like to have no flowers, above all no flowers buried with me. They are too lovely for such a purpose. No singing of hymns or address from anyone. My grave to have my name age and a verse from the Bible chosen by the Rector.

There is generally an interval of twilight as it were during which a painful watch is kept around my bed. I would gladly spare those I loved and who loved me (and they are many) this useless painful scene.

When I have passed away I wish Havell to lock up my room and to allow no one to enter it except for necessary purposes. I might be moved by night to the Church at Milton and remain there till the funeral takes place.

She was buried at Milton Bryan by her friend Lord Alwyn Compton, then Bishop of Ely, and I once came across a letter (I cannot now locate it) describing the funeral and the fantastical grief of Henrietta Synnot. I have hunted in the tangled churchyard of Milton for her grave but have failed to find it. She made a will which was of the greatest importance to me, though I did not know it at the time. She died worth about £20,000. She bequeathed Milton and the East Side house to Henrietta, together with some money, there were legacies to Laura Forster, to my mother, etc., and to me she left £8,000. The interest was to be devoted to my education and when I was twenty-five I was to receive the capital. This £8,000 has been the financial salvation of my life. Thanks to it, I was able to go to Cambridge—impossible otherwise, for I failed to win scholarships. After Cambridge I was able to travel for a couple of years, and travelling inclined me to write. After my first visit to India and after the First World War the value of the £8,000 began to diminish, and later on it practically vanished. But by then my writings had begun to sell, and I have been able to live on them instead. Whether—in so stormy an age as ours —this is a reputable sequence I do not know. Still less do I know how the sequence and all sequences will end, with the storms increasing. But I am thankful so far, and thankful to Marianne Thornton; for she and no one else made my career as a writer possible, and her love, in a most tangible sense, followed me beyond the grave.

Index

[327]

INDEX

INDEX